Children, the Law and the Welfare Principle

This book contrasts and compares the different applications of the law relating to the welfare interests and rights of children in France and Germany. It does so by applying the same matrix of indicators to explore jurisdictional differences between welfare interests and rights in the contexts of public family law (civil – care and protection, etc. and criminal – youth justice, etc.); private family law (matrimonial, adoption, etc.); and hybrid public/private family law (wardship, adoption from state care, etc.). By profiling the nations in accordance with the same indicators it reveals important jurisdictional differences in the extent to which welfare interests or rights determine how the law is currently applied to children in France and Germany.

This volume will be of interest to academics and researchers engaged in law, legal studies, and social policy, and also to policymakers, administrators, and professionals working within child welfare systems.

Kerry O'Halloran, a professionally qualified lawyer, social worker, and academic, has recently retired from 13 years as Adjunct Professor to the Australian Centre for Philanthropy and Nonprofit Studies at QUT, Brisbane. In Northern Ireland he served on the Social Care Tribunal and on a HSS Trust Adoption Panel, has advised the Irish government on law reform matters, and has served in a consultancy capacity to government bodies such as Courts Services (Northern Ireland) and to the Open University in England. His 34 books include many on national and international child care matters.

Children and the Law

The Principle of the Welfare of the Child
A History
Kerry O'Halloran

Children & the Law
Shaping the Modern Welfare Principle in the British Isles
Kerry O'Halloran

Children, the Law and the Welfare Principle
Perspectives from North America
Kerry O'Halloran

Children, the Law and the Welfare Principle
Perspectives from Australia & New Zealand
Kerry O'Halloran

Children, the Law and the Welfare Principle
Civil Law Perspectives from France and Germany
Kerry O'Halloran

For more information about this series, please visit:
Children and the Law: From Welfare to Rights - Book Series - Routledge & CRC Press

Children, the Law and the Welfare Principle

Civil Law Perspectives from France and Germany

Kerry O'Halloran

Routledge
Taylor & Francis Group
LONDON AND NEW YORK

First published 2024
by Routledge
4 Park Square, Milton Park, Abingdon, Oxon OX14 4RN

and by Routledge
605 Third Avenue, New York, NY 10158

Routledge is an imprint of the Taylor & Francis Group, an informa business

British Library Cataloguing-in-Publication Data
A catalogue record for this book is available from the British Library

Library of Congress Cataloging-in-Publication Data
Names: O'Halloran, Kerry, author.
Title: Children, the law, and the welfare principle: civil law perspectives from France and Germany / Kerry O'Halloran.
Description: Abingdon, Oxon [UK]; New York, NY: Routledge, 2024. | Series: Children and the law | Includes bibliographical references and index. |
Identifiers: LCCN 2023041484 (print) | LCCN 2023041485 (ebook) | ISBN 9781032542089 (hardback) | ISBN 9781032542119 (paperback) | ISBN 9781003415688 (ebook)
Subjects: LCSH: Children–Legal status, laws, etc.–France. | Children–Legal status, laws, etc.–Germany. | Child welfare–France. | Child welfare–Germany. | Children's rights–France. | Children's rights–Germany.
Classification: LCC KJE1018 .O43 2024 (print) | LCC KJE1018 (ebook) | DDC 344.4303/27--dc23/eng/20231002
LC record available at https://lccn.loc.gov/2023041484
LC ebook record available at https://lccn.loc.gov/2023041485

ISBN: 978-1-032-54208-9 (hbk)
ISBN: 978-1-032-54211-9 (pbk)
ISBN: 978-1-003-41568-8 (ebk)

DOI: 10.4324/9781003415688

Typeset in Times New Roman
by Deanta Global Publishing Services, Chennai, India

This book is dedicated with much love - as long as we are under the same sky, we shouldn't be sad when we part ways - to my grand daughter, Morgan.

Contents

Acknowledgements

The foundations for this book were laid in earlier publications including *The Welfare of the Child: The Principle and the Law,*[1] *The Politics of Adoption,*[2] *State Neutrality: The Sacred, the Secular and Equality Law,*[3] *Child Care and Protection: The Law and Practice in Northern Ireland,*[4] and in my earlier contributions[5] to this series.[6] Given the not dissimilar subject matter and related caselaw, focused on many of the same jurisdictions, there is inevitably some degree of overlap and I thank the publishers concerned for their understanding.

A sincere debt of gratitude is owed to those who kindly made room in their busy schedules to read and offer comments on draft chapters. In particular I am most grateful to Jörg Reinhardt[7] (Germany) and Blandine Malleavey[8] (France). Of the many others who contributed along the way, special thanks are due to Fabio Macedo[9] and Charlotte Pietri.[10] Their encouragement, support, and advice have meant a lot and this book and its author would have suffered without them.

I am very thankful to Routledge, particularly to Siobhán Poole,[11] for commissioning the book and the series. Responsibility for any mistakes, inconsistencies, or other faults, and for all views expressed, must unfortunately rest wholly with me.

1 Aldershot, Arena/Ashgate Publications, (1999).
2 *The Politics of Adoption: International Perspectives on Law, Policy & Practice* (4th ed.), the Netherlands, Springer, (2021).
3 New York, Cambridge University Press, (2021).
4 Dublin, Thomson Round Hall, (2003).
5 See: *The Principle of the Welfare of the Child: A History*, Routledge 2022; *Children & the Law: Shaping the Modern Welfare Principle in the British Isles*, Routledge 2022; *Children, the Law and the Welfare Principle: Perspectives from North America*, 2023; and *Children, the Law and the Welfare Principle: Perspectives from Australia and New Zealand*, 2023.
6 Series, *Children and the Law* (forthcoming title: *Child Welfare and Rights: A Contemporary Family Law Analysis,* 2024), Oxfordshire, Routledge, 2022–26.
7 Professor, Department of Applied Sciences, Hochschule München, Germany.
8 Professor of Private Law and Criminal Sciences, Child and Family Chair, Université Catholique de Lille, France.
9 Postdoctoral Fellow, University of Angers, France.
10 The CAMELEON Association, France at: www.cameleon-association.org
11 Commissioning Editor, Routledge Law Research.

Acknowledgements

Introduction

'Children are fully-fledged human rights holders'.[1] This is indeed true but there is a world of difference between holding rights and using them. The capacity of a particular child, their opportunity to exercise rights, and the assistance they receive in doing so, will be crucial. If their rights remain inert – unknown to the child, unrepresented by lawyers, or unacknowledged by others – then at best the law will default to address their welfare interests.

This book, like others in the mini-series, endeavours to identify and consider the many ways in which the law now gives effect to children's rights while balancing this with a concern for their welfare interests: it examines differences between the two. A wide range of law is involved. For present purposes, the focus remains very largely confined to the child-specific provisions of family law: the civil jurisdiction, private family law (custody, contact, etc.), and public (care and protection, etc.), together with the criminal jurisdiction (juvenile justice, etc.). However, the environmental context cannot be wholly overlooked: both the rights and the welfare interests of children can be prejudiced by social disadvantage unless this is offset by appropriate and sufficient public services.

Children, the Law and the Welfare Principle: Civil Law Perspectives from France and Germany – the fifth book in this mini-series[2] – examines and differentiates between these two countries as regards the ways in which their laws recognise and give effect to the rights and the principle of the welfare interests of the child. Unlike the previous books, this one deals with countries that are leading representatives of the civil law tradition. As a preliminary it is therefore necessary to consider the differences between the common law and civil law traditions and explore such implications as may arise for children and their welfare interests and rights. Otherwise, the purpose of this book, like the others, is to: understand and explain how the law relates generally to children in both countries; identify characteristic

1 Stated in the 'Foreword' to the *Handbook on European Law Relating to the Rights of the Child* (2nd ed), Council of Europe, (2022), at: https://www.echr.coe.int/documents/handbook_rights_child_eng.pdf

2 O'Halloran, K., *The Principle of the Welfare of the Child: A History*, Routledge, 2022; *Children & the Law: Shaping the Modern Welfare Principle in the British Isles*, Routledge, 2022; *Children, the Law and the Welfare Principle: Perspectives from North America*, Routledge, 2023; and *Children, the Law and the Welfare Principle: Perspectives from Australia and New Zealand*, Routledge, 2023.

DOI: 10.4324/9781003415688-1

jurisdictional differences; and assess their significance. It employs the template of themes previously identified to explore areas of difference and commonality in the relevant law, and the role therein of rights and the welfare principle, as applied to the lives of children in France and Germany.

Part 1 – 'The Civil Law Context' – begins the book with two chapters. Chapter 1 – 'Civil Law and Common Law: Differentiating Characteristics' – identifies and considers the characteristics of these two legal traditions and assesses the significance of differentiating attributes insofar as they impact upon the welfare and rights of children. Chapter 2 – 'Civil Law: France and Germany' – examines the civil law of both countries and again considers the significance of any differences as they relate to children.

Part II – 'France' – is in three chapters. Chapter 3 – 'Policy, Principles, Legislation, and Courts' – outlines the framework of legislation, courts, and regulatory bodies, both domestic and international, which define the role and functions of the principle of the welfare interests of the child. Chapter 4 – 'The Welfare Principle in Contemporary Practice: Public Family Law – Civil and Criminal Jurisdictions' – profiles the contemporary application of the law in that country as it relates to: public family law both civil (child protection, etc.) and criminal (juvenile justice, etc.). Chapter 5 – 'The Welfare Principle in Contemporary Practice: Private Family Law and Hybrid Proceedings' – deals in the same way with private family law (adoption, divorce, etc.); and with the emerging hybrid public/private sector (adoption from the public care system, surrogacy, restraining orders, etc.).

Part III – 'Germany' – again in three chapters (6, 7, and 8) repeats the Part II template to undertake a similar examination of the law as it relates to the welfare of children in Germany. The same chapter structure focuses the material into similar blocks to facilitate a comparative jurisdictional analysis.

Part IV – 'Themes of Commonality and Difference' – in one chapter, 'Themes and a Comparative Jurisdictional Analysis', identifies jurisdictional differences in the law and in the functions of the welfare principle: as applied generally to child welfare/rights issues in France and Germany. It conducts a comparative analysis of the significance of any jurisdictional differences.

The 'Conclusion' closes the book, as did its predecessor, by benchmarking the distinctive characteristics and primary jurisdictional differences against the principles established by the Convention on the Rights of the Child 1989.

Part I

The civil law context

1 Civil law and common law

Differentiating characteristics

Introduction

Unlike its predecessors in the mini-series, this book deals with two countries that represent the civil law tradition. It therefore seems appropriate to start by considering what that difference might mean for the welfare interests/rights of a child. Accordingly, this chapter introduces the civil law tradition,[1] of which France and Germany are two of its leading exponents.

Beginning with a cursory overview of the civil and common law traditions, the chapter then identifies and examines their characteristic differentiating features. It then considers how both legal traditions relate to human rights law in general before focusing on their respective relationships with the rights of children. This brief chapter concludes by assessing the varying contribution of European and international bodies to bridging the gap between the two legal traditions and developing the law relating to the rights of the child.

Modern European Union law and the civil and common law traditions

The welfare interests and rights of European children have for some decades been loosely governed by the principles of the European Convention of Human Rights (ECHR) as interpreted and applied by the European Court of Human Rights (ECtHR), the jurisdiction of which expanded from the 22 countries that constituted the Council of Europe in 1989 to the 47 that did so in 2010, and currently comprises 46 countries (less Russia) with a total population of some 700 million. Other European instruments and fora have been involved, while national legislators and judiciary continue their traditional roles, but increasingly the influence of supra-national law is nudging the ECHR signatory states into a broad consensus on the benchmarks for law, policy, and practice as regards a state's duty of care for its children.

1 The term 'civil law' or *jus civile* refers to the law, rules, customs, etc. governing the citizens of a place: the person, things, and their inter-relationships. It is to be distinguished from *jus gentium* which refers to the law of nations: the legal rules commonly accepted as applying in and between other nations.

DOI: 10.4324/9781003415688-3

Confluence of legal cultures

The European Court of Human Rights sits astride two legal cultures – the British common law and the Continental civil law – the former dating back to the Courts of Chancery in England and underpinning the legal systems of some 80 countries, while the latter is most usually traced to Emperor Justinian in 600 C.E. and is to be found in twice as many countries. The European Convention of Human Rights itself is largely a product of the former having been actively promoted by the U.S. with a strong contribution from Britain.

The ECHR is linked to a common law heritage that includes the Magna Carta, the Bill of Rights of 1689, and the American Declaration of Independence, though undoubtedly it was also influenced by the French Declaration of the Rights of Man 1789. In the immediate aftermath of World War II, the leaders of both nations and others saw the ECHR as a means of binding an inherently unstable Europe to a set of principles and rights that might prevent a repetition of that war. Indeed, Norman and Oborne, perhaps overstating the British pedigree, claim that:[2]

> The truth is that the Convention was framed by British jurists, working within a common law legal tradition stretching back past the US Bill of Rights 1791 to encompass our own Bill of Rights 1689, and the Petition of Right 1628.

The point is fairly made, however, that the ECHR and the rulings of the ECtHR probably owe more to the common law than to the civil law. The latter – with its characteristic hallmarks of codification, rigid judicial application of prescriptive legislative provisions based on abstract norms – can be difficult to apply to complex 'facts on the ground' and arguably leaves little room for a flexible response to newly emerging social norms.

Common law features

The common law was constructed over the centuries[3] from the specificity of High Court writs which eventually amalgamated with the equitable principles forged in the courts of Chancery.[4] The judicial arm of the law retained its independence from its statutory counterpart, with new legislative provisions being interpreted against established judicial precedents, the latter prevailing where any ambiguity could be found.

It would, however, be a mistake to view the common law as one which is clearly defined and uniformly practised throughout the common law world; and, indeed,

2 See Norman, J. and Oborne, P., *The Conservative Case for the Human Rights Act,* Liberty (National Council for Civil Liberties), London, (2009), p 7, at: https://jessenorman.typepad.com/Churchills_Legacy.pdf

3 See, further, O'Halloran, K., *The Principle of the Welfare of the Child: A History*, Routledge, London, 2022.

4 The Supreme Court of Judicature Act 1873 unified the court systems of equity and the common law.

the same observation could be made in relation to civil law. Although, for example, the law in the U.S. and England share the same roots – retaining the same fundamental concepts, principles, and respect for precedents – their versions of the common law now differ significantly. Perhaps, most obviously, in the U.S. the Constitution presides over the workings of the entire system, whereas in England law-making authority rests very largely (if not exclusively) with Parliament. In England there is no judicial equivalent to the U.S. Supreme Court (USSC) – with its capacity to make and change laws, a capacity open to political bias as the judicial bench is formed by political appointments – which continues to be the supreme law-making institution in the U.S. Partly, this is a natural consequence of the difference between what is still a much more centralised legal system and a federated one in which a federal and 50 other fairly independent judicial systems endeavour to achieve a level of conformity with federal legislation. This is a difference replicated, if to a lesser extent, in Australia and Canada where the same federated distribution of authority, governed by a Constitution, positions both countries closer to the U.S. than the English common law model.

JUDICIAL INTERPRETATION IS KEY

As has often been said, 'the common law is judge made law' meaning that the judiciary have always valued a measure of independence from government and from parliament: their capacity to look inwards at the body of accumulated jurisprudence, rather than outwards to follow the latest statutory decree, has been a hallmark of this legal tradition for centuries. Milestone decisions in English law are reported in lengthy judgments, containing carefully crafted judicial arguments for and against propositions, that draw from established sources of authority – both legal and moral philosophy – concluding with a statement of principle agreed to by a majority but also including perhaps equally lengthy statements from any dissenting members of the judicial bench which may, in due course, count for more than the majority decision.[5] The freedom to interpret the law to fit – where possible – the particular configuration of facts brought before the court, and to construe new legislative provisions as far as is feasible to fit with established judicial precedent, is an essential trait of common law judicial practice. Its effect has been well illustrated by many judicial decisions in the U.K.[6] It is less obvious in the U.S. where the USSC has demonstrated a willingness to overturn established judicial authority in compliance with contemporary political exigencies.[7]

Generally, this approach contrasts with that of the civil law judiciary who are more accustomed to applying rather than creatively interpreting the prescribed

5 See, for example, *Liversidge v. Anderson*, [1942] A.S. 206, per dissenting judgment of Atkins LJ.

6 See *Donoghue v. Stevenson*, [1932] AC 562; *Gillick v. West Norfolk & Wisbech Area Health Authority*, [1986] AC 112; and *Re A (conjoined twins)*, [2001] 2 WLR 480.

7 See, for example, *Roe v. Wade*, 410 U.S. 113 (1973); *Dobbs v. Jackson Women's Health Organization*, No. 19-1392, 597 U.S. ___ (2022); and *Windsor v. U.S.*, 570 U.S. 744 (2013).

rules. Where, however, the rules are broadly stated as in some clauses in the German Civil Code[8] then – in the face of legislature inertia – the judiciary have shown an aptitude for substituing their own version of the law to bridge the legislative gap and address an emerging social need.

PRINCIPLES/DOCTRINES

Internal consistency, together with a capacity for continuity – an ability to project a coherent functionality into the future – is essential for any legal system as it is for the future of the society it serves. The common law provides this through reliance on case precedents which allow principles or doctrines that have proven effective in the past to continue to do so in the future. That the welfare interests of a child should be the priority consideration in any decision affecting his or her welfare is one example of such a principle respected through successive generations of judicial judgments, as is the principle (previously part of the 'doctrine of parental rights') that parental responsibility continues throughout childhood.

In particular, moral imperatives were always prominent in the common law as it related to the family: generally as regards marriage, procreation, and child rearing but particularly so in relation to matters of sexuality. The rigidity of values formed generations ago in respect of such matters continue to reverberate through the common law nations and have shaped the polarised attitudes that now constitute the culture wars in the U.S. and elsewhere. The related moralising, initially crystallised by the pro-life/pro-choice confrontation, now extends to gay marriage, transgender matters, assisted death, genetic engineering, DNA patenting, cloning, and stem cell research – issues which contribute to the erosion of family law as a coherent and integrated body of principles and values.

PRECEDENTS

In taking decisions that determine future actions the common law judiciary will be guided by the maxim 'like cases should be decided alike'. As noted by Richard Fitz-Nigel in the 12th century "there are cases where the course of events, and the reasons for decisions are obscure; and in these it is enough to cite precedents".[9] Although, it has to be said, there have also been strong criticisms of a system which might be viewed as weighed down by the 'dead hand of the law' when changes in social mores strongly indicate that continued reliance on precedent is increasingly inappropriate.

Advancing the development of the law by use of analogy – extending the application of a principle proven in one context to the same effect in another – is a distinctive common law characteristic with a long history. For example, a Canadian

8 See, for example, the Civil Code, Article 826: 'Whoever causes injury to another intentionally in a manner offending good morals is bound to repair the injury'.

9 Fitz-Nigel, R., *Dialogues de Scaccario*, 1177–79; cited by Dias, RWM, *Jurisprudence* (5th ed.), Butterworths, London, 1985, at p 56.

judge in the late 20th century creatively found that contemporary free community access to the internet could be analogously justified by the same rationale that permitted free access to public highways in 17th-century England.[10] Such reliance on judicial precedent has become a strong feature of ECtHR rulings which very frequently cite previous decisions of the Court as added justification for the one it has just made.

STARE DECISIS

The doctrine of *stare decisis* ('let the decision stand') essentially requires past case precedents of superior courts to be binding on future judicial decisions on similar matters in all courts. As was once said in its defence, "it is better that the law should be certain than that every judge should speculate upon improvements".[11] It is a very powerful mechanism – almost exclusive to the common law as its civil counterpart gives primacy to every new statutory iteration – and one that by perpetuating the significance of a legal determination places considerable authority in the hands of the judiciary. A precedent on a point of law can only be overuled by specific legislative provision designed to have that effect or by the counter ruling of a superior court.[12]

This is not to imply that the civil law judiciary are mere functionaries, mechanically applying the law as determined by the legislature and as stated in the latest updated Article of the Civil Code. They can and do, if rarely, effect change in the law, but it is through studious reference to legal texts and academic works rather than recourse to case precedents.

Civil law features

Generally traced back to origins in the *Corpus Juris Civilis* issued by the Emperor Justinian in AD 529, this ancient legal system derives from Roman law, as influenced by ecclesiastical teachings and doctrines which shaped its early beginnings during a lengthy gestation in the Romano-Germanic tradition. However, it was the influence of the Napoleonic era in continental Europe that introduced its characteristic logical taxonomy, structured into distinct codes, making a distiction between 'private' and 'administrative' law each with its own separate set of courts, and saw it firmly established in most European countries. As with the common law, it was transferred to the colonies that comprised the empires – Portuguese, Spanish, Belgian, German, Dutch, etc. – of various European rulers and consequently can now be found in many countries on the continents of Africa, the Americas, and Asia. Like the common law, there is no single pure civil law model conforming to

10 *Vancouver Regional FreeNet Association v. M.N.R.*, [1996] 3 F.C. 880.

11 *Sheddon v. Goodrich*, 8 Ves. 491, 497; (1805) 32 ER, 441, 447, *per* Eldon LJ.

12 An example might be the binding effect of the precedent established in *Roe v. Wade* 410 U.S. 113 (1973), coupled with the nullifying effect of *Dobbs v. Jackson Women's Health Organization* No. 19-1392, 597 U.S. ___ (2022): both being rulings by the USSC.

a uniform set of specifications; instead it is represented quite differently in various countries depending on the extent to which it has been influenced by local customs, traditions, and religion, though the same basic set of concepts, categories, and rules prevail in each. Civil law, in keeping with the common law, is now largely secularised – depending on the continuing strength of religion in the various nations – with France and Germany being particularly strong examples of the civil law tradition (see, further, Chapter 2).

JUDICIAL SYSTEM IS MORE ACCESSIBLE

Civil law systems are less centralised than their common law equivalents. Accessibility to the system and indeed to the judiciary is facilitated by a lesser degree of formality and ceremony than that generally found in common law countries; also there are simply more judges in the system. Regional appellate courts allow for swifter processes and provide an administrative supervisory layer that encourages consistency in judicial determinations. The legal system functions in much the same way as any other aspect of French bureaucracy: the judiciary are almost invariably career judges, promoted on merit through the civil service ranks; there is a sense of collective engagement with a decision-making process, with judges meeting with social workers or other relevant professionals outside the adjudicatory forum; the decision reached is unilateral and reported in a judgment that pointedly excludes any mention of dissent.

The fact that in a civil law context less attention is paid to judicial *ratio decidendi* is significant. Judgments, in keeping with the prescriptive nature of the codified rules, tend to be reduced to terse answers to the questions framed in relation to whether or not a particular rule was breached. In France, the rationale for a decision will be briefly stated without any exploration of the relative merits of contesting arguments and usually with no reference to previous judgments on similar issues. In Germany, there is a much greater probability of a judgment including judicial opinions with references being made to academic texts and to previous caselaw.

CODIFICATION

Generally, civil law countries have constitutions structured to recognise and authorise a set of codes that organise their national law (social codes, criminal codes, administrative and tax codes, etc.). These are continuously amended to reflect changes in circumstances and are administered by their respective courts (adminstrative courts for administrative matters, tax courts for tax issues, etc.). The judicial role is, again generally, restricted to applying rather than interpreting the code in relation to each particular set of circumstances. There is little room for judicial discretion, judges look to the codes rather than to caselaw precedents for guidance in decision-making. A civil law system is generally more prescriptive than its common law counterpart.

NO RELIANCE ON PRECEDENT

This hallmark of the common law is – or has been – almost entirely missing from civil law jurisprudence. The rulings of even superior courts have traditionally been treated as not binding on subsequent judicial decisions on the same issue. Civil law judiciary have felt bound to address the particular facts of each individual case and felt free to reverse previous decisions, even to dissent from those made by a superior court, in order to scrupulously ensure the singular justice requirements of each case were met. In recent years, however, this approach has lost a good deal of its doctrinaire attributes: earlier rulings of the *Cour de Cassation* and the *Bundesgerichtshof*, for example, now tend to be treated as a source of authority when similar issues arise.

INDUCTIVE RATHER THAN DEDUCTIVE

A cause – or perhaps an effect – of the above is that there is a distinctively different rationalising approach to judicial decision-making in a civil law context. Inverting the common law approach, the civil law judiciary proceed from the general – deducting from broad statements of rules in the Articles – and apply these to the particular facts of the presenting case, whereas the common law judiciary look to the particular facts first and build up logically and inductively until the facts fit within a governing principle, which then shows the way to an appropriate decision. This may explain why the paramountcy principle is rarely if ever stated as such in the Civil Code nor referred to in judgments, but that would not preclude the judiciary from ultimately giving the welfare interests of a child the same priority weighting and coming to the same conclusion on similar facts as their common law counterparts

Human rights and the civil/common law traditions

When the states of eastern Europe together with others joined the European Union,[13] doubling its membership to 27, they joined a democratic polity, largely based on the civil law, with a multi-layered framework of laws providing for equity, equality, and respect for the fundamental human rights of all citizens. This rights regime, although more extensive, was not unlike that shared by the common law nations which already had an established human rights-oriented legal tradition.

Complementarity of the civil/common law traditions and the ECHR

Although the enlarged membership of the European Union (EU) necessarily increased the overwhelming majority of civil law nations that were signatory states to the ECHR, this did not mean that the tiny minority of common law members

13 In May 2004, Cyprus and Malta joined the EU along with eight Central and Eastern European countries – Czechia, Estonia, Hungary, Latvia, Lithuania, Poland, Slovakia, and Slovenia.

were in any way less committed to the human rights regime. The common law had always placed an emphasis on the rights and duties of the individual. This, perhaps the single most distinctive common law characteristic, grounded the ancient writ of *habeas corpus.*[14] It also found expression in the catchphrase 'no writ no action': the right came first; the petitioner had to fit his complaint within the narrowly defined right/duty prescribed by a particular writ. In short, there was little to distinguish the two legal traditions in terms of their commitment to the rights represented by the ECHR.

Complementarity

Arguably, it would now be a mistake to assume that the common law and the civil law function in parallel as self-contained, wholly separate bodies of law. As far as human rights – particularly those of children – are concerned, they have much in common. Fundamental human rights are embedded in most common law legal systems – inherently, by statute or constitution – reinforced by Article 54 which requires the public bodies of signatory states to ensure their decisions are compliant with ECtHR rulings. Further, while the ECtHR is very much guided by precedent it does not consider itself bound by the rigidity of *stare decisis* and has instead vested in itself a capacity to be flexible and extend recognition to legal rights that it might previously have found unsubstantiated (e.g. rights of gay couples to marry and/or adopt). On approximately 30 occasions the ECtHR has issued a reminder that "The Court must also recall that the Convention is a living instrument which [...] must be interpreted in the light of present-day conditions".[15] This is very much in keeping with the common law approach and does much to bridge the gaps between the two legal traditions and facilitate concerted action to further develop ECHR rights.

THE ECHR, A CATALYST FOR CONVERGENCE

The ECHR has an important role as a stopgap for deficiencies in the domestic law of signatory nations, providing a safety net of imprescriptible fundamental legal rights to catch those victimised by the fault or default of national public bodies. It brings an added and internationally applicable dimension to the largely adjudicative role of those public bodies, which are usually limited in their practice and procedures to adducing facts and applying the prescribed remedies as required by legislative provisions. This core body of rights crosscuts all civil and criminal law, generating principles and standards that have an equal bearing on both judicial and administrative forums. Gradually, over time, as practice across all signatory nations conforms to the stratifying effect of governing principles established by the ECHR, a level of harmonisation is being achieved between the laws of those

14 Mediaeval in origins and first enacted into English law by the Habeas Corpus Act 1679, which continues in effect.

15 See, for example, *Tyrer v. the U.K.*, Application No. 5856/72, (1978), at para 31.

nations. This in turn is having the knock-on effect of introducing a degree of conformity on related social policy matters.[16]

MORE THAN A SAFETY NET

Moreover the Convention is not just an inert safety net, activated only in response to a breach of rights. The ECHR has ruled that the public authorities of signatory nations, in keeping with the Convention ethos and principles, must also act proactively to prevent possible breaches of rights and to promote opportunities for their enjoyment. Convention awareness is generating a culture of respect for rights which transcends the initial minimalist approach that focused on responding to breaches of Articles, instead infusing a deference for rights-compliant standards throughout the social infrastrucure of public bodies such as schools, workplaces, health and social care, judicial systems, etc. A more positive developmental approach is emerging whereby public authorities are now examining their policies and procedures to Convention-proof them so as to pre-empt the circumstances thay may give rise to a potential breach. In short, among the consequences of Convention influence on the shaping of national law is the development or reinforcement of a preventative legal function.

For present purposes, the Convention may be seen as having a threefold functional relevance for the law relating to children. Firstly, some rights in themselves – such as to family life – carry particular implications for that law. Secondly, the differentiation in weighting accorded to these rights – some freestanding and mandatory, others conditional – represents a corresponding differential in the importance attached to the legal functions being given effect and provides a model for similar treatment by signatory nations. Thirdly, the Convention impacts upon the law relating to children by introducing standards as benchmarks for the operation of legal functions. In all three respects, the rulings of the ECHR have brought additional clarity, direction, and emphasis to challenge and shape the domestic law of signatory nations, and ultimately to steer their laws towards convergence.

Broadening the human rights platform in relation to children: a common law/civil law synergy

The range of international instruments giving recognition to the needs, deeds, welfare, and rights of children has been steadily expanding as have the number of complicating provisions that are either vague, very broad, repeat, or differ only slightly from others.[17] In addition, a body of jurisprudence, largely comprised

16 For example, ECHR rulings on the rights of the parties involved in the adoption process (e.g. entitlement of a child to family life and the rights of same gender adopters) are having significant and uniform consequences for how signatory nations define 'family life' and for related social policy adjustments to family support services, etc.

17 See, further, O'Halloran, K., *Children, the Law and the Welfare Principle: European Judicial Perspectives*, Routledge (forthcoming). Also, author acknowledges helpfulness of the *Handbook on*

of ECtHR decisions is constantly growing. As these are necessarily drawn from cases produced in both common law and civil law countries, with the rulings of the Court disseminated throughout the EU, this ongoing process – augmented by rulings of the Court of Justice of the European Union (CJEU) and the United Nations Committee on the Rights of the Child (UN CRC) – is doing much to bridge the gaps between the two legal traditions.

Principles of the United Nations Convention on the Rights of the Child and the ECHR

As of 2023, the United Nations Convention on the Rights of the Child 1989 (UN CROC) had been signed by almost 200 nations including all the major common law (excepting the U.S.) and civil law countries and, of necessity, all signatory states to the European Convention on Human Rights. The latter requires that States Parties, when engaged in the field of children's rights, ensure that their actions are compliant with the provisions of UN CROC.[18] The European Committee on Social Rights (ECSR) has also explicitly referred to UN CROC in its decisions.[19] As both Conventions – and other instruments including the Charter of Fundamental Rights of the European Union, adopted in 2000 – uphold the same core principles relating to the best interests of the child and their right to be heard, it follows that the welfare/rights of the child in the majority of leading civil law and common law nations must become, at least to that extent, gradually aligned with these principles.

A BROADENING CONFORMITY

This process began in Europe with member countries of both legal traditions being required to conform to EU laws on child protection matters in areas such as consumer protection[20] and the free movement of persons.[21] It continued with the introduction of the European Social Charter 1961, as revised in 1996, which recognised children's right to receive free compulsory education (Article 14(2)), prohibited discrimination on grounds of age (Article 21), and banned any child work and

---

European Law Relating to theRights of the Child, (2022), op. cit., as a source of material for this section.

18 See, for example, *Harroudj v. France*, Application No. 43631/09, (2012), at para 42.

19 See, for example, ECSR, *International Commission of Jurists (ICJ) and European Council for Refugees and Exiles (ECRE) v. Greece*, Complaint No. 173/2018, 21 January 2021, para 158; ECSR, *World Organisation against Torture (OMCT) v. Ireland*, Complaint No. 18/2003, 7 December 2004, paras 61–63; ECSR, *Defence for Children International (DCI) v. the Netherlands*, Complaint No. 47/2008, 20 October 2009; and ECSR, *International Federation of Human Rights Leagues (FIDH) v. France*, Complaint No. 14/2003, 8 November 2004.

20 See, for example, Directive 2009/48/EC of the European Parliament and of the Council of 18 June 2009 on the safety of toys, which enforces safety measures for children's toys.

21 See, for example, Directive 2004/38/EC of the European Parliament and of the Council of 29 April 2004 on the right of citizens of the Union and their family members to move and reside freely within the territory of the Member States.

exploitative labour of young people (Article 32). Significantly, the Charter contained a specific provision on the rights of the child (Article 24), which articulates key children's rights principles: the right to such protection and care as is necessary for their well-being (Article 24(1)); the right to express their views freely and to have their views taken into consideration in accordance with their age and maturity (Article 24(1)); the right to have their best interests taken as a primary consideration in all actions relating to them (Article 24(2)); the right to maintain on a regular basis a personal relationship and direct contact with both parents, unless that is contrary to their interests (Article 24(3)); and the right to private and family life (Article 7).[22]

Moreover, the process has also been informed by important instruments adopted by international institutions, such as the Hague Conference on Private International Law and by strategic policy developments such as the adoption of the EU Strategy on the Rights of the Child 2021–2024.[23] The latter, adopted in 2021, included the European Child Guarantee which addressed child poverty and social exclusion through measures in early childhood education and care, education, healthcare, nutrition, and housing. A series of Directives, each addressing an aspect of child protection, were also issued during the period 2011–16. More recently, the Steering Committee for the Rights of the Child, established in 2020 as the successor to the Ad Hoc Committee for the Rights of the Child (2016–2019), now guides the intergovernmental work in progressing the programme 'Building a Europe for and with children' which promotes a holistic and integrated approach to children's rights, mainstreaming child rights across all relevant Council of Europe policy areas. All of this furthered a shared adherence across the common law and civil traditions of EU member states to agreed standards in relation to the welfare interests and the emerging rights of children, a sense of direction constantly reinforced by rulings of the UN CRC, the ECJ, the ECtHR, and the ESCR. The principles established by these bodies, with their equal applicability across both traditions, have necessarily brought those traditions into closer alignment.

ROLE OF THE UN CRC

In terms of bridging the gap between the two legal traditions, as regards their respective approaches to the welfare interests and rights of the child, the role of the UN CRC has been particularly important. By monitoring the implementation of the only international instrument specifically dealing with children's rights and its optional protocols, and by providing guidance on the interpretation of UN CROC

22 See *Handbook on European Law Relating to the Rights of the Child*, (2022), p 22 at: https://www.echr.coe.int/documents/d/echr/handbook_rights_child_eng

23 Note, also, that the Lisbon Treaty 2009 identified the 'protection of the rights of the child' as a general stated objective of the EU (Article 3(3) of the Treaty on European Union [TEU]) and as an important aspect of the EU's external relations policy (Article 3(5) of the TEU).

through its 'general comments',[24] the CRC greatly assists the development of a consensus – not just in Europe but globally – regarding the interpretation and application of children's rights. Its influence in Europe has been apparent in relation to the the standard-setting and treaty-making activities of the Council of Europe: the *Guidelines on child-friendly justice*, for example, was directly informed by a range of CRC provisions. The significance of the CRC in enhancing international awareness of the need to further develop children's rights has been recognised by the ECJ.[25]

ROLE OF THE ECJ

The ECJ from time to time issues judgments concerning children's rights in relation to matters such as migration, foster care, habitual residency, family life, and non-discrimination. It has referred to UN CROC when determining how EU law should be interpreted in relation to children, for example in the *Dynamic Medien Vertriebs GmbH v. Avides Media AG* case,[26] in which it invoked Article 17 of UN CROC, which encourages signatory states to develop appropriate guidelines for the protection of children from media-generated information and material injurious to their well-being.[27] It also referred to Article 3(1) on the best interests of the child in the *M. A. v. État belge* case.[28] ECJ references to UN CROC provisions have increased since the adoption of the EU Charter of Fundamental Rights, as it makes links between the two instruments in the recognition both give to children's rights.

ROLE OF THE ECTHR

No institution has had a greater impact in terms of furthering recognition of children's rights than the ECtHR which has accrued a vast body of jurisprudence over many decades. While, in particular, it has examined many cases under Article 8 of the ECHR (right to respect for private and family life), it has also explored the rights of the child under other ECHR provisions such as the prohibition of inhuman or degrading treatment (Article 3) or the right to a fair trial (Article 6). In some cases, children's rights principles stated in UN CROC have had a profound influence on the ECtHR's reasoning, notably as concerns the Court's interpretation of

24 See, for example, General Comment No. 10 (2007): Children's rights in juvenile justice, CRC/C/GC/10, 25 April 2007; General Comment No. 12 (2009): The right of the child to be heard, CRC/C/GC/12, 1 July 2009; General Comment No. 14 (2013) on the right of the child to have his or her best interest taken as a primary consideration (art. 3, para 1), CRC/C/GC/14, 29 May 2013; General Comment No. 25 (2021) on children's rights in relation to the digital environment, CRC/C/GC/25, 24 March 2021; General Comment No. 24 (2019): Children's rights in the child justice system, CRC/C/GC/24, 18 September 2019.

25 See, for example, CJEU, C-112/20, *M. A. v État belge*, 11 March 2021, para 37.

26 ECJ, C-244/06, *Dynamic Medien Vertriebs GmbH v. Avides Media AG,* 14 February 2008.

27 Ibid., at paras 42 and 52.

28 ECJ, C-112/20, op. cit., at para 37.

Article 6 of the ECHR (right to a fair trial) in relation to the treatment of children in conflict with the law.[29]

ROLE OF THE ECSR

The European Committee on Social Rights rules on the conformity of national law and practice with the European Social Charter either through the collective complaints procedure or the national reporting procedure.[30] It has, for example, ruled on complaints concerning the economic exploitation of children,[31] their physical integrity,[32] the health rights of migrant children,[33] access to education by children with disabilities,[34] children in conflict with the law,[35] and the rights of unaccompanied children.[36]

Conclusion

The common law and the civil law sit alongside each other under the ECHR umbrella as distinct if overlapping systems jointly engaged in protecting ECHR rights. However, the intensive output of the ECtHR over many decades, combined with the rulings of the ECJ, the UN CRC, and other bodies, has done much to narrow the gap between both of these two traditional legal systems. Other developments have also made a contribution to that end. For example the common law has adopted the practice of codifying areas of law, especially as regards tax and commerce legislation and particularly in the U.S.; while the civil law in both France and Germany, perhaps more so in the latter, is demonstrating a willingness to use precedents. Essentially, as time goes on, the differences between the two legal systems are becoming steadily less significant.

29 See, for example, *Maslov v. Austria,* Application No. 1638/03, (2008).

30 See, for example, ECSR, *International Commission of Jurists (ICJ) and European Council for Refugees and Exiles (ECRE) v. Greece,* Complaint No. 173/2018, 26 January 2021

31 ESCR, *International Commission of Jurists (ICJ) v. Portugal,* Complaint No. 1/1998, 9 September 1999.

32 ESCR, *World Organisation against Torture (OMCT) v. Greece*, Complaint No. 17/2003, 7 December 2004; ECSR, *Association for the Protection of All Children (APPROACH) Ltd v. Ireland,* Complaint No. 93/2013, 4 February 2013.

33 ESCR, *Defence for Children International (DCI) v. Belgium,* Complaint No. 69/2011, 23 October 2012.

34 ECSR, *Mental Disability Advocacy Center (MDAC) v. Bulgaria,* Complaint No. 41/2007, 3 June 2008, para 35.

35 ECSR, *International Commission of Jurists (ICJ) v. Czech Republic,* Complaint No. 148/2017, 20 March 2017.

36 ECSR, *European Roma Rights Centre (ERRC) and Mental Disability Advocacy Centre (MDAC) v. Czech Republic,* Complaint No. 157/2017, 17 June 2020.

2 Civil law

France and Germany

Introduction

This chapter sets out to explain the civil law context for the role of the welfare principle in the law relating to children in France and Germany. In conjunction with its predecessor, the purpose of the chapter is to lay the foundations for the more particular comparative analysis of the principle and the law in the two jurisdictions that will follow in the remainder of the book.

It therefore begins with a brief overview of the civil law in both France and Germany, tracing the milestones in its developmental history, before introducing family law and its functions in both jurisdictions. The chapter then goes on to explore family life, the forms it takes, and the law governing its beginning and end. In this way it prepares the ground for the subsequent chapters.

Overview of the civil law

The civil law consists of codified rules, rights, and duties, under an overarching Constitution, administered through a hierarchal infrastructure of first instance and appellate courts. The civil code collates and codifies private laws in systematic fashion to ensure their standardised application. Amendments are by statute which are simply incorporated into the code. The system is so detailed and prescriptive that the judicial role is mainly confined to implementing the law: the proceedings are specified, offences are clearly defined, and the related penalties are fixed; there is little or no margin for interpretation or discretion. Unlike the adversarial basis of the common law system, the civil law approach is inquisitorial: the judge leads proceedings by questioning the parties to determine facts, clarify issues, and rule on compliance or breach of civil code provisions; an approach which, it is sometimes claimed, dispenses with any need for the parties to have legal representatives. Its detailed nature means that each national Code is very much country specific in that it is a product of the customs and culture of that region and is designed to address internal matters. To that extent, and unlike the common law, it has little capacity to transcend national boundaries which clearly has implications for supra-national judicial bodies such as the European Court of Human Rights (ECtHR).

DOI: 10.4324/9781003415688-4

The Civil Code itself – in both France and Germany – is organised by subject with broadly worded clauses allowing a degree of flexibility that provides the judiciary with some – if limited – capacity to respond to emerging social changes.

Civil law systems

France and Germany share not just a civil law culture but also adherence to overarching national constitutions. However, their developmental histories are quite different.

France

The French Civil Code, though not the first of the national civil code systems, was the most thorough and influential. It introduced a national law for all of France to replace the patchwork of regional and municipal laws, charters, and customs. The principles underpinning the French system are drawn from the Declaration of the Rights of Man and of the Citizen[1] while the law is laid down in a codified statute form to be applied by the judiciary. The strong democratic and egalitarian traditions of this nation, developed through its revolutionary experiences of the late 18th century, have done much to shape contemporary family law. Largely redrawn in 1804 and known as the *Code Civil* or *Code Napoléon*,[2] the legislative intent was to establish a body of 'private' law – *droit privé* – to be administered through the judicial courts which were and are divided by jurisdiction: civil and criminal; each presided over by a *juge*, also known as a *magistrat.* This was and remains quite separate and distinct from 'public' or administrative law – *droit public* – administered through its own set of courts known as *les tribunaux administratifs*.

THE FRENCH CIVIL CODE

This addresses matters that concern the private lives and relationships of citizens – such as matrimonial and testamentary issues, inheritance, contract, property, etc. – and is now one of 60 codes.[3] The Civil Code is entirely secular in nature – a significant break with earlier laws – and is devoid of legalistic terminology making it a clearer and more accessible statement of the law than prevails elsewhere. It was devised to constrain the former powers of the judiciary, perceived as often exercised in support of the social elite to which they belonged and from which they owed their appointment, so Article 5 prohibited the judiciary from looking to previous caselaw or abstract principles rather than to the Code for sources of authority.

1 26 August 1789.

2 Formulated by Napoleon to give effect to the principles of the French Revolution, the Code was promulgated in 1804.

3 See, also, the Penal Code, which defines criminal law, and the Family Code, the Civil Code, and the Social Security Code.

OTHER CHILD-RELATED CODES

There are many Codes (see, further, Chapter 3), some of which have a bearing on the welfare interests/rights of children. Of considerable importance is the Code of Social Action and Families (*Code de l'action sociale et des familles*),[4] created in 1953 and formerly known as the Family and Social Aid Code, as it includes the *Aide sociale à l'enfance* child protection responsibilities and authorises out-of-home placements for children admitted to the state care system. The Juvenile Criminal Justice Code (*Code de justice pénale des mineurs*), overhauled in 2021 for the first time since its introduction in 1945, forms the basis for contemporary juvenile justice. The associated Code for Regulating Criminal Proceedings (*Code d'instruction criminelle*) established in 1808, formed the basis for the modern inquisitorial system of criminal courts in France, Article 294 of which mandated the court appointment of a lawyer for anyone without legal representation (see, further, Chapter 4). The Education Code (*Code de l'éducation*), which unites all legislative and regulatory provisions relating to the French educational system, is clearly of importance to children and their families.

CODIFICATION

Codification is not mandatory: large parts of French law are not codified; the *Droit Administratif*, for example, is devoid of codification and is constructed through caselaw. Administrative law in its entirety is a creation of the *Conseil d'Etat*.

Germany

The German Civil Code, or versions of it, preceded the Napoleonic Code in France: the *Codex Maximilianeus bavaricus civilis* was promulgated in Bavaria in 1756, followed by the *Allgemeines Landrecht* in Prussia in 1794, and the West Galician Code in Galicia (then part of Austria) in 1797. The Napoleonic era, however, transferred the French Civil Code to much of the Germanic regions and it was not until the reunification of many traditionally Germanic states in 1871, and the introduction of the *Bürgerliche Gesetzbuch* in 1900, that the German Civil Code was imposed as a unifying legal system throughout Germany and its empire.[5] This instrument codified the private law for the new German empire and subsequently provided a model for national civil codes in many countries as diverse as Greece, Japan, Thailand, and Switzerland.

The Civil Code continued relatively intact throughout the Nazi era, surviving the East/West division and the ultimate reunification of Germany. It has since been amended several times, most extensively in 2002 when 'the Law of Obligations' – one of the five main sections of the Code – was fundamentally reformed.

4 Created by Decree no. 56-149 of 24 January 1956.

5 See, further, Zimmermann, R., *The German Civil Code and the Development of Private Law in Germany*, Oxford University Press, (2006), at: https://ouclf.law.ox.ac.uk/citation/

THE GERMAN CIVIL CODE

The Civil Code has been described as the centrepiece of the German legal system, meaning that it not only provides the main source of authority for civil law issues but it also serves as a reference point for discrete areas of law – such as commercial law – which build upon and refer back to provisions in the civil law. Unlike its French counterpart, the German Civil Code would seem to be more abstract in its terms and thus less prescriptive, allowing for a degree of interpretation which the judiciary have utilised to permit both some flexibility when applying it and some incorporation of precedents.

For present purposes, it is the family law section (*Familienrecht*) which is most important. This is codified in two parts: ss 1297–1588 deals with the law of marriage (including marital property schemes, divorce, and other related issues), and ss 1589–1921 deals with the regulations on the parent-child-relation including descent, legal guardianship, alimony, and other matters.

OTHER CHILD-RELATED CODES

In addition to the Civil Code, a number of other Codes have varying relevance for children and their welfare interests and rights. These include: the Social Code, Book VIII of which relates to Child and Youth Care and governs service provision for children and youths, disabled children and youth, and child protection; and the Criminal Code, particularly s 225 (maltreatment and neglect) and ss 176 cc which relates to child sexual abuse.

Family, the law, and the ECtHR

Core principles have always had a formative influence on the adjudication of family law issues and on the development of its body of law. To that extent, the ECtHR, particularly by embracing United Nations Convention on the Rights of the Child (UN CROC) provisions, has tended to adopt the more principle-led approach of the common law, rather than the codification approach of civil law, as it interprets and applies family law in relation to contemporary relationship issues. What was once little more, in effect, than a law of divorce with attendant issues, has now become greatly more complicated as it adjusts to prioritise a concern for the welfare interests and the rights of children, the furtherance of which requires careful navigation through a maze of competing traditional values, religious beliefs, cultural context, and the demands of public policy. A task for which the guidance of common law principles, rather than the slide rule of the civil law, at times seems more appropriate.

Family law in a civil law context: France

Family law ceased to lie exclusively within the jurisdiction of the Catholic Church and became a secular matter to be addressed by the civil courts in 1791. As such it tends to be largely consolidated within the Civil Code, and also to some degree in the Code of Civil Procedure, within which subdivisions systematically address all related matters and provide a comprehensive taxonomy of associated rules. Most family law matters come within the jurisdiction of the *juge aux affaires familiales*, while matters relating to children fall within the jurisdiction of the *juge des enfants*, and identifying which court will be assigned to hear the case will be determined in accordance with Article 1070 of the Code of Civil Procedure (see, also, Chapter 5).

The family in France

In 2014, a study by the French National Institute for Statistics and Economic Studies found that the 'family' in France tends to take the form of either: a nuclear family (68%), consisting of children living with both parents under the same roof; a single-parent family (21%), where children live with one of their parents; or a blended family (11%), in which children live in a reconstituted family. Interestingly, by 2019, the most common type of French family comprised a couple without children.[6] In recent years, less than half of all French families have marital status.

MARRIAGE

Since the end of the 18th century, while marriages may still be performed in accordance with religious beliefs they have no legal validity. Instead, along with all other aspects of family law, marriage is now defined as 'private' law, a secular matter, to be officiated by a civil ceremony in the town hall.

FAMILY UNITY

The ECtHR has consistently found that family ties may only be severed in very exceptional circumstances and everything must be done to preserve relationships and, if and when appropriate, to rebuild the family.[7] This approach has long been adopted in France. In particular, when it comes to separating mothers from newborn babies, the ECtHR has held that the state justification for doing so must be extraordinarily compelling.[8] Paradoxically, the French state has always regarded the right of such a mother to separate herself from her baby – absolutely and permanently – as quite lawful.

Family breakdown

The Civil Code, Articles 143 to 226, provides rules generally in relation to marriage: of which Articles 212–226 address spousal relationships, Articles 227–309 relate to marriage breakdown, and Articles 203–211 deal with parental obligations

6 See, further, at: https://www.statista.com/topics/6723/families-in-france/
7 *Gnahoré v. France*, Application No. 40031/98, (2000).
8 *K. and T. v. Finland*, Application No. 25702/94, (2001).

(see, further, Chapter 6). The grounds for divorce are: mutual consent, acceptance of the principle of marital breakdown, fault, or breakdown of communal life. In the first instance, when a mutual consent divorce is decreed by a court, a child is entitled to be heard by the judge. Judicial separation is available under the Civil Code, Articles 296 to 308, or a marriage may be annulled on the grounds that essential conditions have not been met (e.g. underage, bigamy, incest, etc.).

As has been pointed out,[9] there is no equivalent in French law to the common law concept of pre-nuptial or post-nuptial agreement, under which parties can contractually, and in advance, organise all the financial consequences of their divorce, together with the administration and allocation of assets and the desired care arrangements for any children, both during the marriage and in the case of divorce. Instead, spouses are free to enter into a marriage contract (*contrat de mariage*), the main purpose of which is to determine their own matrimonial property regime which will govern the couple's marital rights and be applied in the event of a divorce. On marriage breakdown, French law relies on the concept of 'community of assets' to divide spousal property in accordance with the personal assets of each spouse before the marriage and the assets acquired during the course of the marriage, the latter being divided equally.

The Civil Code imposes a duty on both parents (married or not) to contribute to the upbringing of their children, and to financially support them, the amount payable being determined, as elsewhere, in accordance with the parents' income, financial resources, and the child's needs. It continues to be payable after the child reaches 18 years of age until he or she has become self-reliant and, if appropriate, has completed secondary or tertiary/university education.[10]

PROCEEDINGS

The jurisdiction of the *juge aux affaires familiales* to determine family matters is governed by Article 1070 of the Code of Civil Procedure in accordance with which the hearing of proceedings is allocated to one of the 173 *Tribunal Judiciaire* on the basis of the applicant/s residence (*ratione loci*). Given the absence of any equivalent to the common law concept of 'domicile', an applicant's residence has been defined by the *Cour de Cassation* as the place where a person has fixed the permanent or habitual centre of his/her interests.[11] The court considered that this could be ascertained by reference to matters such as: location of the family home, and the place of habitual schooling of the children; an individual's place of work; location of an individual's family, friends, etc.; and the location of their assets.

9 See, further, Thomson Reuters, *Practical Law*, at: https://uk.practicallaw.thomsonreuters.com/6-615-3545?transitionType=Default&contextData=(sc.Default)&firstPage=true

10 The Civil Code, Article 373-2-5.

11 Civ 1st, 14 December 2005, No. 05-10.951. See, also, the Court of Justice of the European Union definition of habitual residence in the case C-523/07 of 2 April 2009.

Law No. 2019-222 of 23 March 2019 radically reformed divorce proceedings by promoting amicable settlements and, wherever possible, transferring proceedings from the court to a process managed by lawyers and a notary (*notaire*).

Children

The main provisions relating to the welfare of children and parental responsibility are to be found in the Civil Code, Articles 371 to 387-6, which in particular states that the separation of parents does not affect the rules and principles governing the exercise of parental responsibility[12] which implies that the separated parents continue to exercise joint parental responsibility over their children. The court may, however, in exceptional circumstances (physical abuse or gross negligence) and in the light of the best interests of the child, grant exclusive and sole exercise of parental responsibility to one of the parents. In the case of divorce, the court will rule on the matter of parental responsibility, residence, contact, and child support. In the case of unmarried parents or civil partnerships, it is theoretically possible for them to separate without any court order being made in relation to their children. In all the above instances, the parents may decide to manage the above matters by way of private agreement (see, further, Chapter 6).

PARENTING ARRANGEMENTS

A change to the law in 2002[13] established that, as a primary principle, in the case of separation of the parents, a shared/alternate residence order should be made in favour of both parents when the circumstances justify it.[14] In most shared residence cases, the child will reside with each parent on alternate weeks. In making an order in respect of a child, particular regard will be had to: the age of the child, the distance between the parents' homes, the availability of both parents and their capacity to communicate, the existence of any parental conflict, and the opinion of the child. The judge will often order that the primary residence of the child be with one parent, and grant the other contact rights, or decide that the non-resident parent's visitation rights will be exercised in a contact centre with possible conditions attached.[15]

When ruling on parental responsibility matters, the judge will have regard to: agreements entered by the parents or the existing status quo; the age, wishes, and feelings of the child; the ability of each parent to fulfil his/her responsibilities and to respect the rights of the other; expert evidence, especially regarding the age of the child; any violence or psychological pressure exercised or existing between the parents; and any welfare reports.[16] If the parents agree on parental responsibility

12 The Civil Code, Article 373-2.
13 Statute n° 2002-305 of 4 March 2002.
14 The Civil Code, Article 372-2-9.
15 Ibid., Articles 372-2 and 373-9.
16 Ibid., Articles 373-2 and 373-11.

matters, the judge will make an order mirroring their agreement, unless it does not sufficiently protect the best interests of the child or one of the parent's consent to the agreement was not given freely.[17]

RIGHTS OF THE CHILD

French law does not recognise the right of a child to be a party to proceedings relating to him or her. However, a child has a right to be heard in all proceedings concerning him/her and can be assisted for this purpose by an appointed legal aid lawyer for child representation (*Avocat d'enfant*). Parents have an obligation to inform the minor child of their right to be heard in all proceedings relating to him/her.

In addition, the child has the right to maintain personal relations with his or her ascendants.[18] Contact rights with other family members or third parties (for example, a stepparent) are at the discretion of the judge, who must, in all circumstances, take into consideration the best interests of the child.

Family law in a civil law context: Germany

The introduction of the Marriage Law and Family Law Reform Act 1976 was an important milestone in the development of family law (even if restricted to West Germany). It returned the law of divorce to the Civil Code and introduced the concept of 'Family Law Courts' with jurisdiction over matrimonial affairs and related matters. Though subsequently amended, the principles and provisions of the 1976 Act continue to provide the basis for establishing and dissolving marital status. Family law, generally, is now to be found largely in the Civil Code, ss 1297 to 1921, and related amendments, but Article 6 of the Constitution is also important, as are many provisions in the Social Code, and so also is the Law Concerning the Proceedings in Family Law Cases and Cases of Non-contentious Matters (*Gesetz über das Verfahren in Familiensachen und in Angelegenheiten der freiwilligen Gerichtsbarkeit*), ss 111 to 270. Family law cases are defined in s 111 of the latter and family law dispute cases are defined in s 112.

The family in Germany

The demographic profile of contemporary Germany is decidedly top-heavy: the elderly proportion of the population is the largest in Europe, globally it is probably second only to Japan; and, with a birth rate of 1.5 children per woman, the European average being 1.58, it has the lowest proportion of children. As they are a scarce resource, children and their welfare interests are highly valued in this society. As contemporary German society has become more pluralistic so also have family

17 Ibid., Articles 373-2 and 373-7.

18 Ibid., Article 371-4.

forms become more diverse. Indeed, the definition of 'family' was expanded in 2017, when a law[19] was passed allowing same-sex marriages and equalising their rights with those of heterosexual couples. While slightly more than half of all families are marital, usually with perhaps one child, the overall numbers of same-sex and single-parent family units are growing as also are the numbers of single adults living independently, who currently constitute more than a third of all households.

MARRIAGE

Marriage in Germany is constitutionally ensured – under Article 6 – of special protection by the state. It is governed by the fourth book of the Civil Code (*Bürgerliches Gesetzbuch*), ss 1297–1588 which endeavours to re-affirm traditional conservative values. As stated in s 1353:

(1) Marriage is concluded for a lifetime. The spouses are mutually bound to a matrimonial community of life.

However, it then goes on to make a significant concession to gender equality and the realities of contemporary social life by pointedly correcting the gender-specific guidance for the stereotyped roles of spouses that had featured in previous provisions relating to marriage. It declares that:

(2) One spouse is not bound to comply with the demand of the other spouse for the establishment of the community, if the demand constitutes an abuse of right or if the marriage has foundered.

As in France, marriage is a strictly secular affair,[20] officiated as a civil ceremony in the town hall. Therefore, a marriage contracted elsewhere on exclusively religious terms will not be recognised in Germany.

FAMILY UNITY

The German Constitution (*Grundgesetz*) assertively protects marriage, family unity, and the welfare interests of children. Article 6 declares that:

1. 'Marriage and the family shall enjoy the special protection of the state'.
2. 'The care and upbringing of children is the natural right of parents and a duty primarily incumbent upon them. The state shall watch over them in the performance of this duty'.
3. 'Children may be separated from their families against the will of their parents or guardians only pursuant to a law and only if the parents or guardians fail in their duties or the children are otherwise in danger of serious neglect'.

19 The law added the following sentence to Article 1353 of the *Bürgerliches Gesetzbuch:* 'Marriage may be entered into for life by two persons of different sex or of the same sex'.
20 The Civil Code, s 1310.

4. 'Every mother shall be entitled to the protection and care of the community'.
5. 'Children born outside of marriage shall be provided by legislation with the same opportunities for physical and mental development and for their position in society as are enjoyed by those born within marriage'.

As a signatory state to the European Convention on Human Rights, Germany respects the right to family unity as being inherent in the right to family life. As a signatory state to UN CROC, it upholds the best interests principle as stated in Article 3(1) which requires Member States, when assessing the best interests of the child, to, in particular, take into account the principle of family unity. Moreover Article 9 states that a child has the right not to be separated from his or her family unless separation is deemed to be in his or her best interests. States are obliged to facilitate the family reunification of unaccompanied minors and to always apply the best interests principle when doing so.[21] In 2021, the ECtHR, in response to a request for advice from the Federal Administrative Court regarding the 'retention of family unity' in the context of migrants seeking refugee status, re-affirmed the importance of this principle.[22] More recently, in 2023, the Court of Justice of the European Union found that the strict requirement to submit an application for family reunification in person meant that, for some people, family reunification was impossible. The Court ruled that it was impermissible for states to insist that applications for family reunification are made in person at a diplomatic post.[23]

Family and family breakdown

The primary statutory sources of law in relation to marriage, marital breakdown, and the welfare of children are: the German Civil Code (*Bürgerliches Gesetzbuch*), ss 1297–1921; the Law Concerning the Proceedings in Family Law Cases and Cases of Non-contentious Matters, ss 111–270; and the Law on Same-Sex Marriages (*Gesetz zur Einführung des Rechts auf Eheschließung für Personen gleichen Geschlechts*). Guidance as to the interpretation of these statutory provisions is provided by the decisions of the regional Courts of Appeal (*Oberlandesgerichte*), the Federal Supreme Court of Justice (*Bundesgerichtshof*), and the Federal Constitutional Court (*Bundesverfassungsgericht*).

DIVORCE

Divorce in Germany is governed by the Civil Code, ss 1564–1568, while related court proceedings are to be found in the Law Concerning the Proceedings in Family

21 *Mubilanzila Mayeka and Kaniki Mitunga v. Belgium*, Application No. 13178/03, (2006) and *Johansen v. Norway*, Application No. 17383/90, (1996).

22 See Case C-91/20, ECLI:EU:C:2021:898, at: https://eur-lex.europa.eu/legal content/EN/TXT/PDF/?uri=CELEX:62020CJ0091&from=IT

23 See Case C-1/23 PPU, at: https://www.infomigrants.net/en/post/48305/no-requirement-to-apply-in-person-for-family-reunification-eu-court-rules

Law Cases and Cases of Non-contentious Matters, ss 133–150. The grounds for divorce are that the marriage has irretrievably broken down.[24] This applies where the spouses have lived apart for either: one year and both of them want the divorce; or three years and one of them wants the divorce; or if conjugal relations no longer exist and cannot be restored.[25] There is no fault-based ground for divorce and it will not be granted if doing so would cause the respondent significant hardship (for example, if he or she was suffering from a severe and deteriorating illness). Judicial separation will be granted: if the spouses are living apart; and/or if there is no 'domestic community' between them and it is clear a spouse does not intend to create this because he or she rejects conjugal community.[26] A marriage may be annulled for the usual reasons of fundamental contractual defect.[27]

PRE-NUPTIAL AGREEMENTS

Unlike France, pre-nuptial or post-nuptial agreements under which parties can contractually, and in advance, organise all the financial consequences of their divorce, have been established in Germany since the Middle Ages.[28] All arrangements concerning the marriage, the matrimonial property rights, and the consequences of a divorce, can be made in a marriage contract.[29] Two decisions – of the Federal Constitutional Court and the High Court of Justice in 2001 and 2004, respectively – introduced the principle that a marriage contract cannot undermine the proper application of the law which could happen if the marriage contract starts with unequal negotiating positions (for example, pregnancy) or leads to an obviously unilateral and unjustified burden on one party. If the contract has undermined the proper application of law, at the date the parties concluded it, then it would be viewed as *contra bonos mores* and therefore invalid.[30]

DISTRIBUTION OF ASSETS

On the breakdown of a marriage each spouse remains the sole proprietor of his or her assets, and also of any assets that he or she has acquired before as well as during the marriage. The principle of community of accrued gains is the statutory regime

24 The Civil Code, s 15651.

25 Ibid., s 1566.

26 Ibid., s 1567.

27 See, further, Martiny, D. and Schwab, D., 'Grounds for Divorce and Maintenance Between Former Spouses', (2002), at: http://ceflonline.net/wp-content/uploads/Germany-Divorce.pdf

28 See, further, Thomson Reuters, *Practical Law*, at: https://uk.practicallaw.thomsonreuters.com/8-575-0676?transitionType=Default&contextData=(sc.Default)&firstPage=true

29 The Civil Code, s 14081.

30 Ibid., s 138. See, for example, the following rulings of the Federal Supreme Court of Justice (*Bundesgerichtshof*):

> *BGH 17.10.2007 – XII ZR 96/05*; *BGH 09.07.2008 – XII ZR 6/07* and *BGH 18.03.2009 – XII ZB 94/06*; and *BGH 29.01.2014 – XII ZR 303/13*.

governing matrimonial assets and means that only the increase in the assets' value is divided equally. A spouse has the right to post-matrimonial maintenance only if he or she has care responsibility for any children and is unable – for reasons of age or health – to find employment or is unable to find employment that offers parity of remuneration with the other spouse. Since the 2008 reforms, maintenance claims can now be time limited and reduced where appropriate.[31] The parent without direct care responsibility must pay child maintenance, the amount of which varies according to their income.

PROCEEDINGS

These are generally held in camera with one judge presiding over the hearing though three will do so if the case goes to the regional Court of Appeal (*Oberlandesgericht*).[32] An ultimate right of appeal lies to the Supreme Court (*Bundesgerichtshof*).[33] As in France, in the absence of any equivalent to the common law concept of 'domicile', an applicant's residence is determined in accordance with where that person has the most social and economic relations, that is, the person's centre of life,[34] as supported by family and professional relationships.

In proceedings concerning care and visitation rights, the parties do not have to be represented by a lawyer. In such proceedings, the court has an obligation to reach an amicable arrangement.

Children

The main provisions relating to the welfare of children and parental responsibility are to be found in the Civil Code, ss 1626–1689b, which in particular states that the separation of the parents does not affect the rules and principles governing the exercise of parental responsibility[35] which implies that the separated parents continue to exercise joint parental responsibility over their children. In the case of unmarried parents or civil partnerships, it is theoretically possible for them to separate without any court order being made in relation to their children. In all the above instances, the parents may decide to manage matters by way of private agreement: court orders for custody, joint custody, or visitation rights will only be made in response to an application from one of the parties. Without an application, the court may, however, in exceptional circumstances (physical abuse or gross negligence, mostly if such are reported to the court by the Youth Welfare Authorities) and in the light of the best interests of the child, grant exclusive and sole exercise of parental responsibility to one of the parents.

31 KG, 13. ZS – FamS – decision of 13 September 2013, 13 UF 94/13.

32 Law on the System of Judicature, s 1191(a) and (b).

33 Ibid., s 133.

34 *Bundesgerichtshof*, FamRZ 2002, 1182 f.

35 The Civil Code, ss 1626 and 1671; see *Zorn*, Das Recht der elterlichen Sorge, 3rd ed. 2016, at p 124 cc.

PARENTING ARRANGEMENTS

German law makes a strict distinction between parental custody, which is the right and duty of parents to care for their child,[36] and the right of visitation. As a rule, if the parents are or were married, they retain, even after separation and divorce, joint parental custody of their children, meaning that they must consult with each other and make joint decisions in relation to all long-term issues in respect to matters such as religion, education, and medical care. Only in very exceptional cases will the courts give one parent sole parental custody (see, further, Chapter 8).

The issue of whether the Civil Code allows the courts to order joint custody, or whether this is only feasible with the consent of both parents, has exercised the judiciary. In 2017, the Federal Supreme Court of Justice stated that the welfare of the child is the sole criterion,[37] consequently it is for the courts to decide without requiring both parents' consent. The judicial transfer of the right to determine residence to one of the parents has no binding effect with regard to a later decision on contact.[38]

As regards unmarried parents, since 2014 an amended version of the Civil Code, 1626(a), states that the parents have joint parental custody if they make a declaration to that effect, if they marry each other, or if the Family Court transfers joint parental custody to them. The amended law provides the father with an opportunity to apply for joint parental custody and the Family Court must make such an order, provided this is in keeping with the welfare interests of the child. There is no longer any legal presumption that paternal custody could be, *per se*, necessarily detrimental to the welfare of the child. Similarly, if an unmarried father has shown sustained interest in the child,[39] he will be granted visitation rights and the right to information concerning the child. Only if this is against the best interest of the child will those rights be refused. However, where the parents are unmarried and have not declared their wish for joint custody, this will only be granted if neither of the parents applies for it. Otherwise, the mother retains sole custody.[40]

As regards visitation rights the rule is that every parent, recognised as such in law, has the right to contact with their own child but without such recognition parental rights are very limited unless there is evidence of sustained interest.[41] Where the parents are separated, regardless of whether they are married, and they cannot agree on contact, either can ask the Family Court to decide on the extent and content of the right of contact. The right, and the form it takes, varies in accordance with the age of the child. In any case the court will appoint a so-called *Verfahrensbeistand*, a kind of guardian for the child.[42] This person mediates

36 The Civil Code, s 16261.
37 *Bundesgerichtshof*, 01.02.2017, XII ZB 601/15.
38 *Bundesgerichtshof*, 27.11.2019 – XII ZB 512/18.
39 The Civil Code, s 1686a.
40 The Civil Code, s 1626 II and III.
41 The Civil Code, ss 1626 III, 1684.
42 *Gesetz über das Verfahren in Familiensachen und in Angelegenheiten der freiwilligen Gerichtsbarkeit*, s 158.

between the parents, speaks with the child, and then makes a recommendation to the judge on the basis of the subjective interests and the welfare of the child, which in most cases is determinative.

RIGHTS OF THE CHILD

In general, a child's right to make independent decisions increases with age.[43] In particular, in the court setting, a child of any age has the right to the services of a guardian (*Verfahrensbeistand*), the appointment of whom is a mandatory duty of the court and once appointed the guardian, as mentioned above, will ascertain and represent the views of the child.[44] If aged 14 or older, the child has a right to be heard directly by the court. If younger, he or she has a right to be heard if either their views are considered to have a bearing on the decision or there are other good reasons for doing so. As a rule even very young children – from three or four years of age – are heard by the court. An inverted right is apparent in the rule that divorce is impermissible if its continuation until the end of the first year of separation is in the interests of the children.[45]

A child has the right to a recognition in law that his or her residence is not necessarily that of the parent or person with care responsibility[46] but may instead be held to be where their lives are centred (determined on the basis of relations to family, friends, and school, etc.),[47] which will most often – but not always – be the same as that of their carer. Some courts assume that the child's residence becomes habitual after six months.[48] Only after reaching the age of 18 can a child make a claim for maintenance on his or her own behalf; until he or she reaches that age any such claim must be made on their behalf by the parent with care responsibility.

Conclusion

While the civil law has evolved somewhat differently in all countries – in response to the influence of national culture, custom, and religion – it has remained essentially a legal system centred on the legislature with the effect that the law is determined more by prescribed provisions than judicial pronouncements. However, codification of the law does not fit very well with the complications and nuances of family life. Other areas of law – relating to companies, insurance, employment, etc. – lend themselves more readily to a systematic and standardised approach. The common law approach, with its reliance on precedents and principles, offers a

43 The Civil Code, s 1626 II.
44 Law Concerning the Proceedings in Family Law Cases and Cases of Non-contentious Matters, s 158.
45 The Civil Code, s 1568.
46 *Bundesgerichtshof*, FamRZ 97, 1070.
47 *Oberlandesgerichte*, Hamm FamRZ 91, 1466.
48 *Bundesgerichtshof* 78, 293, 301; Köln FamRZ 91, 363 f.; Hamm FamRZ 91, 1346; Bamberg FamRZ 96, 1224 f.

good deal more elbow-room for addressing the complexities, and responding to the fluidity, of the many and varied issues afflicting contemporary family life. Indeed, the welfare of the child principle is arguably so socially contextualised by centuries of immersion in the common law and so legally shaped by successive caselaw precedents as to be not wholly comprehensible if viewed solely through the lens of the civil law.

Part II

France

3 Policy, principles, legislation, and courts

Introduction

The Republic of France, a thriving developed nation with a population of some 67 million people, has a legal system based on the civil law under the umbrella of a constitution.[1] The principles underpinning that system are drawn from the Declaration of the Rights of Man and of the Citizen[2] while its basic rules are to be found in the Civil Code.[3] The law is laid down in codified statute form to be applied by the judiciary in what is a unitary state but one in which its regions, municipalities, and *départements* can vary considerably in their interpretation of national law and policy matters. The strong democratic and egalitarian tradition of this nation, developed through its revolutionary experiences of the late 18th century, has done much to shape contemporary family law.

This chapter begins with a brief background history of evolving policy and an explanation of some critical principle. It then outlines both the current legislative framework and the architecture of courts and regulatory bodies, commissions, etc., domestic and international. Its objective is to provide foundations for the following two chapters.

Policy, principles, legislation, and courts

The 'nation-state' concept probably originated in the post-revolutionary ideology of the French Republic. The Declaration of the Rights of Man and the Citizen in 1789 introduced the notion of a social contract, the joint engagement of citizen and state in furtherance of the common good of society, to achieve and maintain the goals articulated in the Declaration. The evolving sense of such a contract – resting on a particularly visceral understanding that citizens and the state are accountable to each other – would seem to have endured and resonates in contemporary laws.

1 See the Constitution of 4 October 1958 and also the preamble of the Constitution of 27 October 1946.
2 26 August 1789.
3 The Code was promulgated in 1804.

DOI: 10.4324/9781003415688-6

Policy

Arguably, there is a distinctive state/citizen relationship in France. The former is perceived by the latter as a largely benign authority – if a bit wayward – responsible for protecting the values and boundaries of society, preserving its cultural heritage, and ensuring the provision of public benefit services. The state would seem particularly supportive of family life, if in its more traditional form, and this is reflected in the twin institutions that have for so long been at the heart of the state's engagement with families and the welfare interests of children – *Aide sociale à l'enfance* (ASE) and the *juges des enfants.*

Background

Laws and government agencies with a specific brief for the protection of children in France are of relatively recent origin.[4]

Initially, as in other countries, the focus was on child labour. Safeguarding children from employer exploitation, from being drawn into the labour requirements of factories and farms, to the detriment of their health and safety, was a readily recognised social issue. The law of 22 March 1841 forbade work by children less than 8 years old and limited it to 12 hours a day for those aged 8–12.[5] By the 1880s, schooling for young children was becoming mandatory nationwide and this imposed further constraints on the availability of child labour. From the closing decades of the 19th century the beginnings of the present child protection agenda and the twin administrative and judicial responses were taking shape.

CHILD PROTECTION: RECOGNITION OF THE NEED

Child neglect and abandonment, a social phenomenon well known to the Church and charitable organisations long before its recognition in law, forms part of the history of all developed nations. In France, the Charity Organisation for Lost Children was founded by Saint Vincent de Paul in Paris in 1638, followed more than a century later by the Lost Children's Hospital in 1761 and by other institutions providing a safe refuge for 'foundlings'.[6]

By the mid-19th century child abuse was beginning to emerge as a significant and unavoidable social issue requiring a legislative response. Until then child neglect, parental chastisement, and child abandonment were prevalent and socially accepted; only abortion, infanticide, and grievous sexual assault constituted crimes

4 See, further, Guedeney, A., 'The Infant Protection System in France: How Does It Work?', *Infant Mental Health Journal*, Vol. 29(1), (2008), pp 5–20.

5 See Gosset, D., Hedouin, V., Revuelta, E., & Desurmont, M., *Child Abuse*, (1997), Masson, Paris.

6 See, further, for example, Grevot, A., 'The Plight of Paternalism in French Child Welfare and Protective Policies and Practices', Paper presented at the Positive Systems of Child Welfare Conference, Waterloo, ON, (2002), at: https://scholars.wlu.ca/cgi/viewcontent.cgi?article=1014&context=pcfp

against children.[7] Judicial statistics show a significant increase in prosecutions for the latter in the mid-19th century: from 1825 through to 1830, an average of 133 persons were tried annually for the rape and indecent assault of minors under the age of 15, reaching 809 from 1876 through to 1880. Awareness of a need to provide legal protection from this and other forms of deliberate harm came in 1852 with the reported case of Celestine Doudet who was found guilty of abuse for administering corporal punishment to five English girls in school. Concern was taken to a new level in 1860 with the public dissemination of research findings into abused and battered children conducted by Ambroise Tardieu, a professor of forensic medicine in Paris, who presented 32 cases of abused children, including 17 under 5 years of age and 5 infants, 18 of whom had died from abuse. He faced strong disbelief from the medical community, particularly when he described the existence of sexual abuse.

From the middle of the 19th century, French law and the French state slowly began to become more concerned with protecting children from abuse and exploitation, as was evident in the laws of 1832 and 1863 against child molestation, which culminated in the law of 1908 banning the registration of children under the age of 19 as prostitutes. There is an argument that this approach was helped by the fact that France recognised the existence and scope of child sexual abuse, even incest, well before its 'discovery' by the common law nations.

CHILD PROTECTION: DEVELOPING A JUDICIAL AND ADMINISTRATIVE RESPONSE

In 1912, the first significant response to the growing public awareness of abused, neglected, and abandoned children came with the appointment of specialist judiciary – the *juge des mineurs* – with a specific jurisdiction for children. Then, in 1935, an important decree on child protection was passed which, by requiring educative assistance or supportive services to parents of children at risk, established what was to become a characteristic indicator of the state/family relationship in France: vulnerable families were to be offered supportive preventative consensual state intervention before – hopefully instead of – coercive child removal and criminal proceedings for child abuse/neglect. Not until 1943, however, during the Vichy administration, was a specialist agency – the *Aide sociale à l'enfance* – instituted to provide social assistance for children. On 2 February 1945, in the immediate aftermath of World War II, a framework of judiciary and courts for children was established together with a framework of protective services – the *Protection maternelle et infantile* (PMI) – for mothers and babies/toddlers.

The role and functions of the ASE, as defined in Articles L221-1 *et seq.* of the *Code de l'action sociale et des familles*, have become of central importance to child protection in France. Its mission, as identified on its website, includes 'prevention and support actions aimed at children and families with psycho-social difficulties

7 See, further, for example, Fuchs, R.G., 'Crimes against Children in Nineteenth-Century France', *Law and Human Behaviour*, Vol. 6, (1982), pp 237–59.

and actions to care for children who, for whatever reason, cannot remain with their families'.[8]

The PMI is a departmental service responsible for ensuring the health protection of mothers and children. As described on its website, it mainly organises consultations and medico-social actions for prevention and follow-up for pregnant women, parents, and children under 6, as well as family planning and family education activities. It also plays an essential role in the care of young children by, for example, training childminders, monitoring and inspecting them, and in the provision of other services for children under six years of age.

In short, the contemporary child protection system in France is a two-tiered system: judicial and administrative. As Blandine Mallevaey explains:[9]

> *The administrative* aspect of child protection is the responsibility of the *Aide Sociale à l'Enfance* (ASE), which is a departmental service whose role includes proposing support measures to parents (the measure will be implemented with their agreement). There are only 3 cases where protection becomes *judicial*: in an emergency, if the administrative measure fails, or if the parents refuse the administrative measure. In such cases, the children's judge will be asked to order an educational assistance measure, which is a judicial child protection measure that is binding on the family. The juvenile court does not intervene in the context of child protection, since it only has civil jurisdiction.

Contemporary policy strands

In France, as already mentioned, the state would seem to have a particularly strong investment in maintaining the fabric of society and this is apparent in its support for the family.

RESPECT FOR PARENTAL AUTHORITY AND BIRTH FAMILY UNITY

The French child protection system has always placed an emphasis on the maintenance of the parent/child bond. In the past this was augmented by a policy in which foster care was used extensively to provide support and respite for families unable to cope for reasons of poor health or poverty. This continued to be the case until the 1970s.

Current policy has been to keep parent–child separation to a minimum. This tends to result in less use of foster care for fear that it will disrupt or displace the birth parent/child relationship. However this can clash with the policy of keeping children safe in situations where the parents are known to be volatile and

8 See, further, at: https://www.diplomatie.gouv.fr/fr/adopter-a-l-etranger/faq-glossaire-textes-de-reference/le-glossaire-de-l-adoption/article/aide-sociale-a-l-enfance-ase

9 Note to author (22 June 2023).

home-based care presents a real risk of harm to their children. In the latter case, children may be entrusted to someone else when their protection so requires (see Article 375-3 of the Civil Code).

INSTITUTIONALISATION

Historically, the state assumed the care of many children abandoned by their parents due to the latter's poverty. These *pupilles de l'État* were housed in institutions and generally remained there for the duration of their childhood, though adoption – then as now – remained a possibility as there was no parent to object or whose consent would be needed.

Currently, institutional care remains very much in use, unlike in most other developed nations where it is considered harmful to a child's psycho-social development. The continued reliance on institutionalisation was regretted by the United Nations Committee on the Rights of the Child (UN CRC) in its 2023 communique.[10] Following a decision to provide out-of-home placement, a child is now most often sent initially to an institution for further assessment; he or she will rarely be placed directly into foster care. Young infants are often kept in institutional settings (albeit smaller in scale, better staffed, and with more attention given to the psychological needs of children than formerly)[11] for long periods of time. Recently this practice has been altered by the introduction of amendments to the Civil Code allowing the *juge des enfants* to entrust a child to the other parent or to another member of the family.[12] This may alleviate the risk of extended placements producing correspondingly extended attachment issues.

STATE PRE-SCHOOL PREVENTATIVE INTERVENTION

Childcare – an important element in any nation's preventative intervention strategy – is heavily subsidised in France: the state funds approximately 80% of the costs, and all cities, towns, and some villages have a local crèche (compared with an approximately 40% state subsidy in the U.S.). Because it is so affordable, the service is often accessed for quite young children; many are enrolled at two-and-a-half years of age.

Also, of considerable significance, are the multi-disciplinary health teams located in every *département* and which provide a free public health screening service on at least three occasions for every child below the age of two years. Across France, these doctor-led teams with responsibility for the health and the detection of abuse and neglect of infants, visit public daycare centres and public

10 See, further, at: https://www.diplomatie.gouv.fr/en/french-foreign-policy/united-nations/news-and-events/news/news-2023/article/united-nations-the-un-committee-on-the-rights-of-the-child-welcomes-the

11 Appel, G., 'An Attempt to Eradicate Deficiency in a Nursery', *Neuropsychiatrie de l'enfance et de l'adolescence*, Vols 4–5, (1982), pp 257–62.

12 See amendments introduced by the law of 7 February 2022 on child protection.

kindergartens. They have pediatricians, obstetricians, mental health physicians, and others available to assist as required, and all are trained to detect evidence of neglect or abuse. They provide an invaluable first line of defence in detecting a need for child protection.

JUGE DES ENFANTS: THE TWIN CIVIL AND CRIMINAL JURISDICTIONS

France has a singular approach to children who, for whatever reason, come before the courts. Their needs and deeds are viewed as symptoms of family vulnerability or dysfunction which requires 'education' in the form of assistance from social workers, psychologists, and other state-employed experts in family dynamics. Accordingly, the *juge des enfants* exercises both a civil and criminal jurisdiction and since the extension of the judicial remit in 1958 to include *assistance éducative*,[13] they have also had wide powers to direct supportive state assistance to vulnerable families. The thrust of the 1958 ordinance was both preventative, to encourage the judiciary to divert children away from possible future involvement in the criminal justice system, and protective of family unity in that it made available judicial options to avoid the withdrawal of paternal authority. The judicial jurisdiction in family proceedings is, however, restricted to public law issues.

The French approach is also singular in the way the legal system relates to children. There is no courtoom as such; the judge conducts proceedings in his/her office where all parties, including the child, are encouraged to speak directly to the judge. Legal representation is rare and the judge's role is less adjudicative but more that of a mediator whose aim is to encourage parents and child to consent to the appropriate steps needed to address the presenting issues. Moreover, the judicial role continues beyond the initial decision-making as he or she continues to manage the case thereafter, until such time as further intervention is not required, which may be some years after the initial hearing (see, further, below).

Principles

The principles guiding the state approach to the welfare interests and rights of children are generally those of a traditional nature and compatible with maintaining the integrity of the family unit.

The paramountcy principle

In 1997, the *Conseil d'Etat* ruled that Article 3(1) of the United Nations Convention on the Rights of the Child (UN CROC) – the child's interest must be a paramount consideration – was directly applicable to French law. However, this conflicts with

13 The *Cour de cassation* has ruled that jurisdiction in respect of *assistance éducative* proceedings is exclusive to the *juge des enfants* and has denied the *juge aux affaires familiales* any jurisdiction to order educational measures.

traditional presumptions favouring family unity and maintenance of the parent/child bond. It conflicts also with Article 375-1 of the Civil Code which states that the *juge des enfants* 'shall always strive to obtain family's consent to the measure envisaged'. Given that in many cases the child is before the *juge des enfants* due to parental abuse or neglect, when the interests of parents and child are clearly not synonymous and the associated measures will be correspondingly divergent, there cannot be any aggregated concept of 'family' consent. If paramountcy is to prevail then traditional presumptions and Article 375-1 will have to give way.

More recently, the CRC, in its 2016 report, acknowledged that the principle of the best interests of the child had been raised to the constitutional level and that the *Cour de cassation* and the *Conseil d'Etat* had jointly agreed on its paramountcy weighting. However, the Committee remained concerned that the right was not sufficiently integrated in practice and was not always properly assessed and applied in all government actions and decisions. It suggested that there should be a requirement for prior evaluative studies to be conducted to assess the impact of government bills and public investment on the welfare interests of children.

PARAMOUNTCY: CHILD CONSENT

The *Cour de cassation* has ruled that a judge has to 'take into account the feelings expressed by the minor and failing to do so is a ground for cassation' but 'is not bound by their expression'. This applies in particular to proceedings before the family court (relating to the exercise of parental authority, the child's residence, visiting and accommodation rights, etc.) in which the child 'may' be heard by the court.[14] On the other hand, as part of the educational assistance procedure before the *juge des enfants* (child protection issues), the judge is obliged to hear the child capable of discernment[15] and must therefore summon the minor to be heard, failing which the decision may be annulled. In addition, the Act of 7 February 2022 strengthened the *juge des enfants* obligation to hear the child as part of the educational assistance procedure by stipulating that he or she 'must systematically conduct an individual interview with the child capable of discernment at the time of his or her hearing'.[16]

A child's consent is also relevent in the context of adoption. Articles 345 and 361 of the Civil Code now provide (for plenary and simple adoptions, respectively) that the adoption of every child aged 13 or older is conditional upon the prior consent of that child. Article 348-3 requires the consent to be given before a notary public in France or abroad or before the diplomatic authorities abroad. If the child is a *pupille de l'État*, parental consent is instead given by the *Aide sociale à l'enfance*.

14 The Civil Code, Article 388-1.

15 The Code of Civil Procedure, Article 1182 para 2.

16 The Civil Code, Article 375-1. Author acknowledges advice from Blandine Mallevaey on this matter (note to author, 22 June 2023).

PARAMOUNTCY: ADOPTION

There is no suggestion in the Civil Code or other laws that the welfare interests of the child concerned are to be accorded a paramount legal weighting in adoption proceedings: Article 353-1 of the Civil Code is limited to stating that the court can only order an adoption if it is in the child's best interests. Indeed, the continuance of the '*accouchement sous X*' practice would in itself indicate that paramountcy has no part to play in adoption, as does the fact that every year only a small proportion of the childcare population exit state care by way of that route. Such facts caused the CRC, in its 2016 report, to urge 'the State party to ensure that the paramountcy of the best interests of the child is strictly observed regarding adoptions'.[17]

The parental rights principle

Paternal authority was abolished in France in 1970 when the term *puissance paternelle* in the Civil Code was replaced by *autorité parentale*.[18] Parental authority – defined by Article 371-1 of the Civil Code as 'a set of rights and duties, the purpose of which is the welfare of the child' – then replaced the concept of 'paternal authority' and was held to be inherently vested equally in both parents.[19] Despite this, the CRC, in the above-mentioned report, expressed concern that French law continues to refer to 'parental authority' which, as the Committee points out, is not conceptually compliant with the rights of the child and suggested that it be replaced by a term such as 'parental responsibility'.[20]

INALIENABLE

Parental rights are held to be inalienable but, arguably, the legacy of '*accouchement sous le secret*' and its continued role in adoption, illustrates quite the opposite: the continuing right of a mother to absolutely and irrevocably relinquish all parental rights would seem to be at odds with any interpretation of 'inalienability'. Moreover, as the challenge to maternal anonymity was unsuccessful in *Odièvre v. France*[21] – when the European Court of Human Rights (ECtHR) ruled that denying children given up at birth the right to later discover their biological parents' identity did not violate the European Convention – it remains the case that technically parental rights, at least in this context, weigh heavier in law than the welfare interests of the child. Also, and again supporting the traditional parental rights principle, there have been cases where the claims of a non-custodial but genetically linked parent have been found to be more closely aligned with a child's welfare interests than those of the person bearing actual day-to-day care responsibilities of a parent.

17 CRC/C/FRA/CO/5, at para 55.
18 See 4 June 1970 Law No. 70-459 as amended by the 4 March 2002 Law No. 2002-305.
19 Ibid.
20 CRC/C/FRA/CO/5, at para 49.
21 *Odièvre v. France* [2003] 1 FCR 621.

For example, in *Mandet v. France*[22] the Court deemed that the child's best interests did not necessarily lie where the child perceived them to be (i.e. in maintaining the established filiation and preserving emotional stability), but rather in establishing his 'real' (i.e. genetic) paternity.

PARENTAL RESPONSIBILITY AND CORPORAL PUNISHMENT

The CRC in its 2016 report expressed regret that France had declined to implement an earlier recommendation that it prohibit corporal punishment. It recommended explicitly prohibiting corporal punishment in all settings, including in the family, in schools and day care settings, and in alternative care and reiterated 'that no violence against children is justifiable and that corporal punishment is a form of violence, invariably degrading and preventable'.[23] Not until 2019 did France become the 56th country to achieve a full legal prohibition of all forms of corporal punishment of children in all settings with the passing of the Bill entitled *interdiction des violences éducatives ordinaires*.[24]

SHARING PARENTAL RESPONSIBILITIES

The principle of 'joint custody' – *garde conjointe* – is at the heart of French family law and applies regardless of marital status. It may be interpreted in the broad sense, as the joint exercise of parental authority, or in the narrower sense, as indicating that the child's residence may alternate between the home of each parent. In essence it means that both parents take all the important decisions affecting the child together and each plays an equal part in the child's life – their education and the provision of direct care and protection – for the duration of childhood.

The permanency planning principle

Permanency planning requires a placement to be one that ensures, as far as possible, that the child has a secure, stable, and loving family to support them through childhood and beyond, and to give them a sense of security, continuity, commitment, identity, and belonging. In the U.K. and the U.S. – if not more generally – the term 'permanency planning' is interpreted as meaning adoption, usually non-consensual: this would almost certainly be the presumption in relation to infants or young children who have suffered parental abuse, and would at least be a consideration for older children.

22 Application No. 30955/12, (2016).

23 Op. cit., at para 44. See, also, CRC/C/FRA/CO/4, para 58.

24 The law of 10 July 2019 on the prohibition of ordinary educational violence added to Article 371-1 of the Civil Code, which defines parental authority, that this authority must be exercised without physical or psychological violence. See, further, Council of Europe at: https://www.coe.int/en/web/children/corporal-punishment

For a French child in need of an out-of-home placement, the question of permanency planning will arise, if at all, on entry to the care system when the professionals concerned formulate the child's *projet pour l'enfant* (care plan). At that point the adoption option would be the automatic first choice where parental consent is available or is unnecessary, which would be the case if the child is one of the few designated *pupilles de l'État* or *sous le secret*. Otherwise, permanency planning – as it is known in the U.S. and the U.K. – most probably has no part to play. The alternative presumption in France is that the child will return to his or her family of origin and the *projet pour l'enfant* will be guided by that objective.

The proportionality principle

Both the proportionality principle and the margin of appreciation rule are regarded by the ECtHR as important mediatory mechanisms for reconciling differences in culturally determined national law with the broadly applicable standards established by the European Convention on Human Rights (ECHR). Given the particular culturally derived laws in France – for example, those relating to filiation and *sous le secret* – it is unsurprising that the principle has assumed a significant role in this country.

The singularity of its significance for French family law was illustrated by the *Mennesson* case[25] which triggered the first ever request from any nation to the ECtHR for an advisory opinion.[26] This concerned two children born in California through a surrogacy arrangement and the commissioning French couple's subsequent inability to obtain recognition in France of the parent/child relationship legally established between them in the U.S. The advisory opinion, delivered five years after the case was determined, considered – among other matters – the question of proportionality, and concluded that the French denial of recognition was not proportionate when it came to the children as the effect of that denial was far reaching in terms of their identity and legal status and was not compliant with their welfare interests. France had violated their right to respect for their private lives.

Legal system: legislation, courts, and representation

The Republic of France has a legal system that dates from Napoleonic times and which is naturally coloured by the socialist ethos of that time. Additionally, as a leading member of the Council of Europe, a signatory state to all major legislative instruments, and subject to the rulings of supra-national courts – particularly those of the ECtHR – France accommodates and contributes to an ever-growing layer of modern jurisprudence.

25 *Mennesson v. France*, Application No. 65192/11, (2014).
26 See ECHR 132 (2019).

Legislation: international law

France has signed and ratified the United Nations Convention on the Rights of the Child 1989[27] and its two Protocols.[28] The *Cour de cassation*, in a 10 March 1993 decision, ruled that the Convention did not have a direct effect, i.e. it only creates obligations for member states and therefore cannot be invoked directly by a party in a family proceeding. However, the administrative court, *Conseil d'Etat*, decided on 22 September 1997, that some of the provisions of the Convention were directly applicable, especially Article 3(1). Since 2005, the *Cour de cassation* has recognised the direct applicability of certain provisions of the International Convention on the Rights of the Child, in particular Articles 3.1 and 12.2. Subsequently, in *Harroudj v. France*,[29] the ECtHR ruled that the Convention must be interpreted as incorporating UN CROC which is also explicitly referenced by the European Committee of Social Rights.[30]

In addition, France has signed and ratified: the Hague Convention on Protection of Children and Cooperation in Respect of Intercountry Adoption 1993;[31] the Optional Protocol to the Convention on the Rights of the Child (2016); the Optional Protocol to the International Covenant on Economic, Social and Cultural Rights (2015); the Convention on the Rights of Persons with Disabilities and its Optional Protocol (2010); and the Council of Europe Convention on Action against Trafficking in Human Beings (2008). It has also signed the European Convention on the Exercise of Children's Rights (2008) and has signed but has yet to ratify the International Convention on the Protection of the Rights of All Migrant Workers and Members of Their Families (see, further, Chapter 1).

Legislation: domestic law

The hierarchy of French laws are ranked, in descending order of importance, as *lois organiques* (institutional acts akin to the Constitution), *lois ordinaires* (ordinary acts akin to statutes), and *ordonnances* (measures issued by government akin to regulations).

27 Signed and ratified on 26 January 1990.

28 Signed and ratified in 2000. The Optional Protocols on the sale of children, child prostitution, and child pornography, and on the involvement of children in armed conflict, as well as the ratification of ILO Convention No. 182 concerning the Prohibition and Immediate Action for the Elimination of the Worst Forms of Child Labour.

29 Application No. 43631/09, (2012) at para 42.

30 See *International Federation of Human Rights Leagues (FIDH) v. France*, Complaint No. 14/2003, (2004).

31 Signed on 5 April 1995 and ratified on 30 June 1998.

THE CONSTITUTION

The Constitution of France 1958,[32] as amended, incorporates the Declaration of the Rights of Man and of the Citizen 1789. For present purposes, it may be noted that a significant section of the Constitution is devoted to 'social welfare' which declares the entitlement of citizens in need of state support. This has since been augmented by reforms in 1930, 1932, 1946, and 1998 which have had the effect of extending social security to almost all citizens and in theory should ensure that vulnerable families receive assistance.

THE FRENCH CIVIL CODE 1804: PART VIII

This section of the Civil Code, subject to ongoing amendment, deals in some detail with parental authority, its exercise, the intervention of the family affairs judge, etc. It also deals with *assistance éducative* (i.e. child protection measures before the *juge des enfants*) and matters of adoption (Arts 343–60) and guardianship (Arts 361–70).[33]

STATUTE N° 2022-219, 21 FEBRUARY 2022

This legislation amends the Code of Social Action and Families and the Civil Code to further enable the legal grounds for recourse to adoption and to strengthen the status of 'wards of the state'.

STATUTE N° 2022-140, 7 FEBRUARY 2022

Dealing with child protection, this law amends the Social Action and Family Code, the Civil Code, and the Social Security Code to provide enhanced protection and support for children from the child welfare system (ASE).

STATUTE N° 2022-300, 2 MARCH 2022

This statute strengthened parental control over their child's internet access. It introduced 'terminal equipment intended for the use of online public communication services giving access to services and content likely to harm the physical, mental or moral development of minors'.

STATUTE N° 2021-478, 21 APRIL 2021

This statute was introduced to protect children from sexual crimes and incest. It amends the Penal Code by creating new sexual offences of which children can be victims.

32 Also known as the Constitution of the Fifth Republic. The first constitution was published in 1791 following the overthrow of the absolute monarchy that had perpetuated the *ancien regime*.

33 See, further, at: https://www.napoleon-series.org/research/government/code/book1/c_title08.html

STATUTE OF 11 SEPTEMBER 2019

This essentially created the current legislative part of the Juvenile Criminal Justice Code by replacing the law of 2 February 1945 in relation to child offenders. It restated the general principles applicable to juvenile justice, including: the primacy of educational over punishment; the special nature of juvenile justice; and the tapering of responsibility depending on age, with the age of criminal majority still set at 18. It introduced a 'presumption of non-discernment' for delinquent minors under 13 years of age.

STATUTE N° 2016-297, 2 MARCH 2016

Entitled 'Regarding the Protection of Children', this statute pursues the objectives initiated by the law of 5 March 2007 to

> contribute to the knowledge of the population of minors and young adults in danger benefiting from a child welfare benefit or a judicial measure of child protection, as well as that of the activity of child protection services; and to facilitate the analysis of the coherence and continuity of the actions implemented for the benefit of minors, their families and young adults under the protection of children.

One of the most noteworthy provisions of the Law concerns the payment of the back-to-school subsidy that the government pays to low-income families with children – *L'allocation de rentrée scolaire* – which will in future be paid into special government savings accounts for every minor in state care until he or she reaches the age of majority. Also, under Article 37, it directs that the court must appoint an *ad hoc* administrator to represent the interests of any minor in state care.

STATUTE N°2013-404 OF 17 MAY 2013

This legalised same-sex marriage and provided parity of legal status with heterosexual marriage.

STATUTE N° 2013-595 OF JULY 2013

This statute was for organising and planning the public school reform.

STATUTE N° 2013-711 OF AUGUST 2013

This redefined trafficking in persons to better capture the different forms of exploitation, including those involving children.

STATUTE N° 2012-301 OF MARCH 2012

This regulates the transmission of information for monitoring children in danger.

STATUTE N° 2007-293 OF MARCH 2007

The legislative intent was that this statute would reform child protection law by establishing the subsidiarity principle: the primary rights and responsibilities for ensuring the well-being of children was recognised to be that of their parents; the role of the state was to assist the parents and work in partnership with them; but it would intervene in situations of urgent risk to children and/or when parents were unco-operative. A centralised agency (CRIP) was established to gather information and co-ordinate professional roles in respect of children at risk.

In 2016 the CRC blamed the slow implementation of this statute as the cause of increased cases of children left at risk of domestic violence and unprotected at home and urged that it be speedily implemented by public authorities at all levels, including in terms of prevention, identification of children at risk, and quality of care interventions.[34]

STATUTE N° 2007-308 OF 5 MARCH 2007

This statute, amending Article 388-1 of the Civil Code, provides that 'the discerning child has the right to express his/her view in any judicial proceeding that concerns him/her. The hearing of the child (always in private) cannot be refused by a judge where this hearing is at the child's request'. As Francoz-Terminal comments, this was "a reform that greatly strengthened the right of a child to be heard and to express his/her views before a judge".[35] Though being heard is, of course, quite different from being able to make a meaningful contribution to decision-making.

STATUTE N°2005-744 OF 4 JULY 2005

The reforming statute aimed to improve the support to adopters, especially those engaged in intercountry adoption, and created the *Agence Française de l'adoption*[36] to assist such adopters. It strengthens the assistance and support given to adopters, once children have been entrusted to their care, by introducing mandatory post-adoption service provision to be delivered either by the adoption service of the local authority or by the *Agence Française de l'adoption.*[37]

Statute n°2004-1 of 2 January 2004

This established the *Observatoire national de la protection de l'enfance* (ONPE) which gathers and collates information on matters relating to child protection.

34 Op. cit. at para 49.

35 Note to author (20 December 2013).

36 See, further, at: www.agence-adoption.fr/home/

37 An alternative view of the impact of this law has been expressed by *Terre des Hommes* which asserts that:

> "Since the passing of a law on 4 July 2005, the involvement of the French Central Authority in 'strictly private' adoptions with non-contracting states has noticeably diminished. The situation is therefore highly alarming". See Lammerant, I. and Hofsetter, M. (eds) *Adoption: At What Cost?*, *Terre des Hommes*, Lausanne, Switzerland, 2007, at p 12.

STATUTE N° 2002-305 OF 4 MARCH 2002

This amended the parental responsibility provisions in Articles 371 to 387 of the Civil Code by providing a new definition for *autorité parentale*: a collection of rights and duties in respect of the child's welfare interest.[38] This reform also modernised the exercise of parental responsibilities.

STATUTE N° 2000-549 OF 15 JUNE 2000

This, the Education Code, compiles all laws and regulations in the field of education and higher education. It defines the general principles of education, its administration and organisation, and is of central importance to French youth. It was recently amended – by lois n° 2022-299 of 2 March 2022 to combat school harassment.

STATUTE N° 66-500 OF 11 JULY 1966

This statute, the basis of modern adoption, introduced the two legal forms of adoption that now exist in France: plenary adoption which severs the links between the child and its birth family and creates a new set of parental relationships; and simple adoption which institutes a second set of relationships with the adopting parent/s without severing the links with the family of origin. Whereas previously *legitimation adoptive* was restricted to two non-separated spouses, *adoption plénière* now became available to an unmarried person. Moreover, consensual adoption for both 'legitimate' and 'illegitimate' children was introduced for circumstances where both mother and father have given their consent. Pascale Salvage adds "Since 2005, France has suppressed the terms 'legitimate, natural, illegitimate'. As far as adoption is concerned, the only difference that remains is that unmarried couples cannot adopt in common".[39]

STATUTE N° 56-149, 24 JANUARY 1956

This, the all-important and much amended Code of Families and Social Action, compiles all legislative and regulatory provisions with a bearing on social action and the family.[40] It specifies and defines the administrative measures intended to provide various forms of support to families. The Code was amended by Law No. 2022-140 of 7 February 2022 to provide enhanced protection and support for children in the child welfare system (ASE).

38 The Civil Code, Art. 371-1.

39 Note to author (19 June 2020).

40 See, further, at: *Code de l'action sociale et des familles* (C.A.S.F.) at: https://www.legifrance.gouv.fr/affichCode.do?cidTexte=LEGITEXT000006074069&dateTexte=20190508, *archived at* https://perma.cc/H7BU-RVD7

STATUTE N° 45-174 OF 2 FEBRUARY 1945

This foundation stone of the juvenile justice system substituted *assistance éducative* instead of accountability and punishment as the basis for the response of the system to child offenders.

STATUTE OF 28 MARCH 1882

Known as the Jules Ferry law (Article L131-2 of the Education Code) this guaranteed freedom of instruction by giving parents the choice of how their children are educated.

Courts

The French court system was subject to major structural reform in 2020 which amalgamated and reorganised the lower tiers. Essentially, though still complex, it is in two hierarchical halves: the 'judicial courts' with civil jurisdiction including on matters of personal status; and 'administrative courts', the *tribunaux administratifs,* which deal with matters of public administration law. The following is a bare outline of that system insofar as it relates to children.

Judicial courts

The jurisdiction of these courts includes proceedings concerning children – matrimonial, divorce, adoption, etc. – and these are heard within a hierarchy of courts presided over by the *Cour de cassation.* Access to the courts is facilitated by a more generous system of legal aid than is generally available elsewhere and would seem to be readily available.

COUR DE CASSATION

This, the Supreme Court of Appeals, sits at the apex of the court structure. It is not strictly an appeal court as it does not reconsider the facts of a case; instead it takes referrals from lower courts and either confirms or quashes decisions on the basis of their accuracy in terms of a correct interpretation of the law.

COUR D'APPEL

This appeal court hears appeals from decisions taken in the courts of first instance – on both public and private law matters – from which there is a fundamental right of appeal. There are a total of 36 such courts, locally based providing a relatively prompt appeal process thereby facilitating consistency in judicial decision-making, each organised into specialised chambers. An appeal may lie from this court – *en cassation* – to the *Cour de cassation.*

FIRST INSTANCE COURTS

These are organised according to civil or criminal jurisdiction and further divided in accordance with financial tariffs and gravity of offence.

Administrative courts

These deal with matters of public law. Issues relating to the French state, administrative bodies, etc. are processed through the administrative courts or *tribunaux administratifs*, the most superior of which is the *Conseil d'État*.

CONSEIL D'ÉTAT

This court was established in 1799 and has a double jurisdiction: as a court of first instance and as a court of appeal, neither of which have any direct bearing on children and their welfare/rights.

COUR ADMINISTRATIVES D'APPEL

Created in 1987, these determine appeals against decisions delivered in the administrative courts.

TRIBUNAUX ADMINISTRATIFS

These are ordinary courts of first instance with a largely civil jurisdiction (they also have a criminal jurisdiction restricted to misdeamours). They deal with public law issues that are outside the remit of the specialist courts.

Specialist courts

There are several specialist courts. Children and issues concerning their welfare interests – civil or criminal – will be brought in the first instance before the *juge des enfants*. Family matters, where issues lie between parents, will most often be heard before the *juge aux affaires familiales.*

JUGE DES ENFANTS

Initially appointed by an ordinance of 2 February 1945 to deal with young offenders, the jurisdiction of the *juge des enfants* is now defined by Article 151-3 of the *Code de l'organisation judiciaire* which states that the threshold of judicial intervention is evidence of danger to a child under the conditions specified in Article 375. Essentially, this confers a twin civil/criminal jurisdiction.

This is a very child-friendly judicial legal system. No formal application to the judge is necessary: parents, guardians, and children can invoke the jurisdiction of the *juge des enfants* directly and very informally by letter, phone-call, or by coming in person to court and requesting an appointment. Formal procedures are restricted to agencies, government officials, etc. The hearing is also very informal, taking place in the judge's office – never in a courtroom – conducted in a problem-solving rather than interrogative manner, and is very short.

JUGE AUX AFFAIRES FAMILIALES

The jurisdiction of this family court judge is largely confined to private law disputes. As Blandine Mallevaey explains, this judge:[41]

> has broad jurisdiction over the exercise of parental authority in a wide range of disputes: delegation, deprivation of the exercise of parental authority, disputes over the child's religion, health, schooling, etc., proceedings relating to the determination and residence of the child and rights of access and accommodation, etc. Since 2012, the court has also acted as a guardianship judge for minors, and is therefore responsible for guardianship and the emancipation of minors.

All issues regarding a child's maintenance or education, for example, are brought before this court under Article L213-3 of the *code de l'organisation judiciaire*.

Representation for children

Article 389 of the Civil Code, which recognised parents as not only having parental responsibilities in respect of their child but as also being his or her legal representatives, was repealed in 2015. Consequently, children are now parties to proceedings before the *juge des enfants* though not before the family court. As mentioned above, proceedings before the *juge des enfants* have always been deliberately informal, but following the 2015 reforms a child with party status is now entitled and more likely to be represented by a lawyer, but such representation has to be formally requested, it is far from mandatory. As Blandine Mallevaey comments "the time has come to consider the systematic appointment of a lawyer to accompany the child in educational assistance matters".[42] The previous informality and consensus management of hearings may well have made for a more child-friendly forum – more comprehensible and engaging for the subject – but it may also, conceivably, have diluted some basic principles of justice.

Article 1183 of the *Code de Procédure civile* gives the judge a discretionary power to order any kind of assessment (medical, social, psychological, or other professional contribution) regarding the welfare interests of the child. This will usually be the responsibility of the *Service Educatif Auprès du Tribunal* (S.E.A.T.).

41 Note to author (22 June 2023).
42 Ibid.

THE CHILD IN COURT

Under Article 388-1 of the Civil Code the *juge des enfants*, though not the family court judge, has a duty to hear any child – *capable de discernement* – in cases of educational assistance unless their age or state of mind does not allow it. The Act of 7 February 2022 strengthened the obligation of the *juge des enfants* to hear the child as part of the educational assistance procedure by stipulating that he or she 'must systematically conduct an individual interview with the child capable of discernment at the time of his or her hearing'.[43] The family court judge is not obliged to summon the child for a hearing. The latter has a right to be heard only if he or she so requests and provided that he or she is capable of discernment.[44]

CONSENT OF CHILD

Article 388-1 of the Civil Code now states that where a child wishes to be heard before the *juge des enfants* then their request must be granted. However, in its 2016 report the CRC remained concerned that little progress had been made to systematically ensure respect for the views of the child in all relevant contexts of life. It was concerned that the hearing of a child in legal proceedings was subject to a written request, and that the *juges des enfants* had dismissed such requests on such flimsy grounds as that they were poorly written. The Committee expressed further concern that children in vulnerable or marginalised situations, such as children in administrative placement and children with disabilities, were often not consulted in matters concerning them.[45]

Where the child is older than 13, then his or her personal consent is mandatory for both a plenary[46] and a simple adoption.[47]

Other official and regulatory bodies

France has much the same range of agencies, bodies, and commissions – including in relation to human rights – as can be found in most other contemporary developed nations. It should also be noted that a Secretary of State for Children was created in 2019.

43 The Civil Code, Art. 375-1.

44 See Mallevaey, B., *Audition et discernement de l'enfant devant le juge aux affaires familiales*, (2019), at: https://www-jac-cerdacc-uha-fr.translate.goog/audition-et-discernement-de-lenfant-devant-le-juge-aux-affaires-familiales-b-mallevaey-sous-la-direction-2018/?_x_tr_sl=fr&_x_tr_tl=en&_x_tr_hl=en&_x_tr_pto=sc

45 CRC/C/FRA/CO/5, at para 29.

46 See the Civil Code, Art. 345.

47 See Art. 360 *in fine* of the Civil Code: *L'adoption simple est permise quel que soit l'âge de l'adopté.* (…) *Si l'adopté est âgé de plus de treize ans, il doit consentir personnellement à l'adoption.*

AIDE SOCIALE À L'ENFANCE (ASE)

This organisation, branches of which are to be found in all *départements*, is of central importance to the welfare interests of French children. Its services are as defined by Article L221-1 of the code of social action and families (supplemented by the law of 5 March 5 2007 reforming child protection) and include: provision of material, educational, and psychological support to minors and their families in difficulty; facilitation of the social integration or promotion of young people and families; provision of urgent protection for minors in difficulty; provision for minors in the care of the service, in collaboration with their family or their legal representative; and preventative interventions to prevent ill-treatment of minors. Recent amendments to the Social Action and Family Code, the Civil Code, and the Social Security Code by the law of 7 February 2022 promise to ensure that the ASE will provide greater protection and support for children.

L'OBSERVATOIRE NATIONAL DE LA PROTECTION DE L'ENFANCE (ONPE)

In 2016, this lead agency for researching, disseminating, and advocating in relation to child protection matters replaced the *Observatoire national de l'enfance en danger* which was established in 2004.

AGENCE FRANÇAISE DE L'ADOPTION

Established on 18 May 2006, this agency is ostensibly a public body, accredited to mediate in all Hague-compliant countries and such other countries with which France has a partnership agreement, as the Minister may determine on a case-by-case basis. It is seen as having a dual status as both a state agency and an accredited body.

DÉFENSEUR DES ENFANTS

The national office of *Défenseur des enfants*, broadly equivalent to an Ombudsman, was established in 2000 and is recognised by the United Nations Committee on the Rights of the Child as the organisation designated to ensure that these rights are respected. It aims to ensure that the interests of the child have priority over all others. In 2016 the CRC expressed concern regarding the insufficient resources and visibility of the Defender of Children within the Defender of Rights, and the fact that the State party does not systematically consult the Defender of Children on bills affecting children's rights and does not sufficiently follow up on its reports and recommendations.

The *Défenseur* has the power to refer matters to the *Président du Conseil Général* and to the *procureur*.

Other

UNICEF, in its 2022 report,[48] claimed that 'existing public policies on children are numerous but very scattered, which hinders their legibility, effectiveness and visibility'. However, in its 2023 communique, the UN CRC welcomed the introduction of the new office of Secretary of State for Children and paid special tribute to the national strategy on prevention and the protection of children.[49]

Conclusion

In France, the state assumed its present primary role as a benign intervener in family affairs in the aftermath of World War II. The basic foundations of the French system for protecting the welfare interests of children were all put in place then and continue to function in much the same way. The main government agency – the *Aide sociale à l'enfance* – was established in 1943 to provide direct social assistance to children, and to families for the benefit of children, and its community-based offices are now to be found in every one of France's 101 *départements*. This agency is supported by the *Protection maternelle et infantile* which was established in 1945 with a specific brief to provide health care services for young mothers and their children before and for some years after the birth of their child. Perhaps of greatest importance, however, was and is the office of the *juge des enfants*. This was launched in 1945 with a twin brief for children involved with the civil and criminal jurisdictions of the law. In an interesting contrast with their common law counterparts, this judge is authorised to take direct case management responsibility for children found to be in need of care and protection or to be juvenile offenders.

The above institutional infrastructure – together with the provisions of Part VIII of the Civil Code, the Social Welfare and Family Code, and the Criminal Code – as reinforced by international law, provides the basic framework for applying the law relating to children in France.

48 See *Droits des enfants en France* (2022), at: https://unicef.hosting.augure.com/Augure_UNICEF/r/ContenuEnLigne/Download?id=480588C0-E8CD-4A6A-B8D8-80AAA060B4C4&filename=SynthDroitsEnfantsFrance2022_final_pages.pdf

49 See, further, at: https://www.diplomatie.gouv.fr/en/french-foreign-policy/united-nations/news-and-events/news/news-2023/article/united-nations-the-un-committee-on-the-rights-of-the-child-welcomes-the

4 The welfare principle in contemporary practice

Public family law – civil and criminal jurisdictions

Introduction

French family law – more so than its common law counterpart – treads an uneasy path between on the one hand emphasising and respecting the privacy of the family and the authority vested in parents to manage family affairs and, on the other, holding parents accountable for any failure in their responsibilities. The difficulties in managing that balance are most acute when it comes to weighing the needs and deeds of children against the interests of others in the fields of child protection and justice, respectively, which is the subject of this chapter.

The chapter deals with the public law as it relates to French children. It is in two parts: first the civil law (child protection, etc.); then the criminal (juvenile delinquency, etc.). It begins with a consideration of the state/family relationship, with state consensual intervention, the legal requirement to support vulnerable families, and the agencies and services available. It then considers the grounds for coercive intervention, the threshold of harm to a child that requires the state to investigate standards of parental care and protection. It examines the process whereby the responsibility for a child in need of care or protection transfers from parent to state and assesses the options then available in terms of out-of-home care for the child concerned. There is a particular focus on the state duty to rehabilitate a child with his or her family of origin. Attention is also given to the problems associated with unaccompanied migrant minors and trafficking. The second part of the chapter explores the legal system as it relates to child offenders. It considers preventative and remedial forms of intervention, the role of the *juge des enfants*, and the representation provided to offenders, and it identifies the custodial and community-based disposal options available to the court. It assesses the part played by the welfare principle relative to the requirements of justice.

Public family law: civil jurisdiction

The social construct of 'family' as defined in French law is quite singular. For legal purposes the rules and proceedings relating to family matters are to be found in the Civil Code, as significantly amended, but the Code itself is a product of the Napoleonic era and is conceptually rooted in the revolutionary ideology that gripped France at the turn of the 18th century. Central to the meaning then attached

DOI: 10.4324/9781003415688-7

to 'family' is the concept of 'filiation'.[1] This continues to be of fundamental significance in family law.

The concept of 'filiation' is socially rather than genetically determined. The law gives effect to this by ensuring that status relationships are ascribed, rather than automatically acquired, and puts in place rules governing how and why it may be conferred. So, French citizenship is not simply a consequence of being born in France, nor is French ethnicity seen as synonymous with its borders (it accommodates the *Quebecois*, for example, but not necessarily all resident Algerians or others with their own distinct ethnic orientation). Filial attachment with the ancillary right to claim the family name does not automatically come as a birthright (mothers can choose not to acknowledge their children). Family law has to be seen in this context: matters of individual and cultural identity, the role of the family unit in society, and the acquisition of status-based relationships are more socially determined than genetically prescribed.

Parents and state

On the whole, French family law manages conflict between the interests of child, parents, and state by giving primacy to the facilitative role of *assistance éducative* and placing this under the jurisdiction of the *juge des enfants* (whose jurisdiction is restricted to public law issues). Should consensual intervention fail, issues will return to the *juge des enfants* who will then exercise the court's coercive intervention either through the civil jurisdiction (to determine whether parental authority should be removed) or through the criminal jurisdiction (whether the alleged criminal activity is that of parent or child). The combined effect of Articles 2(1) and 6(2) of the Basic Law is to place an obligation on the state to assure children and adolescents that they will receive adequate and safe parental care. As is stated in Article 375-1 of the French Civil Code the *juge des enfants* 'shall always strive to obtain family's consent to the measure envisaged'. It is an important characteristic that distinguishes the French approach from most of the common law jurisdictions but is not dissimilar to that adopted in other European nations.[2]

Prevention: consensual intervention

This is the first of three possible stages of state intervention in family affairs on child welfare grounds. In keeping with a traditional French policy of state support to maintain family unity – rather than the U.K. emphasis on mediation and rescuing

1 See, further, Fulchiron, H., 'Egalité, Vérité, Stabilité: The New French Filiation Law after the Ordonnance of 4th July 2005', *The International Survey of Family Law*, Jordan Publishing, Bristol, 2006, pp 203–216.

2 See, further, Eglin, M., 'Judicial Child Protection in France and England: A Comparative Approach', (June 2001), at: https://www.afmjf.fr/Judicial-child-protection-in.html

the most vulnerable on family breakdown – this *assistance éducative*[3] intervention stage aims to invest the resources necessary to reinforce parental coping capacity and avoid future child protection measures. The legal duty to provide preventative services, as well as child care and protection, falls to the *Aide sociale à l'enfance* (ASE), a centrally managed but locally based state child protection service, which currently has national care responsibility for some 300,000 children. The ASE is supported, in the early years of pre- and post-childbirth, by the *Protection maternelle et infantile* (Maternal and Child Protection agency).

State duties to support families in need

In 1958, Article 375 of the French Civil Code was extended to allow the *juge des enfants* to order support for parents in the form of *assistance éducative* measures (*aide éducative en milieu ouvert*) when the health, the safety, or the morality of a minor is in danger, or when the conditions of his/her 'education' are gravely compromised. This extension replaced the former discretionary power of state authorities to offer assistance and is indicative of the state/parent relationship: there is a strong legal presumption that the care and protection of children is a family rather than state responsibility; the latter has a duty to take all possible measures to support parents in coping with their responsibilities; and the authority to direct consensual supportive intervenion duty rests with the courts rather than with government social services departments, as in the U.K.

SERVICE PROVISION

Aide éducative à domicile (AED) is the government agency responsible for providing educational and psychological support to parents to help them cope with the needs of their children. Laws of 1986 and 1989 require social workers and psychologists to provide assistance such as managing conflicts between parents and children, overseeing housekeeping budgets, school attendance, etc. There is a strong legal presumption that a child should remain in his/her family and that the latter should receive state support 'in order to overcome the material and moral difficulties it encounters'. That support may include the voluntary placement of a child in state care on a temporary basis for family respite reasons and parents may apply to a court for the exercise of parental authority to be delegated to the ASE for that purpose.

Interestingly, in circumstances where parental neglect is due to or associated with mismanagement of social benefits – *tutelle aux prestations sociales* (welfare payments, rent, etc.) – then French law provides that the *juge des enfants* may appoint a *tuteur* to administer those benefits in the interest of child welfare and to take such steps as may be necessary to improve the children's standard of living and to advise the family on rehabilitative measures.

3 The ordinance of 23 December 1958 created the modern concept of *assistance éducative* (assistance in upbringing).

SAFE HAVENS

The first such facility – *ruota degli esposti* – was, perhaps, established at the hospital in Marseilles in 1188 though other sources indicate that *tours d'abandon* or 'foundling wheels' were introduced by Saint Vincent de Paul in 1638 in Paris. Although officially prohibited in 1904, they had become irrelevant with the acceptance of the *accouchement sous X* procedure which continues to be the legally accepted means whereby a mother may anonymously relinquish her child.

Under Article 381-1 of the French Civil Code (Article 350 before the law n° 2016-297, 14 March 2016), an abandoned child is one who has been in the care of a private person, or an institution, or the ASE, for a full year during which the parents have shown no interest in him or her. At the end of that period the court must issue a declaration of abandonment unless the parents have been prevented from taking care of the child 'by any cause' (Law 2016-297, 14 March 2016). In almost all cases the child was in the care of the ASE, and the declaration gives him or her the status of *pupille de l'État*.

Protection: coercive state intervention

Under Article 371-2 of the French Civil Code parents are vested with the authority to 'protect the child in his/her safety, health and morality. They have in his/her respect a right and duty of custody, supervision and education'. Under Article 222-17 of the French Criminal Code any 'failure by the legitimate, natural or adoptive father or mother, without a legitimate reason, to comply with their legal obligations to the point of seriously endangering the health, safety, morals or education of their minor child' is a criminal offence.

Duty to promptly intervene

The *inspecteur de l'Aide sociale à l'enfance* will assess where there is evidence of 'danger' to a child and will refer the situation to the *procureur*, who may decide to invoke the jurisdiction of the *juge des enfants* or, in cases of serious abuse, will initiate the prosecution of suspected offenders.

The European Court of Human Rights (ECtHR) has found the French state to be culpable for failing to effect prompt intervention resulting in preventable harm.[4] For example, in *Association Innocence en Danger v. France* and *Association Enfance et Partage v. France*[5] it was severely censored for not providing unaccompanied migrant minors with access to health care services (see, further, below). So, also, in *Affaire A.L, v. France*,[6] which concerned a child who was only four months old when contested proceedings began but was six-and-a-half years old when they concluded. These protracted proceedings were found to have been wholly prejudi-

4 Note, however, that France launched a Global Action Plan 2015–2017 for the protection of children.
5 Application No. 15343/15, (2020).
6 Application No. 13344/20, (2022).

cial to the claims of the genetically linked applicant and to have compromised the welfare interests of the child.

MANDATORY REPORTING

The law 'Regarding the Protection of Children'[7] amended the Penal Code to broaden the scope of provisions that punish the failure to notify authorities when a crime has been committed. Previously, anyone who knew of neglect or abuse of a child of 15 years of age or younger was required to inform the police or other government authorities or risk a fine and up to 3 years in jail. The law now requires everyone, including close relatives of a perpetrator, to notify the authorities of any crime committed against any child (i.e. someone below the age of 18).

MULTI-AGENCY CO-OPERATION

Over the years there has been a good deal of criticism regarding the French child protection system, mainly as regards the availability of national statistical data and failures in inter-agency collaboration. There would seem to be much truth in the observation that:[8]

> Our system is generous and ambitious: it uses many different agencies and experts, and it offers many different pathways of care, but it succeeds only rarely in undertaking coordinated and efficient action, both protective and effective, over time. Apart from some isolated research, the different systems (i.e., services, preschool, health, psychologists, PMI, midwives, child mental health services, ASE, family judges, and judges for children) do not know much about each others' efforts in terms of child protection and may not collaborate about a particular child if they do not wish to do so.

Investigation

This, the second stage of state intervention on grounds of child welfare, becomes operational where there is evidence of sustained parental neglect. To determine whether or not such grounds exist the *juge des enfants* will normally request that an inquiry be undertaken.

INVESTIGATION AND EDUCATIONAL ORIENTATION (IOE)

This is the term used for what is a routine assessment of the child, their family, and the circumstances giving rise to concern which is conducted by a licensed

7 Statute n° 2016-297, 14 March 2016.

8 See, further, Guedeney, A., 'The Infant Protection System in France: How Does It Work?', *Infant Mental Health Journal*, Vol. 29(1), (2008), pp 5–20 at p 16.

agency. It comprises educational, social, psychological, and psychiatric reports regarding the child and their parents. In practice, these reports tend to be descriptive, with little evaluation and rarely any assessment of the child's attachments. They are seldom based on clinical observation of the child with parents, nor are structured situations with free play or developmentally appropriate tasks typically used. Developmental testing of infants is rare.

JUGE AUX AFFAIRES FAMILIALES

At this point a referral may be made to the *procureur* for court protection – rather than to the ASE for preventive measures – who will, if the facts so warrant, submit a prosecution to the *juge aux affaires familiales.* Under the Act of 8 January 1993 the *juge aux affaires familiales* (whose jurisdiction covers divorce, custody, and contact), is authorised to hear an application – either made jointly by parents and authorities, or by the latter alone where parents are deemed to have lost interest in their child for more than one year.

JUGE DES ENFANTS

Where the investigation reveals child protection concerns then the *juge des enfants* assumes responsibilty for the case. In relation to the ensuing judicial hearing, Eglin makes the following very interesting observation:[9]

> The focus of French proceedings is not on the abuse but on the partnership between the judge and the family. This is particularly illustrated by the fact that parents and children can directly invoke the *juge des enfants*' jurisdiction. Therefore, the circumstances in which the French *juge des enfants* intervenes are by nature different from those that fulfil the threshold criteria. It makes the French system close to a defence of the birth family and parents' rights ideology, where families and social services consider the *juge des enfants* as a protective father.

Eglin views this patriarchical approach as more oriented towards problem solving than decision-making: while 'in England, the paramountcy of the welfare of the child dictates to courts their course of action, in France, the whole system is constructed so as to promote the upbringing of the child by his/her parents'.[10] It certainly seems quite different from that practised in the common law nations where a pronounced adversarial process focuses on a forensic assessment of threshold of harm criteria and the judicial role is then necessarily more adjudicative (despite many claims that the U.K. system is investigative rather than adversarial). The

9 See, Eglin, M., 'Judicial child protection in France and England: a comparative approach', (June 2001), at: https://www.afmjf.fr/Judicial-child-protection-in.html

10 Ibid.

judicial hearing determines whether there are grounds to warrant the removal of parental responsibilities and their transfer to the ASE, or occasionally to another 'fit person' (now more likely to occur following the law of 7 February 2022*)*.[11] Such a transfer of parental responsibilities is determined by evidence of 'danger' to the child rather than parental fault (well-intentioned but ineffectual parental care is sufficient to satisfy the 'danger' criterion) and is anticipated to be on a short-term basis while every effort is made to restore effective parenting arrangements. It is also only made 'after hearing the child when the latter is capable of discernment'.[12]

In its 2016 report the Committee on the Rights of the Child (CRC) expressed deep concern about the absence of official statistics and the existence of reports documenting 'child battering'[13] and estimated that in France two children die each day, potentially attributable to domestic violence. It was concerned about the lack of a comprehensive strategy addressing all forms of violence against children and the high and increasing incidence of domestic and gender-based violence. It was also deeply concerned that parents who have been convicted of serious offences, including murder, against one or more of their children were allowed to retain their parental responsibility, thereby putting the rights to life, survival, and development of their other children at risk. The Committee recommended that France establish a national database on all cases of violence against children, including ill-treatment, sexual abuse and neglect, domestic violence, harassment, and bullying.[14]

Care proceedings

The *Tribunal de grande instance* (civil court) can order the removal of parental authority when parents put the health, security, morality, or education of their child in danger, or do not meet their responsibilities in relation to a child previously placed under an *assistance éducative* measure. This, the third stage of state intervention on child welfare grounds, is intended to protect a child from a clear danger of future parental abuse, or parental inability to ensure adequate protection from a known risk to their welfare interests, on a long-term basis. There is much evidence indicating that French children are in need of such protection. In 2020, for example, there were almost 40,000 officially recorded cases of child sexual abuse, 80% of which were against girls.[15] In 2021, 310,525 children were taken into state care which is much the same as in 2020.[16] There is also evidence that care proceedings are often delayed and are failing to keep up with the flow of children requiring protection. As the Justice Ministry has acknowledged, the situation deteriorated in

11 Amending the Civil Code, Art. 375-3.
12 Ibid.
13 Kempe, H., et al., 'The Battered-Child Syndrome', *Child Abuse & Neglect*, Vol 9 (2), 1985.
14 CRC/C/FRA/CO/5, at paras 27, 42, and 43.
15 See, Statista Research Department, (2022), at: https://www.statista.com/statistics/1246288/monthly-number-sexual-assaults-minors-reported-france/
16 See, further, *Les chiffres clés en protection de l'enfance* at: https://onpe.gouv.fr/system/files/publication/fs_chiffres_cles_pe_2021.pdf

2021: 'the increase in the average length of time it takes to implement courts' decisions in child protection cases is real'.[17]

CARE PLAN

A care plan, or *projet pour l'enfant*, is finalised by the judge after the authorities and the parent/s have explored and tested the options and agreed a way forward. Although it is not a legal requirement, the judge is expected to state the objectives of the plan and to give directions to the ASE on how they are to be achieved. The judge may choose to place the child either with the ASE, giving that agency discretion to place where it considers appropriate, or direct a specific placement in an educational or health institution.

EMERGENCY PROTECTION ORDER

Emergency protection is authorised under Article 375-5 of the Civil Code which allows the judge to order interim measures. In cases of urgency, Article 1184 of the *Nouveau Code de Procédure civile* does not require the judge to hold a hearing prior to ordering such protection. However, the *Procureur* has a duty to invoke the *juge des enfants*' jurisdiction within eight days. Emergency measures can last up to six months and can be renewed.

ASSISTANCE ÉDUCATIVE ORDER

An *assistance éducative* measure can last up to two years and is the option most frequently used by the *juge des enfants.* As there is no limitation on the number of renewals, this order may in practice remain in place for the duration of childhood.

This option, permitted under the policy of *service d'adaptation progressive en milieu naturel*, allows a child to return home as part of an intensive professional investment designed to improve parenting skills. It may require attendance at a supervised parent and child residential placement, an *accueil sequential*, which allows for a time share arrangement between family home and a specialised training unit. Article 375-2 of the Civil Code identifies this as the preferred placement: 'every time it is possible, the minor must remain in his/her current environment'. Alternatively, the judge may decide to protect the child by directing his or her removal from the parents, either placing the child with one parent, in a *foyer* (i.e. a residence) or a *pouponnière* (i.e. a day nursery), or in foster care.

The judge has a wide discretion to attach conditions such as 'resorting to an education or health institution, or having a professional activity'. Once issued, the order is normally given effect by the ASE which, before taking any decision, will ascertain the opinion of the child and obtain his/her parents' written opinion.

17 See, *Le Monde*, (15 May 2022), at: https://www.lemonde.fr/en/france/article/2022/05/15/france-s-deteriorating-child-protection-system-causes-long-delays_5983559_7.html

If parents are opposed to the decision taken by the ASE, they can apply to the *juge des enfants* for a variation of the decision. The two-year duration of the order remains under the managment of the same *juge des enfants* and will do so until the child reaches 18 years of age, unless terminated by a *plus-lieu à assistance éducative* order on the basis that the child is no longer in danger. During this time the parents retain all their rights, except those of 'custody' (a term no longer in use), and are consulted about decisions concerning the kind of placement and its location.

State care

In 2015 the French child care population was 295,357, a rate of 20.1% of all children under 18,[18] an increase from 2010 when the equivalent figures were 273,000 or some 19% of all children, and a dramatic increase since 1990 when they were 112,800 and 8% respectively. This increase has been noted by the CRC which has expressed concern regarding 'the growing number of children separated from their family, as ordered by the judiciary, particularly affecting children whose families live in poverty'.[19]

Foster care: partnership, rehabilitation, and concurrent planning

France, to a greater extent than the U.K., has a strong traditional preference for maintaining family ties. Consequently, it has relied on foster care as a more appropriate option than adoption for furthering the welfare interests of a child in state care. However, the relatively high proportion of the child care population in institional facilities has been a matter of concern to the CRC which advocates that the state should instead 'support and facilitate family-based care for children wherever possible, and establish a system of foster care for children who cannot stay with their families'[20] – a recommendation which avoids mentioning non-consensual adoption as a means of achieving family-based care.

INSTITUTIONAL RECEPTION AND ASSESSMENT

Initially, a child who has suffered abuse or neglect is most often placed in a residential facility where their particular needs will be profiled. They are very seldom sent direct to a foster home and indeed may never go there. The traditional reliance on residential facilities as the primary resources for children admitted to state care is shrinking less rapidly in France than in most other developed nations. In 2010, approximately 53% of children in state care were fostered and some 38.6% were in residential care, a distribution that had been fairly consistent for the previous decade. As of 2020, slightly less than half of the child care population (47%) were in foster care.

18 See, further, at: https://onpe.gouv.fr/chiffres-cles-en-protection-lenfance
19 Op. cit., at para 53.
20 See at: CRC/C/FRA/CO/5, at para 53.

FOSTER CARE

In its 2023 report to the UN CRC, the French authorities estimated the number of children in foster care as approximately 230,000.[21] It should be noted, however, that French statistical data in relation to child protection matters is difficult to find and at times difficult to understand.

Foster families – *familles d'accueil* – have been trained, paid, approved, registered, and regulated by the ASE since 1977. The numbers of children accommodated with foster families is distinctly low relative to other developed nations and of those so placed only a small proportion would seem to be in kinship placements (in 2007, an estimated 7% of children in care were placed with family members[22]). The reason for this is possibly policy driven: rather than replace the birth family with a foster or adoption family, a child in state care is placed in the neutral environment of a residential facility, thereby keeping open the possibility of reunification of a child with their family of origin. Parents are seldom stripped of their legal status and responsibilities. However, it should be noted that the law of 7 February 2022 has strengthened the probability of an increase in kinship placements.

Maintaining links between a foster child and their family of origin is a necessity, not only because the majority of the birth parents retain their parental rights and responsibilities, but also because Article 375-7 para 2 of the Civil Code gives parents a 'right of correspondence and visit'; this contact right is thus clearly assigned to parent rather than child. The CRC has expressed concern that some 'placement decisions are not taken with a view to ensure continuity of a child's familiarity with his or her surroundings, foster carers and environment'. It criticises 'the few opportunities for children to contact and meet with their families, at the geographic distance between the family home and the institutional care' and urges the authorities to 'facilitate the rehabilitation and social reintegration of children', adding, also, that there is 'insufficient consideration of the views and the best interests of the child when decisions on alternative care are made by the child welfare service (ASE)'.[23]

PARTNERSHIP AND REHABILITATION

Once in foster care, as Guedeney has noted, 'the principle of reunification with the biological family still applies, even though the parents may have made little

21 See, further, at: https://www.ohchr.org/en/news/2023/05/experts-committee-rights-child-praise-france-outreach-patrols-supporting-families

22 See, Thoburn, J., 'Globalisation and Child Welfare: Some Lessons from a Cross-National Study of Children in Out-of-Home Care', University of East Anglia Social Work Monographs, (2007), at: https://www.researchgate.net/publication/265357214_Globalisation_and_Child_Welfare_Some_Lessons_from_a_Cross-National_Study_of_Children_in_Out-of-Home_Care

23 CRC/C/FRA/CO/5, at para 54.

progress and even though the child may have developed strong attachment bonds to the foster family'.[24] This is corroborated by Eglin who explains:[25]

> Even in the most serious cases, the *Aide Sociale à l'Enfance* will always attempt to "repair" the relationship, in the belief that the child will never thrive if the damage is not repaired. If it is not possible, placements are usually designed to allow parents to retain a place in the child's life and to avoid depriving the child of his/her birth family.

This policy, referred to as 'the ideology of maintaining the parent–infant relationship at all costs' has been criticised. It is alleged that:[26]

> there is no systematic effort to listen to the child's feelings about the separation, to assess the child's understanding (or lack of understanding) of the situation, or to evaluate the ways in which contact with the parents helps or hinders the development of the child. Decisions rendered by judges who are informed by experts or by professionals of various agencies may not necessarily be based on the best knowledge available in the field, be it regarding attachment, infant development, or assessment of infants and parents. This is particularly true in the assessment of the parenting capabilities of individuals with mental disorders, when considering the suspension or resumption of parents' supervised visits with their children, or in cases of divorce when there are decisions regarding joint custody and shared time for infants

Nevertheless, the principle of maintaining or restoring the parent/child relationship has been established for some time[27] and confirmed by recent judicial rulings in the context of the problem of unaccompanied migrant minors.[28] There is a firm policy of family reunification, wherever feasible, for every child taken into state care. This is why out-of-home placements are on a temporary basis: placements authorised by *juge des enfants* and given effect by the *Aide sociale à l'enfance* in foster homes or in institutions cannot last more than two years, though in practice they are often renewed for a further two-year period. Indeed, the *Cour de cassation* has ruled that an out-of-home placement cannot be maintained unless justified in accordance with Article 375 of the Code. Article 375-2 emphasises the importance of using the *assistance éducative* procedure to correct the functioning of the family so that it is better able to protect the child. Indeed, the judge has a duty to regulate contact with

24 See, further, Guedeney, A., 'The Infant Protection System in France: How Does It Work?', *Infant Mental Health Journal*, Vol. 29(1), (2008), pp 5–20, at p 14.

25 See Eglin, M., 'Judicial Child Protection in France and England: A Comparative Approach', op. cit.

26 See Berger, M., *The Failure of Child Protection Services*, Dunod, Paris (2003).

27 See statute law in 1984 requiring planning for family reunification.

28 See *Mugenzi v. France*, Application No. 52701/09, (2014), a ruling on the right of family unity for refugees in France which confirmed a principle of wider application including for children in state care.

parents – a duty which, the *Cour de cassation* has advised, should not be delegated to the ASE – though, unlike in the U.K., this contact is not treated as a right of the child which is due to French law giving insufficient recognition and weighting to the separate welfare/rights of the child. The judge may allow the child to stay with his/her family for extensive periods of time (several weeks). This usually occurs as a preparatory stage to full rehabilitation of the child with his/her family.

Where a child in state care, under an *assistance éducative* measure, has had no contact with their parents for a full year then – following the required ASE application to the court – the child will be deemed to have been abandoned, unless good reason can be shown as to why the parents are not and will not be in a position to resume care responsibility. The court may then issue a declaration of abandonment.

Wards of the state

Pascale Salvage explains that a child is a *pupille de l'État* if: 1) his parents are unknown; 2) his parents have consented to his or her adoption when they put him or her in the custody of the social welfare; 3) he is an orphan without family; 4) there has been a declaration of abandonment in court; or 5) if he or she has been declared a ward after parental rights have been withdrawn by the court.[29] The two most common categories are 1 and 4. The majority of the children in the care of the local ASE are not *pupilles de l'État* and are not adoptable without their parents' consent which has caused the CRC to deplore 'the situation and status of children abandoned *de facto* but not *de jure* to ASE'.[30] Falling from 24,000 in 1977 to 7,600 in 1987, the number of wards of the state had stabilised at approximately 3,300 in 1997 but had declined further to 2,347 in 2010 though subsequently increased marginally to 2,626 by 31 December 2016.[31] In 2021 there were 3,965 *pupilles de l'État*, a significant increase of 14.5% on the previous year.[32]

Residential care

In France, a relatively high proportion of children in care are in residential facilities; indeed, a survey once concluded that 'France had the highest total of young children under three in institutional care in the E.U.'.[33] In 1990, of 112,800 children in care, 32% were in various forms of institutions.[34] In 2002–03 more than 2,000 children, all less than three years of age, were in residential units.[35] By 2007, of the

29 Note to author (19 June 2020).

30 Op. cit., at para 53(b).

31 See, further, at: https://onpe.gouv.fr/chiffres-cles-en-protection-lenfance

32 See, further, *Les chiffres clés en protection de l'enfance* at: https://onpe.gouv.fr/system/files/publication/fs_chiffres_cles_pe_2021.pdf

33 See Chou, S., and Browne, K., 'The Relationship Between Institutional Care and the International Adoption of Children in Europe', *Adoption & Fostering*, vol. 32(1), 2008, at p 47.

34 See Initial report to CRC, 1993.

35 See Chou, S., and Browne, K., op. cit., at p 44.

121,400 children in care, some 39% were in various forms of residential care. As of 2020, some 37% of the French childcare population were in such accommodation and a further 16% were in other non-foster home facilities, such as kinship placements and sheltered appartments. Orphanages, including those provided by SOS Children's Villages, are a long-established and socially accepted form of residential care for children. It has been said that:[36]

> problems which are common to institutions worldwide also are apparent in French institutions. They include rapid staff turnover and infants staying for very long periods, with no assessment regarding the effects of separation. Their care shifts among many different caretakers as they await the judge's decision regarding whether the child's parents are able to take care of the child again or if the child should be sent to foster care

In its 2016 report the CRC expressed its concern regarding cases of ill-treatment of children with disabilities in institutions and the insufficient independent monitoring of such institutions.[37] As Guedeney challenges: 'France must decide if institutions can ever be good enough for infants, or if they should be closed and children placed in foster family care, even in emergencies'.[38] In fact, however, the reliance on residential care is set to increase: as of 2022, the authorities had decided to create two new children's homes, though they will not be completed before 2024.

SECURE ACCOMMODATION

Due to a lack of facilities to contain children who harm themselves and refuse protection, the Ministry of Justice promoted the creation of *centres éducatifs renforcés* (CEF), where highly qualified teams of social workers and psychologists work intensively with young people. They mainly house young offenders. Article 375-4 of the Civil Code empowers a judge to direct that a child should attend an educational or health institution, and the *Cour de cassation* has interpreted this as allowing the judge to instruct the ASE to place a child in a specified setting.

Adoption

Under Article 347 of the Civil Code, the following may be adopted: children in respect of whom the mother and father or the Family Council have validly consented to adoption; wards of the state (found children, orphans,[39] and those whose

36 See Guedeney, A., 'The Infant Protection System in France: How Does It Work?', *Infant Mental Health Journal*, Vol. 29(1), (2008), pp 5–20, at p 14.

37 CRC/C/FRA/CO/5, at para 40.

38 Op. cit., at p 16.

39 Only those orphans without any extended family members able to undertake guardianship responsibility and therefore entrusted to Child Welfare Services.

parents having been deprived of all parental responsibility[40] are then entrusted to the ASE as *pupilles de l'État*); and children declared abandoned under the conditions noted above and provided for in Article 350. Overseas children may also become the subject of adoption by French adopters (see, further, Chapter 6).

DOMESTIC VOLUNTARY ADOPTION

The distinction between plenary and simple adoption has always given the French adoption process a different profile from other countries, particularly those belonging to the common law tradition. In French law, adoption is essentially a consensual process. Once the child's filiation to both parents has been established, their consent is necessary, unless grounds exist for this to be dispensed with (see, further, Chapter 6).

ADOPTION FROM STATE CARE

Conceptually this is problematic in France where parental ties have been regarded as legally inviolable, except in the most extreme circumstances.

Article L224-4 of the Social Welfare and Family Code governs the adoption of children from the public care system. Once declared a ward of the state, law 2016-297 requires that the child be placed for adoption if this is considered to be in their best interest.[41] This is not always achieved. In 2001, only 1,195 wards had been placed in a family with a view to adoption. By the end of 2003, out of 2,882 such wards (average age two years and ten months), only 1,009 were so placed; by 2010 this was true for about one-third but by 2016 nearly half were placed in families for adoption. If not placed within the first few months of becoming wards, children are unlikely to be so later on: 78% of placements occur within the first six months and 95% within two years. So, for example, in 2010 some 45% of children had been adopted within a year of their being warded. In aggregate, 68% of children exit from the status of ward via adoption.[42] In 2021 there were 613 adoptions of *pupilles de l'État*, which was 4% more than in the previous year.[43]

In practice, adoption from public care is confined to the small minority of children designated wards of the state though this may be altered by the law of 21 February 2022 which amends the Code of Social Action and Families and the Civil Code to secure recourse to adoption and to strengthen the status of 'wards of the state'. The latter are fostered with a family approved for adoption or for whom the

40 See Article L224-4 of Social Welfare and Family Code.

41 Article L225-1, as amended in 2016.

42 See, further, ONED at www.oned.gouv.fr-contact@oned.gouvr.fr.
It reports that in 2010 children were adopted as opposed to 714 in 2009. These children were very young (77% less than one year old) and were adopted through para 1 of article L224-4 of the CASF (73%) and by a *département*-registered family (84%$).

43 See, further, *Les chiffres clés en protection de l'enfance* at:
https://onpe.gouv.fr/system/files/publication/fs_chiffres_cles_pe_2021.pdf

foster family has submitted an adoption application. They must share the home of their future adoptive parents for at least six months before the plenary adoption decision[44] (see, further, Chapter 6 for 'adoption from state care').

Unaccompanied migrant minors, detention, and trafficking

According to the UNICEF 2022 report,[45] 'since 2012 at least 33,786 children have been detained', mostly in Mayotte, a French overseas territory highly exposed to irregular immigration from Comoros. It adds that in all probability the country has a significant population of clandestine child migrants. In its report to the UN CRC, the French authorities estimated the number of unaccompanied minors in the state in 2022 as approximately 41,000.[46]

The ECtHR, in *Popov v. France*,[47] noted that the United Nations Convention on the Rights of the Child encourages states to take appropriate measures to ensure that a child seeking to obtain refugee status enjoys protection and humanitarian assistance. The CRC, however, in its 2016 report, was doubtful about the French authorities' commitment to this policy and expressed concern regarding 'the situation of migrant children, particularly unaccompanied migrant children'.[48]

Rights and welfare interests

The right of children – including unaccompanied migrant minors – to be reunited with their parents is well recognised in France.[49] It is a right with application when such a child is found in France, and when a child's parents are facing deportation from France. Reunification of a child with their parents is often crucial to safeguarding their welfare interests.

In 2016 the CRC found that the French authorities 'do not sufficiently consider the best interests of the child as a guiding principle in all initial assessment processes and subsequent arrangements'. It drew attention to the fact that the circular of 31 May 2013 (for equitable distribution of services provided to unaccompanied migrant children) had been 'partially annulled by the *Conseil d'Etat* decision of January 2015 resulting in insufficient quality of care and protection of children and refusals by certain municipalities to provide such protection'.[50] It also noted the 'precarious situation of children and their families in refugee camps … such as in

44 Article 345 of the Civil Code.

45 See *Droits des Enfants en France* (2022), at: https://unicef.hosting.augure.com/Augure_UNICEF/r/ContenuEnLigne/Download?id=480588C0-E8CD-4A6A-B8D8-80AAA060B4C4&filename=SynthDroitsEnfantsFrance2022_final_pages.pdf

46 See, further, at: https://www.ohchr.org/en/news/2023/05/experts-committee-rights-child-praise-france-outreach-patrols-supporting-families

47 Application Nos. 39472/07 39474/07, (2012).

48 Op. cit., at para 69.

49 *Mugenzi v. France*, Application No. 52701/09, (2014).

50 CRC/C/FRA/CO/5, at para 73.

Calais and … the refusal by authorities to register children and the insufficiency of venues and services to provide them with appropriate and adapted protection'.[51] Efforts are being made to alleviate the plight of children in such camps. Currently three specialist foster care agencies – *Fondation Grancher*, the *Service d'accueil familial du département de Paris*, and the *Service d'accueil des Mineurs Isolés Etrangers du département du Pas-de-Calais* – are attempting to provide services for unaccompanied migrant children.

In this context the case of *International Federation of Human Rights Leagues (FIDH) v. France*,[52] was important. It concerned Articles 13 (the right to social and medical assistance) and 7 (the right of children and young persons to social, legal, and economic protection) of the European Social Charter and the prohibition against discrimination. The complainant alleged that recent reforms of the *Aide médicale de l'Etat* (State medical assistance) and to the *Couverture maladie universelle* (Universal sickness cover) deprived a large number of adult and child migrants of their right to medical assistance.[53] The complaint cited several differences between the arrangements made for the exercise of the right to medical assistance by French children and those made for the exercise of the same right by the children of illegal immigrants, including the provision of spectacles and dental prostheses, and admission to the medical assistance scheme after a certain time. The Committee held that legislation or practices that deny entitlement to medical assistance to foreign nationals, even if they are there illegally, are contrary to the Charter. It found a violation of Article 17 on the basis that medical assistance to the illegal immigrant children in France is limited to situations that involve an immediate threat to life and that children of illegal immigrants are only admitted to the medical assistance scheme after a certain time. The decision in effect placed an obligation on the authorities to ensure that unaccompanied migrant children had equality of access to national social and health care services.

DETENTION

In total there have now been 11 ECtHR rulings against France for its detention of migrant minors, a practice described as a 'flagrant lack of humanity'. In the course of its rulings on three cases in 2023 the Court did not mince its words:[54]

> Taking into account the age of the minors, including an infant, the accommodation conditions at the Mesnil-Amelot detention centre and the duration of the detention, the Court considers that the competent authorities have subjected them to [inhuman or degrading] treatment. Having regard to the

51 Ibid., at para 75.

52 Complaint No. 14/2003, (2004).

53 Author is advised that the situation has since improved: free emergency medical aid is now available for persons in 'irregular siruations', even if there is some debate about its maintenance (note from Charlotte Pietri, 11 July 2023).

54 *Affaire A.C. et M.C. v. France*, Application No. 4289/21, (2023).

> inseparable bonds between a mother and her eight-month-old baby, and the emotions they share, the Court considers that the same is true [...] in the case of the applicant A.M., emphasising moreover that she was alone with her three minor children.

In 2022, a national report on detention centres and facilities revealed that 94 children were still detained in administrative detention centres (CRA) in Metropolitan France and 2,905 in the Mayotte CRA alone. In addition, at least 129 unaccompanied children were detained in the CRAs in Metropolitan France even though a juvenile court had not yet made a decision on their situation. It has been estimated that since the first ruling against France in 2012 for inhuman and degrading treatment, more than 35,000 children have been locked up in detention centres.[55] It would seem that despite very many repeated ECtHR condemnations, the French authorities are determined to persist in a policy that disregards the welfare interests and rights of tens of thousands of children.

TRAFFICKING

France is a signatory nation to the Palermo Convention[56] – the only universal, legally binding instrument on combatting human trafficking, particularly as regards women and children – and is also party to the Optional Protocol to the Convention on the Rights of the Child on the sale of children, child prostitution, and child pornography. Domestic law, specifically Article 225-4 of the Penal Code, criminalises sex trafficking and labour trafficking.

France has reported that its recent efforts in giving effect to the Convention have included:[57]

> opening a new children's shelter that could accommodate trafficking victims and adopting a national action plan (NAP) for children exploited in commercial sex, including child sex trafficking. The government established a new unit of eight investigators specializing in the exploitation of children in commercial sex, which included child sex trafficking, as well as a cooperation mechanism for victim assistance on police operations with a civil society network.

Nonetheless, the UN Special Rapporteur on Trafficking in Persons, Especially Women and Children was sufficiently concerned about the issues that arose in two

55 See, further, at: https://www.statewatch.org/news/2023/may/detention-of-children-european-court-of-human-rights-rules-against-france-11-times/

56 The supplementary protocol to the United Nations Convention against Transnational Organized Crime, General Assembly resolution 55/25 of 15 November 2000 (known as the 'Palermo Convention'). France also ratified the Council of Europe Convention on Action Against Trafficking in Human Beings (**known as the 'Warsaw Convention') in 2008.**

57 See U.S. Department of State, *2022 Trafficking in Persons Report: France* at: https://www.state.gov/reports/2022-trafficking-in-persons-report/france/

cases concerning France to make an *Amicus Curiae* submission to the ECtHR in 2021,[58] in which she made the important point that 'the recruitment, transportation, transfer, harbouring or receipt of a child for the purpose of exploitation shall be considered trafficking even if this does not involve any of the means.[59] In other words, consent is irrelevant regardless of whether any means have been used'.[60] Given that many of the young women and girls soliciting in France, as elsewhere, find themselves in that situation as a result of voluntarily migration, followed by exploitation, it is clearly important that their status as victims be respected. As the Rapporteur expressed it, 'States have a positive obligation to take operational measures to protect victims, or potential victims, of trafficking'.[61]

Moreover, the U.S. 2022 report identifies significant failings in French efforts to protect the welfare interests of the children involved, mentioning that:

> police continued to arrest and prosecute child victims of forced begging and forced criminality and deport undocumented migrants … funding for victim assistance decreased compared with the prior year and was generally insufficient. Furthermore, the government again did not take effective steps to address the 3,000 to 4,000 unaccompanied Comorian children at risk for sex and labour trafficking in Mayotte.

Particularly worrying is the reference to 'the significant increase in children exploited in commercial sex in the past few years, which NGOs estimated to be between 10,000 and 15,000 predominantly French girls, in April 2021', which caused the national rapporteur to publicly urge the government 'to adopt a clear criminal policy against the sexual exploitation of children'.[62]

Public family law: criminal jurisdiction

The criminal jurisdiction for children can probably be dated to the end of World War II when the ordinance of 2 February 1945 introduced the first *juges des enfants* who exercised both civil and criminal jurisdictions.[63] This legislation, which continues in force, was based on the principle that educative measures – or welfare considerations – had to take precedence over punitive ones. It was an approach

58 See Mullally, S., 'Submission by the UN Special Rapporteur on Trafficking in Persons, Especially Women and Children, in the Cases of *H.F. and M.F. v. France* (App. No. 24384/19) and *J.D. and A.D. v. France* (App. No. 44234/20) before the European Court of Human Rights', (2021). Available at: https://ssrn.com/abstract=3933138 or http://dx.doi.org/10.2139/ssrn.3933138

59 Citing Council of Europe Convention on Action against Trafficking in Human Beings (n 3) Art. 4(c). See also Palermo Protocol (n 18) Art. 3(c).

60 Ibid., at para 16.

61 Ibid., at para 19.

62 Op. cit.

63 The criminal and civil jurisdictions being authorised by the 1945 Ordinance and Articles 375 ff. of the French Civil Code, respectively.

that has led through a succession of youth justice reforms to a continuing welfare orientation in the 21st century.

The system

The *juges des enfants*, exercising their dual jurisdiction, remain the centrepiece of the legal system as it relates to children, which falls within the responsibilities of the *Protection judiciaire de la jeunesse* (PJJ), a nation-wide state service for juveniles. However, serious offences committed by 16- to 18-year-olds are now tried by the Juvenile Assize Court composed of three professional magistrates and a jury of citizens. This court can either order educational measures, impose fines and prison sentences, or offer the option of restorative justice. The fact that judges, diagnostic social workers, and social workers in education share the same office accommodation must facilitate teamwork and the co-ordination of professional expertise. This has not, however, prevented the CRC from recommending that France 'establish specialized juvenile court facilities and procedures'.[64]

Age of criminal responsibility

Article 122-8 of the French Criminal Code states that it is for a judge to determine whether a child has attained a sufficient degree of discernment to be held criminally liable for their actions: in effect a child, however young, may be found to have such discernment, though this must be proven.[65] From the age of 10 a child may be tried in a criminal court and from the age of 13 will be treated in law as an adult. In its 2016 report the CRC expressed regret that the age limit had not been raised and recommended that it be established at 'not below the age of 13 and requiring the child's capacity of discernment'.[66] In its 2023 report to the CRC, the French authorities advised that revised juvenile justice legislation introduced a legal definition of 'discernment': minors were not held responsible if found to have a lack of discernment, and all minors were presumed to not have sufficient discernment until proven otherwise.[67]

CHILDREN IN COURT

The *Tribunal de grande instance* (criminal court) can order the removal of parental authority where parents have been sentenced for a crime committed in relation to their child, whether the child was perpetrator or victim. Otherwise, children

64 Ibid., at para 82.

65 See ruling of the Criminal Division of the final Court of Appeal, (13 December 1956).

66 CRC/C/FRA/CO/5, para 81 (citing previous similar recommendation at CRC/C/FRA/CO/4, para 98).

67 See, further, at: https://www.ohchr.org/en/news/2023/05/experts-committee-rights-child-praise-france-outreach-patrols-supporting-families

accused of offences appear before the *juge des enfants* in his or her office where proceedings are conducted in a child-friendly manner (see, further, Chapter 4).

The binary distinction between civil and criminal jurisdictions has become somewhat blurred in recent years as legislators attempt to address the increase in criminal activity of young children. Since the adoption of the Law of 9 September 2002 – setting automatic minimum sentences for repeat offenders – *juges des enfants* have imposed 'educational sanctions' (Article 15-1) on children aged 10 to 13 which represent an intermediate stage between punishment and welfare considerations. In addition, the Law of 5 March 2007 on the Prevention of Delinquency, primarily targeting young offenders, has introduced a fast-track procedure whereby a young offender can be immediately brought before the judge. It also assigns more responsibility to civic authorities, specifically mayors, to develop preventative strategies that might reduce levels of delinquency. These laws have given the judiciary more discretionary powers, in cases of juveniles between 13 and 18 years of age, than is generally available to their counterparts elsewhere in Western Europe. In 2021, a total of 111,666 minors became subject to both the civil and criminal jurisdictions of the *juges des enfants*, a 9% increase on the previous year.[68]

ROLE OF THE WELFARE PRINCIPLE

The influence of the welfare principle can be seen, for example, in the fact that educative measures are imposed more frequently than imprisonment. It is also apparent in the recourse in recent years to restorative justice, which 'constitutes any measure allowing a victim along with the perpetrator of the offence to participate actively in the resolution of the difficulties resulting from the offence, and in particular in reparation for the harms of any kind resulting from its commission'.[69] This was initially introduced by Law No. 2014-896 of August 15, 2014 and subsequently amended by successive judicial reforms and young offender management policies.[70] This optional alternative to criminal proceedings offers a more welfare-oriented approach to offending, allowing a child to avoid being burdened by a criminal record.

There are also indications to the opposite effect: suggesting that welfare considerations are either not being allowed to influence the justice process or are doing so but the consequences are not very positive. One example of the former is revealed in the CRC's recommendation in its 2016 report that the authorities should 'refrain from treating children above 16 years of age as adults'.[71] An example of the latter might lie in the fact that the reoffending rate among minors is higher than among adults. However, recidivism is a difficult issue in France as elsewhere and there is

68 See, further, *Les chiffres clés en protection de l'enfance* at: https://onpe.gouv.fr/system/files/publication/fs_chiffres_cles_pe_2021.pdf

69 *Gouvernement de la République française*, 2020, Article 10-1. See, also, Circular of 15 March 2017 (*Ministère de la justice*, 2017).

70 See *Code de la justice pénale des mineurs*, Articles L13–4 and L112–8.

71 Op. cit.

little evidence that it would be reduced by a greater or lesser welfare orientation, just so long as in either case minors who commit an offence are not regarded 'as beyond redemption'.[72]

Court orders: community sentences

At the lighter end of the tariff of sanctions for convicted offenders are a menu of educative measures – including warnings, a requirement to remain at home, or supervision provided by the probation service – any one or combination of which might be imposed by the *juge des enfants.* These have become slightly more punitive since the 2002 law which introduced additional non-custodial sanctions including 'educational sanctions' for children aged 10–18 such as fines, confiscation, prohibition from entering specified places or facilities, attendance at training courses, and other forms of restitution and compensation.

Court orders: custodial sentences

The Perben Law of 2002 initiated a policy change towards juvenile offenders that emphasised accountability and consequences for deviant behaviour. It amended Article 2 of the 1945 Ordinance to introduce other penalties for those aged 13–18. It also provided for the creation of centres for *l'enfance délinquante.* These are 'closed educational centres' for minors subject to a judicial supervision measure or given suspended sentences subject to a period of probation; most are persistent offenders who have already been sentenced in criminal proceedings. Young offenders who do not comply with 'educational sanctions' – under the Law of 9 September 2002 – can be placed in such centres. Moreover, once they have reached the age of 13, minors can be given a prison sentence.

The CRC, in 2016, recommended that 'detention is only used as a measure of last resort and for the shortest possible period of time' and 'that children are not detained together with adults'.[73]

Child victims

The CRC recommendations in its 2016 report included that 'children who witness offences are provided with the same procedural guarantees as child victims' and 'guarantee that bans on defendants approaching or contacting victims are implemented and allocate resources to protect victims from secondary victimization, retaliation, or intimidation'. It also noted that 'although engaging in child prostitution is a criminal offence, clients are not always prosecuted' and 'the rape of a child, although a crime in the Penal Code, is often re-qualified as sexual aggression'. It

72 See, further, Roumajon, Y., *Ils ne sont pas nés délinquànts* (They were not born delinquents), R. Laffont (publisher), (1981).

73 Op. cit.

urged the authorities to 'ensure that all child victims receive appropriate and secure legal, social, educational and medical assistance'.[74]

Conclusion

Public family law relating to children has both a civil and criminal jurisdiction but in France, unlike the common law countries – and some others – there is not such a clear distinction between the two.

State intervention on child welfare grounds – the civil jurisdiction – is either consensual or coercive; in both, the *juge des enfants* may play a key role, and again the distinction between the two may be blurred. In the former instance, the legal and social policy emphasis is very much on providing *assistance éducative*[75] by delivering the resources necessary to reinforce parental coping capacity and avoid future child protection measures. In the latter, *assistance éducative* measures may also be used due to the well-established principle of maintaining or restoring the parent/child relationship[76] and the policy of using those measures to correct the dysfunctioning of the family. In both instances the service delivery duty falls to the *Aide sociale à l'enfance*, with support if appropriate from the *Protection maternelle et infantile*, but service provision may be directed by the *juge des enfants* who may specify the type of service needed. The use of such measures has been strengthened by the law of 7 February 2022. An *assistance éducative* measure can last for up to two years, may be renewed indefinitely, and may be subject to conditions such as attendance at a training facility.

State intervention on child offence grounds – the criminal jurisdiction – is again focused on amelioration of family difficulties; the emphasis is on child welfare rather on accountability and punishment. Again, the *juge des enfants* plays a central role in legal proceedings and may have recourse to *assistance éducative* measures. State intervention in the French family – whether consensual or coercive, on civil or criminal grounds – would seem to focus more on repairing family functioning than on the needs or deeds of the child in isolation.

74 Ibid., paras 83–6.

75 The ordinance of 23 December 1958 created the modern concept of *assistance éducative* (assistance in upbringing).

76 See statute law in 1984 requiring planning for family reunification.

5 The welfare principle in contemporary practice

Private family law and hybrid proceedings

Introduction

The public-private dichotomy in law can perhaps be seen in terms of: public law which establishes relations of verticality where legislation, legal status, and the authority of institutions, courts, and regulatory bodies are all hierarchically ranked; and private law characterised by the legal horizontality of personal relationships, identity concerns, and the navigation of reciprocal rights and duties, etc.[1] In recent decades and in all modern developed nations this dichotomy has been severely disrupted. Partly this has been due to a receding state being supplanted by civil society: traditional hierarchical structures being displaced by new mediatory mechanisms for brokering conflicts in public and private interests; the role played by a rapid expansion in professionalism, managerialism, and globalisation has clearly had an impact. So, also, has the pressure brought to bear on national cultural norms by the principles imposed by supra–national laws and courts, not least of which has been the fragmentary effect of human rights.

Family law in France has not escaped the erosion of that dichotomy. In keeping with the fading significance of the traditional heterosexual marital family as the bedrock of a stable society, the law has developed a functionality that transcends the rigidity of a public/private polarisation. This chapter begins by examining private family law and then the growing area of public/private family matters. It considers firstly the law relating to founding a family, before considering how the law relates to family breakdown, paying particular attention to the legal weighting given to the welfare interests and rights of the child. This is followed by a broad consideration of the state's public service responsibilities for child welfare. The chapter concludes with a review of hybrid proceedings, such as adoption from state care, identifying and assessing the public and private strands, and their implications for child welfare/rights.

1 See van den Berge, L., 'Rethinking the Public-Private Law Divide in the Age of Governmentality and Network Governance', *European Journal of Comparative Law and Governance*, Vol 5(2), 2018, pp 119–143.

DOI: 10.4324/9781003415688-8

Founding a family

As the European Court of Human Rights (ECtHR) established in *E.B. v. France*,[2] Article 8 of the European Convention on Human Rights (ECHR) does not in itself confer a right to found a family nor to do so by way of adoption. As it then explained, the existence of 'family life' is in fact a pre-condition for the operation of Article 8[3] (see, further, Chapter 3).

Family life

French family life has been recognised in many different forms. In *Gas and Dubois v. France*[4] the ECtHR found that it existed in the relationship between two women who were living together and had entered into a civil partnership, with the child conceived by one of them by means of assisted reproduction being parented by both. In *Boughanemi v. France*[5] it was found that the relationship between two siblings constituted family life. The ECtHR in both *Mennesson v. France*[6] and *Labassée v. France*[7] found that Article 8 was applicable because the commissioning couple had acted as the parents of the children from the time of the latters' birth and lived with them in a way that constituted family life: there was 'an effective personal link' ('*de facto* family life')[8] between the private life of the children and the determination of their legal affiliation (see, further, below). In France, as elsewhere, there are many different ways of forming a family.

Adoption

Governed by the Civil Code,[9] Articles 343–60, adoption in both plenary and simple forms is available but subject to somewhat archaic rules such as that adopters must be childless and not less than 50 years of age. A full or plenary adoption order – equivalent in almost all respects to the common law version – is the one most usually granted and is irrevocable.[10] Simple adoption is appropriate when the subject is the birth child of a spouse; the other spouse, as applicant, is then only eligible for a simple adoption order during the lifetime of their spouse; the order does not terminate the child's legal ties with their family of origin. In a simple adoption, the adopted child becomes a member of his new family but retains some legal bonds with his family of origin, has inheritance rights in respect of both families, and does not automatically acquire the nationality of the adopters. A simple adoption order

2 Application No. 43546/02, (2008).
3 Ibid., at p 18.
4 Application No. 2595/07, (2010).
5 Application No. 22070/93, Reports 1996-II, no 8, p 593, 22 EHRR 228.
6 Application No. 65192/11, (2014).
7 Application No. 65941/11, (2014).
8 See, also, *C.E. & A.L. v. France,* Application Nos. 29775/18 and 29693/19, (2022) at para 49.
9 See, further, at: https://www.napoleon-series.org/research/government/code/book1/c_title08.html
10 Article 359 of the French Civil Code.

can be revoked but only in exceptional circumstances and only after a full judicial hearing.[11]

Accouchement sous le secret

Traditionally, a woman's right, under Article 341 of France's Civil code, to give birth anonymously was known as *accouchement sous X* (births by an unidentified person) because the birth mother was recorded on the birth certificate issued in the maternity hospital as 'X' and the child was referred to as '*né sous X*'. Now, records simply refer to an 'anonymous delivery' and to the mother as 'X'.[12] The right to anonymity, added to the Civil Code in 1993, has existed in one form or another since 1793 when, under the National Convention of the French Revolution, secret pregnancies and births were protected by law.[13] It is the absence of recognition by the mother of the child (denial of filiation or dis-affiliation) to whom she had given birth anonymously, that removes the necessity to obtain her consent for the child to be taken into state care.[14]

This right was examined by the ECtHR, in *Odièvre v. France*,[15] when it decided in favour of upholding the right of anonymity. As was explained in that case:[16]

> The *mater semper certa est* rule has not found acceptance in French law. There is an ancient tradition in France that enables newborn babies to be abandoned in accordance with a set procedure. The practice can be traced back to the time of Saint Vincent de Paul, who introduced the use of the *tour*, a sort of revolving crib housed in the wall a charitable institution. The mother would place the child in the crib and ring a bell. On that signal someone on the other side of the wall would cause the *tour* to pivot and collect the infant. The aim of Saint Vincent de Paul in setting up the Foundlings Home (*Euvre des Enfants trouvés*) in 1638 was to prevent infanticide, abortion and babies being exposed.

In January 2002 the right was modified by the introduction of the Act of 3 December 2001 (*loi n° 2001-1235*) which, among other measures, eliminated the

11 Article 345 of the French Civil Code.

12 Article 341-1 of the Civil Code, introduced in 1993, precludes a child born to X from establishing any legal tie to the mother, even if her identity should be discovered. The law has been relaxed somewhat by Statute n° 2009-61 of 16 January 2009. See, also, Article 325 of the Civil Code. The legal claim is available to the child where he/she has no legal filiation at all and no *de facto* parent-child ties. But in practice this almost never happens for X children since almost all are adopted within their first ten months. Therefore the claim is barred due to the establishment of the adoptive filiation link.

13 Statute of 27 June 1904 and Decret-Loi of 2 September 1941. Also, see, Donovan, K., 'Real Mothers for Abandoned Children', *Law & Society Review*, 2002, p 1.

14 See Article L224-4, point (1), of the Social Action and Families Code.

15 [2003] 1 FCR 621. Also, see *Kearns v. France* Application No. 35991/04, ECHR, 10.01.08.

16 Ibid., at para 15.

discrimination in inheritance rights that traditionally disadvantaged children 'born out of wedlock'.[17] This, in conjunction with improvements in the social consequences for unmarried mothers, resulted in far fewer babies '*nés sous X*' (or *sous le secret*) becoming *pupilles de l'État* (wards of state) as a first step to adoption. Nonetheless, generally some 500–50 babies a year are voluntarily relinquished by their parents, taken into care, and adopted, usually within 12 months. By 2021 the numbers had fallen to 390, a 25% drop from the previous year.[18]

The virtual absence of adoption in a child care context (although a few are adopted, this is almost invariably by their foster parents, with only a handful becoming otherwise available to domestic adopters), together with the dwindling availability of '*sous le secret*' children and wards of the state, has meant that effectively adoption in France has for some time been largely interfamilial (by step-parents or kinship) or intercountry in nature.[19]

As in other developed western nations, the use of adoption by a parent or relative of a child in order to legally consolidate a reformed family unit, is well established. Article 345-1 of the Civil Code provides for the plenary adoption of a child by the spouse of the child's parent while Article 360 provides for the simple adoption of a child by the parent's spouse.

Step-parent adoptions, and most adoptions by relatives, tend to be simple rather than plenary in nature.[20]

Welfare interests

Only certain categories of children are eligible for adoption: on a private law basis, those whose parents have voluntarily relinquished them to the state for adoption and whose consent is available; and in public law, *pupilles de l'État* (children of the state, i.e. with no known parents) with consent of the authorities, and those for whom there has been a judicial declaration of abandonment (see, further, below). The adoption gateway is thus only accessible to those children whose parents are dead, or their whereabouts are unknown, or who have consented to adoption. In effect, parental circumstances rather than child welfare interests determine whether a French child becomes available. The fact that the children entering the process are then placed with prospective adopters who have been assessed, and will be supported by the authorities, for that purpose, is clearly conducive to promoting their welfare interests.

17 Note that the marital status of parents no longer determines the legal status of their children: whether married or not their child will have exactly the same legal status. See Ordonnance n° 2005-759 of 4 July 2005, as since ratified by the Statute n° 2009-61 of 16 January 2009.

18 See, further, *Les chiffres clés en protection de l'enfance* at: https://onpe.gouv.fr/system/files/publication/fs_chiffres_cles_pe_2021.pdf

19 See, further, Halifax, J., 'Why are there so many international adoptions in France?', at: http://www.uea.ac.uk/swp/icar2/pdf's/Halifax99.pdf

20 See, further, Robcis, C., *The Law of Kinship: Anthropology, Psychoanalysis and the Family in France*, Cornell University Press, Ithaca, NY, 2013.

Consents for adoption

Adoption in France is almost exclusively a consensual process: the consent of the parent/s is a necessity other than in exceptional circumstances. The consent to place for adoption a child who is the subject of an '*accouchement sous X*' process, is given by the appropriate state authority. Such a placement, by virtue of the provisions of Article 352 of the Civil Code, constitutes a bar not only to the return of the child to the mother but also to any declaration of filiation or recognition. The consent of a child aged 13 or older is a pre-requisite for his or her simple adoption but not, curiously, for a child of the same age in a plenary adoption.

'Open' adoption

As illustrated by the legacy of '*accouchement sous le secret*' there is little in the way of a culture of 'openness' in the French adoption process. This was evident in *Odièvre v. France*[21] when the ECtHR ruled that denying children given up at birth the right to discover their biological parents' identity did not violate the European Convention. The lack of openness is also apparent in domestic adoptions by the requirement – when the child is under two years of age and is not related to the adopter by kinship or marriage – that he or she be delivered to a child welfare service or to a duly authorised body for adoption. This provision[22] is designed to avoid direct contact between the biological family and potential adopters.

Step-parent adoption

A large proportion of annual adoptions are by step-parents: but these are 'simple' rather than 'plenary'. Unlike many common law countries, the law in France has resisted allowing step-parents to use the full legal status of adoption as a means of usurping the legal standing of a birth parent: this is probably because of the complications arising for filiation. The applicant step-parent must be married to the birth parent of the child to be adopted.[23] This use of adoption as an addendum to divorce, consolidating the reforming of families and constituting a significant generator of domestic adoption proceedings in this as in all modern western nations, has in France been very largely confined to 'simple' adoptions.[24]

Post-adoption contact

Because French law accommodates both plenary and simple adoptions, post-adoption contact is not such an issue as in other countries. If ongoing contact between

21 *Odièvre v. France* [2003] 1 FCR 621.
22 Article 348-5 of the French Civil Code.
23 See Article 343 of the Civil Code. The law is to be amended.
24 See Zachia Belmmoktar, info stat justice n° 175, fév. 2020, *L'adoption de l'enfant du conjoint en 2018.*

the child and his or her birth family is seen as important and all parties are in agreement, then the adopters are channelled towards simple adoption.

Intercountry adoption

Article L225-17 of the Social Welfare and Family Code states:

> Persons entrusted with a foreign child with a view to his or her adoption shall apply for the authorisation contemplated in Articles L225-2 to L225-7 of this Code.

In 1997, a total of 3,528 children from 70 countries were adopted into France. In 2003, of the 4,500 children adopted, almost 4,000 (90%) were born abroad.[25] By 2019, only 421 children (615 in 2018) from five countries were adopted by French parents. In its 2016 report the Committee on the Rights of the Child (CRC) expressed concern regarding 'the high number of intercountry adoptions involving countries of origin that are not party to, nor comply with, the safeguards of 1993 Hague Convention on Protection of Children and Co-operation in respect of Intercountry Adoption'.[26] The fact that a growing proportion of intercountry adoptions are from non-Hague compliant countries, correspondingly increases the risk to the welfare interests of the children involved and likewise increases the probability of a public law intrusion into what is otherwise very largely a private law process.

Cultural/religious affinity

Again, the fact that French law offers a choice between plenary and simple adoption means that if maintaining cultural/religious links is a priority for relinquishing parents then prospective adopters will be restricted to a simple adoption. This would also be the case in 'kafala' arrangements where Muslim adopters would be expected to maintain contact with and ensure the adoptee continued the Islamic cultural/religious commitment of the birth parents. Intercountry adoption, on the other hand, is plenary in nature and no legal guarantee can be given that the child's cultural heritage will be respected and maintained by the adopters.

Reproductive rights: abortion, surrogacy, IVF, etc.

In France, as in other modern western nations, advances in medical science have greatly affected the balance between wanted and unwanted births and thereby increased the proportion of children who are much wanted and the probability that their welfare interests will therefore be promoted.

25 See, further, at: www.diplomatie.gouv.fr/fr/adopter-a-l-etranger/la-mission-de-l-adoption/les-statistiques-de-l-adoption

26 Op. cit., at para 55.

Abortion

The introduction of legal access to abortion in the 1970s had a dramatic effect on the number of babies termed '*nés sous X*', or '*sous le secret*', born to anonymous mothers and available for adoption. The abortion law reduced the number of such infants from an estimated 10,000 babies a year to between 500 and 600 reaching 700 in 2010, 610 in 2017, and down to 500–50 by 2020[27] (see, further, below). Abortion is legal only up to 12 weeks[28] (as opposed to 24 in the U.K.). In the years spanning the end of the 20th and beginning of the 21st centuries the rate of abortion plateaued at approximately 225,000 in 2010. In 2021, France had an abortion rate of 15.5 per 1,000 women aged 15–49.[29]

Currently, the law defines abortion as a routine elective medical procedure freely available within the first 14 weeks of pregnancy (extended from 12 weeks in 2022) and legally permitted at any time during a pregnancy if the mother's life is in grave danger, or if a serious abnormality is detected in the foetus. Such is the extent of the accommodating approach in France that it would seem this nation is preparing to become the first to enshrine abortion as a constitutional right.[30]

IVF

In 2021 the law which had restricted IVF treatment to heterosexuals was extended to same-sex couples and single women. This equality legislation brought France into alignment with most other European nations and will clearly increase the number of wanted births and thereby increase the probability of more children having their welfare interests promoted.

Surrogacy

Surrogacy is not merely unavailable but since 1991 it has been legally prohibited.[31] Indeed, the legal position has hardened in recent years which has pushed what would otherwise be a private law matter into the public law arena (see, further,

27 See, for example, Lefaucheur, N., *Etude – enfants nés sous X*, CNRS-IRESCO, Paris, 2000 and further, at: https://www.onpe.gouv.fr/

28 See article L2212-1 of the *Code de la santé publique*. Note also the ruling in *Conseil constitutionnel* June 27, 2001, # 2001-446 DC which rejected a challenge that such a raising of the legal threshold permitted "eugenic practices" by allowing more time for identifying foetal anomalies and so facilitating the selection of children to be born.

29 In 1955 there were 1,170,143 abortions; 550,127 in 1985; 343,024 in 1995; 341,588 in 2001; 190,363 in 2011; 224,300 in 2018; and 223,000 in 2021 (see *Institut National des Etudes Demographiques*, 'INED').

30 See, further, at: https://www.theguardian.com/world/2022/nov/24/france-moves-closer-to-making-abortion-a-constitutional-right#:~:text=France%20has%20moved%20a%20step,to%20voluntarily%20end%20a%20pregnancy"

31 Under article 16.5 of the Civil Code, such contracts are null and void. The *Cour de cassation* in 1991 invalidated a decision of lower jurisdictions giving effect to surrogacy by creating a filiation link between the child and the wife of the biological father after the completion of such a contract.

below). A surrogacy contract is null and void, and violations are punished by civil and criminal sanctions (civil sanctions by Articles 311-25, 325, and 332-1 of the Civil Code and criminal sanctions by Articles 227-12 §3 and 227-13 of the Penal Code). Any couple making an agreement with another woman that she will bear a child, impregnated by means of artificial insemination, and surrender it on birth to the couple will be prohibited from adopting that child. Since 2010, French courts have consistently denied recognition to surrogate contracts and to any right-to-adopt children born abroad from surrogate mothers.

However, although surrogacy is still prohibited in France, the *Cour de cassation* ruled in 2015 that children born to surrogate mothers should be legally recognised and registered and in the same year the *Conseil d'Etat* decided to grant nationality to such children. Further, in 2019 the *Cour de cassation* decided that if the child is born in a jurisdiction where surrogacy is lawful then, on return to France, his or her birth certificate must be re-issued and the spouse of the birth father (man or woman) will be registered as the second parent, without having to adopt the child.

The 2014 case of *Mennesson v. France*[32] was something of a milestone in French law relating to surrogacy. The ECtHR then considered the refusal of French authorities to register children brought to France following completion of surrogacy arrangements in the United States violated the children's right to family life. Ultimately, the Court relied on the principle of the welfare interests of the child in its determination that it would violate those interests to deny the children the legal status of filiation and citizenship, particularly as there was a genetic link between father and child (see, further, below).

Surrogacy and the welfare interests of the child

In the above *Mennesson* case, while the Court found no violation of the applicants' right to respect for family life, concluding that they were not prevented from enjoying family life in France, it attached great importance to the best interests of the children, particularly as the man to be registered as their father was in fact their biological father. To deny a child legal affiliation when biological affiliation is established and with the parent claiming full recognition, was judged not to be in the children's best interests: those interests would be best served not just by legally consolidating their family life but also affirming their right to an authentic genetic identity. The Court therefore found a violation of Article 8 in respect of the 'private life' of the children.

In 2019 the *Cour de cassation* sought and obtained from the ECtHR an opinion concerning the recognition in domestic law of a legal parent-child relationship between a child born through a gestational surrogacy arrangement abroad and the intended mother.[33] The Court advised that French domestic law should provide

32 Op. cit.

33 Request No. P16-2016-001 (April 2019). See, further, at: https://hudoc.echr.coe.int/eng#{"itemid":["003-6380799-8365006"]}

a possibility of recognition of a legal parent-child relationship with the intended mother, designated in the birth certificate legally established abroad as the 'legal mother'. However, the child's right to respect for private life within the meaning of Article 8 did not require such recognition to take the form of entry in the register of births, marriages, and deaths of the details of the birth certificate legally established abroad; another means, such as adoption of the child by the intended mother, might be used provided that the procedure laid down by domestic law ensured that it could be implemented promptly and effectively, in accordance with the child's best interests.

More recently, in *Affaire A.L. v. France*,[34] the ECtHR considered a domestic, and therefore illegal, surrogacy arrangement which had resulted in the surrogate mother giving the child not as agreed to the unmarried same-sex couple (one with a genetic link to the child) with whom she had an arrangement, but to a married heterosexual couple – one of whom promptly registered himself as the child's father – for financial profit. Following several years of litigation, during which the child lived with the married couple, the genetically linked applicant's claim was rejected on the grounds that the child now had an established family life. The Court found that while the French courts' refusal to legally establish the paternity of the genetic father amounted to a violation of his right to respect for his private life, nonetheless at this stage the six-year- old child's best interests could only be served by translating the married couple's parenting status from *de facto* to *de jure*. In contrast to *Mennesson*, the child's right to a genetically validated identity was not deemed to be a core component of their best interests.

Sexual orientation and gender transitioning

Requests for gender transition, reflecting much distress among the children concerned and their parents, have greatly increased in recent years in France[35] as elsewhere in Europe: probably by a multiple of five since 2012, perhaps constituting what has been described as 'this epidemic-like phenomenon'.[36] All countries so affected have taken, or are in the process of taking, responsive measures.[37]

The relevant law in France is in the process of change. In 2010, this country became the first in the world to declassify gender dysphoria as a mental illness, meaning that a child expressing a wish to change their gender no longer had to receive psychiatric assessment and treatment. Further, since 2017 it has been possible to change gender identity without undergoing sex reassignment surgery,

34 Application No. 13344/20, (2022).

35 See, further, Eliacheff, C. and Masson, C., *La fabrique de l'enfant-transgenre* (The Making of the Transgender Child), L'OBSERVATOIRE (publisher), 2022.

36 The National Academy of Medicine report, 'Medicine and gender transidentity in children and adolescents', (2022), at: https://www.academie-medecine.fr/la-medecine-face-a-la-transidentite-de-genre-chez-les-enfants-et-les-adolescents/?lang=en

37 Countries such as Spain (2023) and Ireland (2015) are among the 11 European countries that – as of 2023 – had introduced legislation permitting gender identity change by self-declaration.

enforced sterilisation, or receiving any medical diagnosis. France allows the use of puberty blockers or cross-sex hormones with parental authorisation and without any age limitations; it also permits surgical treatments, specifically mastectomy, which is allowed in France at the age of 14, and surgeries relating to external genitalia.

A report published in 2022 by the National Academy of Medicine warned that:[38]

> Whatever the mechanisms involved in adolescents – excessive engagement with social media, greater social acceptability, or influence by those in one's social circle – this epidemic-like phenomenon manifests itself in the emergence of cases or even clusters of cases in the adolescents' immediate surroundings. This primarily social problem is due, in part, to the questioning of an overly dichotomous view of gender identity by some young people.

In the same year a law was introduced to prohibit parents and professionals from refusing to facilitate a child's decision to undergo a gender-transitioning process, and to heavily penalise those who do so. The law provides for 'the total or partial revocation of parental authority' of any parent who attempts to prevent their child's gender transition. This law is to be reinforced by the introduction of a new crime into the Criminal Code criminalising anyone who practises 'conversion therapies' to change a person's sexual orientation, even at their request.

The law makes no distinction between minors and adults, although the problems faced by each group are clearly different. The prohibition against 'conversion therapies' would appear to include the care of minors genuinely suffering from gender dysphoria and might therefore prevent them receiving professional assistance. Also, while no longer requiring proof of surgery or medical interventions, trans persons will still need to go before a court in order to have their gender marker – birth certificate entry – changed, though changing the first name can be done by the registry office.[39]

Child's consent

Children may access gender-affirming treatment – such as puberty blockers and hormone replacement treatment – at any age on the basis of their consent. Accessing surgical procedures will require parental consent until the child concerned is at least 14 years of age.

Welfare interests

The more 'affirmative' French approach must ease the pressure on uncertain children facing the challenge of the transitioning process and the scepticism of others.

38 Op. cit.

39 See *A.P., Garçon et Nicot v. France*, Application Nos. 79885/12, 52471/13 et 52596/13, (2017).

However, the relative ease with which the process may be commenced – with puberty blockers perhaps being authorised for those aged as young as 10 and hormone bombardment and surgical operations as early as 15 – may well lead more to commit to the process, including some who may later regret having done so. As is pointed out in the above-mentioned 2022 report by the National Academy of Medicine, 'the side effects of hormone therapy, such as impact on growth, bone fragility, risk for sterility, emotional and intellectual consequences, and, for girls, symptoms reminiscent of menopause' are in themselves very serious. For those who do come to have regrets following completion of their gender reassignment treatment, the adverse impact on their welfare interests can be devastating. This was among the findings reported by the French Academy of Medicine in a 2022 study on the subject which also noted that in the period 2010–2020 the number of children who intended to change their gender increased by a multiple of 8.[40] Nonetheless, the fact that legal recognition can be obtained without the necessity for irreversible surgery – although many will want physiological transformation – must be in keeping with the welfare interests of the many children spared traumatic intervention and the few for whom a reversal of the process may eventually be desired.

Children and reconstituted families

Parenting decisions in the context of family reconstitution – post-family breakdown arrangements for child care, rights of step-parents, etc. – occupy a growing proportion of court time in all developed nations and often give rise to issues concerning the welfare/rights of the children involved.

Family disputes

Private family law disputes are dealt with in adversarial proceedings by the *juge aux affaires familiales*. The concept of parental responsibility – which replaced the traditional legal terms 'custody' and 'joint custody' in 1987 – is now firmly embedded in French family law, and is accompanied by a legal presumption that this responsibility is jointly shared by both parents (see, also, Chapters 1 and 4). In cases of urgency, proceedings may be fast-tracked – *procédure accélérée au fond* – such as when domestic violence is involved. An appeal from a *juge aux affaires familiales* can be lodged up to one month after the decision.[41] What is conspicuously missing from the legal landscape of private family law disputes – as it is from its public law counterpart – is any equivalent to the range of issue-specific court orders, proceedings, and matching bodies of associated caselaw that characterise

40 See, further, at: https://civilek.info/en/2022/05/05/in-france-children-curse-the-genderless/

41 Except for fast tracked proceedings (Article 481-1 of the *Code de procédure civile*) for which the time limit is 15 days.

family law disputes in a common law context.[42] The civil law tool-box is applied afresh to every new case, the codified provisions fitted to address each particular configuration of facts, seemingly without reliance on past precedents nor any need to establish future guiding principles.

Matrimonial proceedings

Marriage rates in France are the lowest in Europe. Whereas in 1970 there were almost 400,000 marriages, by 2009 the numbers had fallen to just 250,000 and had reached 244,000 in 2022.[43] The number of unmarried couples has quadrupled to around 2 million in the last two decades aided by the introduction of the *pacte civil de solidarité* (PACS) under law no. 99-944 of 15 November 1999 which protects the individual rights of each party and entitles partners to share property rights and to enjoy income tax benefits

The low marriage rate is accompanied by a high divorce rate, which more than doubled from 142,000 in 1980 to 290,000 in 2002, before falling back to 133,909 in 2010 and falling steeply to 57,437 in 2020.[44] It is estimated that more than a third of marriages now end in divorce. The divorce rate is higher in urban areas and, as Guedeney has noted, in Paris it has risen to 50% of married couples who have children less than five years of age. This has led to an increase in the number of children referred to juvenile judges for protection when the parents contest their divorce procedures. In a growing number of situations, a parent accuses the other of maltreatment or of sexual abuse, all of which impacts adversely on the welfare interests of very many children.[45]

DIVORCE, NULLITY, JUDICIAL SEPARATION, AND RELOCATION

As in other developed nations, due to the delay and high costs involved in contested proceedings, by far the majority of applications for divorce/nullity or judicial separation are settled by agreement between the parties, in which case they may draw up a formal parental agreement in respect of proposed child care arrangements to which the court will give only the most cursory attention before assenting. In the event of the parents failing to reach agreement they may have recourse to mediation services and if that fails then it will fall to the *juge aux affaires familiales* in contested proceedings to establish an arrangement that is most conducive to protecting the welfare interests of the child or children concerned (see, also, Chapter 1).

42 This difference may well be a legacy from the traditional common law approach: the writ was all-important, they were standardised, finite in number and each was specifically prescribed; a plaintiff had to ensure that his/her claim fitted within the terms of the writ. There was no equivalent in civil law.

43 See, further, at: https://www.statista.com/statistics/464239/total-number-marriages-france/

44 See, further, at: https://www.statista.com/statistics/465782/number-of-divorces-france/

45 See, further, Guedeney, A., 'The Infant Protection System in France: How Does It Work?', *Infant Mental Health Journal*, Vol. 29(1), (2008), pp 5–20.

Family law in France, unlike in other countries such as the U.K., does not provide legislative directions on the specific issues to be addressed – a 'welfare checklist' – to guide the judiciary and other regulators when making decisions regarding contested prenatal care arrangements or on other matters affecting the welfare interests of a child.[46] Based on the history of each parent's direct care of their child, the relative merits of their proposed future care arrangements, and the wishes of the child, the judge will first establish that both parents must retain their responsibilities for the child throughout his or her childhood. The judge will then make decisions regarding: the child's future residence, the visiting rights and shared care arrangements of the non-custodial parent, maintenance, and other ancillary matters.

PARENTAL RESPONSIBILITY DISPUTES

Such disputes may arise and be addressed in the course of divorce proceedings or arise later in the event of disputes about parenting arrangements. It is mandatory to then hear the views of any child who has reached the age of discernment. Parental disputes may of course occur at any time following the legal dissolution of a marriage or partnership and require the court to rule on contested issues – such as where the child is to live, relocation of parent and child, visitation rights, their education, medical treatment, etc. – which will require the parents to return to court where the same process of judicial decision-making as above will be followed. There would seem to be no equivalent to the sophisticated menu of court orders, functionally differentiating aspects of parental responsibilities, such as would be issued at the conclusion of equivalent proceedings in common law jurisdictions. Instead the principle is that both parents must take joint responsibility for determining all issues, bearing in mind that for one parent to prevent the other from exercising his or her right of access and accommodation constitutes a criminal offence. Other principles – perhaps constituting a recognition of children's rights – may also come into play. One such principle, rule, or right is that siblings should not be separated. There is, at the very least, a strong presumption that siblings, even half-siblings, should not be separated unless there is clear evidence that this would be in their best interests.

If parents cannot agree, they must refer the particular issue to the judge who will rule on that matter. In the case of an intractable parental relationship, the judge may determine that it would be in the interest of the child to assign the exercise of parental authority exclusively to one of the two parents.

COURT ORDERS

In the absence of a range of private family law orders, there are three public law protective measures which allow for the appointment of individuals to take responsibility for managing the affairs of someone deemed legally or medically unfit to

46 Paradoxical really, given that the civil code characteristically 'codifies' judicial application of the law while the common law equally characteristically does so in a discretionary manner.

do so. These measures are guardianship, curatorship, and protection of the court. Only guardianship has any particular relevance for children and if the appointment is made by a testator in their will (testamentary guardian) then it is a purely private law matter. If made by a judge – *juge des tutelles* – usually to manage the child's estate and general financial affairs, then it will have public law dimension (see, further, below).

The welfare principle in contemporary practice: public/private family law

Since the closing decades of the 20th century a 'shrinking state' has done much to affect the public/private balance which, since the emergence of the *Première République* in 1792, has politically tilted towards the former.[47] State withdrawal from direct public benefit service provision has been accompanied by growth in the non-governmental contribution, featuring: de-centralisation of government, increased regulatory controls, government colonisation of the nonprofit sector, and government services being delivered by proxy via charities and other civic society entities. This has caused, or at least been accompanied by, a shift in functionality from both the public and private sectors in general – as also in family law – to a growing centre ground where hybrid public/private activity is now flourishing.

Public service matters

In France, the sixth richest country in the world and the standard bearer for egalitarianism, 21% of its children in 2018 lived in households where the standard of living was below the poverty threshold.[48] The question arises – what responsibility does the state bear for the suffering it causes – by action or inaction – to the welfare interests of its children?[49]

An answer of sorts was, perhaps, provided nearly a century-and-a-half ago when five-year-old Agnès Blanco was severely injured by a cart belonging to a state-owned factory in Bordeaux.[50] The company successfully rejected any liability: a civil action for damages could not lie against 'servants of the state' engaged in public service duties; private law proceedings could only be brought against

47 In recent years, state coercive intervention has become more salient in the face of Isis terrorist attacks and social protest led by the *Gilets Jaunes* and others against state-imposed taxes, pension constraints, etc.

48 *Droits des Enfants en France* (2022), at: https://unicef.hosting.augure.com/Augure_UNICEF/r/ContenuEnLigne/Download?id=480588C0-E8CD-4A6A-B8D8-80AAA060B4C4&filename=SynthDroitsEnfantsFrance2022_final_pages.pdf

49 See, further, Behrendt, L., *Achieving Social Justice*, The Federation Press, Sydney, 2003.

50 TC 8 February 1873, *Blanco*, D.1873.3.17. M. Blanco brought an unsuccessful suit against the prefect of the department of the Gironde, as representing the state, for a declaration that the state was civilly liable under Articles 1382, 1383, and 1384 of the Civil Code. See, further, Bell, J. and Lichère, F., *Contemporary French Administrative Law*, Cambridge University Press, Cambridge, 2022.

private not state entities. The state would seem to be continuing to rely on this principle – that it cannot be civilly accountable for any harm caused to children in the performance of its public service duties – as offering a viable defence to harm resulting from the manner in which it delivers contemporary public services.

Poverty

'France is not rich enough, in terms of children, that it might neglect anything that can help them become healthy persons',[51] an observation that continues to ring true some eight decades after it was first pronounced, as a reminder that more needs to be done.

UNICEF, on International Children's Rights Day in November 2022 published a report on the rights of children in France in which it concluded that France is struggling to guarantee even the most basic rights for children in vulnerable situations.[52] According to the study, 21% of French children live below the poverty threshold, with nearly 5,700 living in shanty towns in mainland France, 30,000 housed in hotels – a solution deemed unsuitable for family life – while 1,600 have no accommodation. A 2022 report[53] on early childhood and poverty estimated that more than 2 million people have turned to food aid distribution in France, 17% of whom have a dependent child under the age of three; and a third of young parents turned to food aid for the first time in the winter of 2021.[54] Even allowing for distortions caused by the Covid pandemic, these reports substantiate the concerns expressed earlier by the CRC in its 2016 report which, while welcoming the adoption of the Multi-Year Poverty Reduction and Social Inclusion Plan, regretted 'the situation of 20% of children living in poverty and the large numbers of homeless children'. Contrary to the policy articulated in the Plan, the Committee highlighted the 'cases of forced evictions of Roma children and their families, without alternative relocation and without notice'.[55]

Employment

In 2021, the UN International Year for the Elimination of Child Labour, France announced to the International Labour Organisation (ILO) its intention to become a 'pioneer country' in the elimination of child forced labour. It had already made a start with its law of 27 March 2017 which created an obligation for multinationals to take the necessary action to end child labour practices domestically and internationally.

51 See the explanatory statement of the 2 February 1945 Ordinance No. 45-174 on juvenile justice.
52 Op. cit.
53 See *Break Poverty* (2021), at: https://breakpoverty.com/en/an-intolerable-increase-in-early-childhood-poverty-as-a-result-of-the-health-crisis/
54 See, also, Organisation for Economic Co-operation and Development, *Growing Unequal? Income Distribution and Poverty in OECD Countries,* Paris, 2008.
55 Op. cit., at para 69.

MIGRANT MINORS

There is an obvious potential for foreign children to be exploited, in breach of Article 4 of the ECHR, by being used as forced labour. This was illustrated in *C.N. and V. v. France*[56] which concerned the forced-labour claims of two sisters of Burundian origin taken to live with their aunt and her family in France and accommodated for four years in the basement of the house in allegedly very bad conditions. The older sister did not attend school and spent all her time doing household chores and taking care of her aunt's disabled son. The younger sister attended school and worked for the aunt and her family after school. Both complained to the ECtHR that they had been held in servitude and subjected to forced labour. The ECtHR found that the first applicant had been subject to forced labour as she had to work seven days a week, with no remuneration, no holiday, and with no likelihood of change. The ECtHR further found that the state did not meet its positive obligations, since the legal framework in place did not offer effective protection to victims of compulsory labour.

While it is impossible to know how representative this case is – of undocumented migrant minors being exploited under threat of exposure to the authorities – it is indicative of the potential for such practices to be sustained, hiding in plain sight but under the radar of relevant regulatory bodies.

Health

The CRC, in its 2016 report, expressed concern at 'the inadequacy of resources and general deterioration of specialized child health personnel, services and structures'. It also noted: the persistent excessively high level of infant mortality; the number of migrant children without a valid residence permit who continue to experience difficulties in exercising their right to health services; the high rates of mental health and psychosocial disorders, particularly among teenagers where the rates of voluntary pregnancy terminations are also high; and the curious fact that 'children are not allowed to be accompanied by parents when hospitalized'.[57] The reference to infant mortality rates is a matter of particular concern. In 2022, research findings showed that after a rapid decline in the infant mortality rate until 2005, the trend slowed down and the rate has steadily increased from 2012 onwards by 0.04 deaths per 1,000 live births per year.[58] According to Eurostat data, this trend has resulted in France ranking 25th in Europe, with 3.8 deaths per 1,000 live births in 2019.[59]

56 Application No. 67724/09, (2012).

57 Op. cit., at para 61.

58 See Trinh, N. et al., 'Recent Historic Increase of Infant Mortality in France: A Time-Series Analysis, 2001 to 2019', *The Lancet*, (2022), at: https://www.thelancet.com/journals/lanepe/article/PIIS2666-7762(22)00032-1/fulltext

59 See, further, at: https://ec.europa.eu/eurostat/databrowser/view/DEMO_MINFIND__custom_2268533/default/table?lang=en

The CRC and other treaty bodies have repeatedly expressed concern regarding the medically unnecessary and irreversible surgery and other treatment that is routinely performed on intersex children.[60] That this is a continuing issue was evidenced in the 2021 non-governmental organisation report to the International Covenant on Civil and Political Rights committee[61] which, in its opening sentence, states that 'all typical forms of Intersex Genital Mutilation are still practised in France, facilitated and paid for by the State party via the public health system (*Sécurité Sociale – Assurance Maladie*)'.

Education

The CRC, in its 2016 report, was concerned about 'the large deterministic role that the socio-economic origin of children plays on school achievement' noting that 'some children, including Roma children, unaccompanied migrant children, and children living in precarious housing face numerous difficulties to be enrolled in ordinary schools or canteens, with cases of refusal by municipalities'.[62] This continues despite the growing body of caselaw dealing with discrimination in access to education.[63]

Although Article 17(2) of the European Committee of Social Rights (ECSR) permits a distinction to be made between children with and without disabilities, nevertheless it has been determined that the norm should be to integrate children with disabilities into mainstream schools, where arrangements are made to cater for their special needs, and specialised schools should be the exception.[64] Worryingly, the CRC in 2016 found it necessary to advise the French authorities that they should 'ensure that children with autism are not subjected to forced institutionalisation or administrative placement and that parents are no longer subjected to reprisals when refusing institutionalisation of their children'.[65] The ECtHR, in *Dupin v. France*,[66] affirmed the basic right of autistic children to education while the ECSR, in *International Association Autism Europe (IAAE) v. France*,[67] ruled that it should be the norm to integrate children with disabilities into mainstream schools, in which arrangements are made to cater for their special needs, and specialised schools should be the exception. In an interesting addendum to the CRC concern regarding 'forced institutionalisation', it is worth noting that in 2022 the French

60 CRC/C/FRA/CO/5, para 47-8. Also see, CAT/C/FRA/CO/7, paras 34-35; and CEDAW/C/FRA/CO/7-8, paras 18e-f + 19e-f

61 See NGO Report (for LOIPR) to the 6th Periodic Report of France on the International Covenant on Civil and Political Rights at: https://intersex.shadowreport.org/public/2021-CCPR-France-LOIPR-NGO-Intersex-IGM.pdf

62 Op. cit., at para 71.

63 See, for example, *Dupin v. France,* Application No. 2282/17, (2018).

64 *International Association Autism Europe (IAAE) v. France*, Complaint No. 13/2002, (2003).

65 CRC/C/FRA/CO/5, at para 60.

66 Application No. 2282/17, (2018).

67 Complaint No. 13/2002, (2003).

authorities instituted rules that virtually prohibit homeschooling. Ostensibly, and probably in reality, the reason for this initiative was to obstruct any home nurturing of radical Islamisation but the effect is to also constrain the good intentions, and up until now the wholly acceptable standard of practice, of very many ordinary parents. It constitutes a small but significant shift from the private realm of family law choices to public law mandatory compliance.

Discrimination

Discriminatory attitudes and behaviour can often adversely impact children's welfare interests and rights such as those of migrants or those 'born out of wedlock'.[68] In its 2016 report, the CRC expressed concern regarding the ongoing discrimination against children in many areas including the continuing racial discrimination and stigmatisation in relation to Roma children.[69]

CHILDREN WITH DISABILITIES

The Committee in its above-mentioned report drew attention to 'the persistent discrimination against children with disabilities, especially children with multiple disabilities, in their access to education, regarding equality with others, including during recreation, extracurricular activities, in school facilities, and vocational training'. It expressed regret that 'the law provides for a system of special units within mainstream schools for children as young as three; that some children with disabilities are institutionalized, some are still in segregated schools, and others drop out of school as a result of a lack of accommodation and support'. Reiterating earlier comments, it urged the authorities to 'effectively adopt a human rights- based approach to disability without delay' and 'to take immediate measures to ensure that the rights of children with autism, especially their right to inclusive education, are respected.'[70]

INHERITANCE RIGHTS

The ECtHR has dealt with discrimination against children in a variety of situations including discrimination in the context of rights of inheritance. In *Fabris v. France*,[71] for example, the applicant complained that he had been unable to benefit from a law introduced in 2001 granting children 'born of adultery' identical inheritance rights to those of legitimate children, a law passed following the ECtHR's judgment in *Mazurek v. France*[72] in 2000. The Court held that the legitimate aim of protecting the inheritance rights of the applicant's half-brother and half-sister did not outweigh his claim to a share of his mother's estate. In this case, the difference

68 *Mazurek v. France*, Application No. 34406/97, (2000).
69 CRC/C/FRA/CO/5, at para 23.
70 Ibid., at para 57, citing General Comment No. 9 (2006).
71 Application No. 16574/08, (2013).
72 Application No. 34406/97, (2000).

in treatment had been discriminatory, since it had no objective and reasonable justification. The Court found that it was in breach of Article 14 of the ECHR taken in conjunction with Article 1 of Protocol No. 1 to the ECHR.

RELIGION AND SCHOOLS

Religious discrimination in the classroom, often conflated with freedom of expression, has given rise to a steady stream of legal issues. In *Dogru v. France*[73] and *Kervanci v. France*,[74] for example, the ECtHR upheld the expulsion of two girls, aged 11 and 12, from schools where they had refused to remove their Islamic headscarves during physical education classes. The ECtHR found that the purpose of the restriction on applicants' right to manifest their religious convictions was to adhere to the requirements of secularism in state schools. Additionally, according to the national authorities, wearing a veil, such as the Islamic headscarf, was incompatible with sports classes for health and safety reasons. The ECtHR deemed this reasonable, as the school balanced the applicants' religious convictions against the requirements of protecting the rights and freedoms of others and the public order. It considered that such state action to restore religious anonymity in the classroom was not a violation of the private right to manifest one's religion under Article 9. Accordingly, it concluded that the interference with the freedom of the pupils to manifest their religion was justified and proportionate to the aim pursued. It therefore found no violation of Article 9 of the ECHR.

Legal proceedings, processes, and court orders

In all developed nations, children have become an increasingly precious and scarce resource – due to inexorable demographic trends, falling fertility rates, the demands of new family forms, and other factors – which is apparent in the proportion of court time now taken up with contested custody claims. One area of family law where the disputes are indicative of private/public tensions is adoption from state care. The varying degree to which the developed nations are prepared to facilitate this process offers a revealing insight into a significant contemporary social trend.

Adoption from state care

Article L225-2 of the Social Welfare and Family Code states:

> Children in State care may be adopted either by persons given custody of them by the children's welfare service wherever the emotional ties that have been established between them warrant such a measure or by persons granted authorisation to adopt.

73 Application No. 27058/05, (2008).
74 Application No. 31645/04, (2010).

Of all the children in state care who may in theory be eligible for adoption it is really only possible for those who fall within the ambit of Article L224-4 of the Social Welfare and Family Code. Only for that very small minority, who have been so abused by their parents that the latter have been judicially stripped of their responsibilities, can it be said that their welfare interests may be promoted by entry to the adoption process.

In France, the fact that adoption of children from the public care system is not a policy objective is reflected in the statistics: in 2021 of the 310,525 children in care only 613 – *pupilles de l'État* – were adopted.[75] A clear distinction is drawn between filiation (biological or adoptive relationships) and child protection: the latter is focused on options to support families in need, by means of education, control, and assistance measures, that enable parents to protect their children. Child care adoptions are restricted to 'wards of the state' and largely confined to children who are young and healthy. As has been observed:[76]

> France encourages the adoption of younger children … but also regards successful integration into a foster family as a satisfactory form of permanence. All children in care in France, irrespective of age and status, must by law be put up for adoption as rapidly as possible once it becomes clear that return home is no longer a possibility.

In practice, the children concerned are much more likely to spend their childhood in long-term foster care or in an institution than with adopters.

CONSENT

Where a child is a ward of the state or is otherwise in the public care system and the parents have not given their consent to adoption, then this may be provided by the local council responsible for the child. No consent is needed for the adoption of children for whom the courts have issued a declaration of abandonment.[77] The court may grant an adoption order if it determines that consent has been unjustifiably, or abusively, refused by one or both of the birth parents, or if they are disinterested in the child, or if they are at risk of endangering the child's health or morality.[78] The consent of the child to be adopted is a mandatory legal requirement for adoptees aged 13 or older.[79] Only a small proportion of 'wards of the state' are adopted: in 2018 this was the outcome for 647 such children.

75 See, further, *Les chiffres clés en protection de l'enfance* at: https://onpe.gouv.fr/system/files/publication/fs_chiffres_cles_pe_2021.pdf

76 See Selwyn, J., and Sturgess, W., 'International Overview of Adoption: Policy and Practice', University of Bristol, 2000, at p 37.

77 Articles 381-1 and 381-2 of the French Civil Code.

78 Article 348-6 of the French Civil Code.

79 Article 348-5 of the French Civil Code.

POST-ADOPTION STATE SUPPORT

Lois n° 2005-744 of 4 July 2005 introduced a duty to offer post-adoption support services to assist adopters. Each *département* is now required to make available post-adoption support services for all parties of both domestic and intercountry adoptions. Responsibility for service provision rests with either the adoption service of the *département* or the *Agence Française de l'adoption*. Organisations such as CLSC Plateau Mont Royal offer various post-adoption services, free of charge, in the form of group sessions and individual counselling. Adoption Counselling and Advisory Services (COCAs) are available to provide post-adoption support. Nonetheless, by 2016 the CRC remained concerned regarding the 'insufficient support to adoptive parents and other family members in the adoption of children with specific needs, namely due to their age, siblings, disability or illness', causing it to recommend that the authorities 'ensure that adoptive parents and families are provided with adequate specialized adoption support'.[80]

POST-ADOPTION INFORMATION ACCESS

The identity of birth parents will not be disclosed to an adoptee if the parents formally requested confidentiality at the time of the birth and have not officially retracted that request. Until the 1960s, an estimated 10,000 babies a year were '*nés sous le secret*', or born to mothers who had exercised their right to anonymity and left no trace of parental identity on their children's birth certificates or on any other official records.[81] Although the numbers have since decreased appreciably, reaching 664 in 2009, 666 in 2019, and 550 in 2018, such anonymous births may, obviously, compromise the welfare interests of the adoptees by denying them knowledge of their birth family. This has resulted in a situation where an estimated 450,000 people have been deprived of origins information: officially edited out by the French state.

This entrenched right of parental veto, endorsed by the decision in *Odièvre v. France*,[82] illustrates the public/private dichotomy in contemporary French adoption law. It concerned the applicant's unsuccessful assertion that the French system of anonymous births prevented her from accessing information about her natural mother. She argued that "her request for information about strictly personal aspects of her history and childhood came within the scope of Article 8 of the Convention" and that "[e]stablishing her basic identity was an integral part not only of her 'private life', but also of her 'family life' with her natural family, with whom she hoped to establish emotional ties".[83] The French Government countered that "no

80 Op. cit., at para 55.

81 The exercise by any woman of this right, which is enshrined in Article 326 of the Civil Code and which the legislature has to date shown no intention of reconsidering, is governed by the provisions of Article L222-6 of the Social Action and Families Code, as amended by the Act of 22 January 2002.

82 Application No. 42326/98, (2003).

83 Ibid., at para 25.

family life within the meaning of Article 8…existed between the applicant and her natural mother", on the basis that "the applicant had never met her mother, while the latter had at no point expressed any interest in the applicant or regarded her as her child".[84] This finding illustrates the strong differentiation between French law and that of the U.K. and most of Europe on this matter.

The legal guarantee of maternal anonymity with the inevitable accompanying identity issues for the children concerned has been a matter of ongoing concern to the Committee on the Rights of the Child.[85] The Committee noted the introduction of the law adopted on 22 January 2002 relating to the right to know one's origins,[86] and allowing mothers who have a baby in secret to place their name in a sealed envelope thus leaving open the possibility to decide later in life if they wish to meet their child or not. This option, however, is entirely discretionary.

The limited factual information recorded on an adoptee's original birth certificate, the process for gaining access to it, and the extent of information required to be kept on agency files, combine to make it difficult for an adoptee or birth parent to obtain a full factual picture of the adoption to which they were parties. However, the general rule is that an adopted child has a right of access to all the documents in his or her administrative file, upon request if the child is of age, otherwise via his or her legal representative. The *Conseil national pour l'accès aux origines personnelles* is the government agency responsible for managing the discovery of origins information and co-ordinating searches for records held by the *Aide sociale à l'enfance* (ASE) and adoption agencies, though this is clearly difficult in relation to children *nés sous le secret* or abandoned. Children whose identity was known before adoption can access that information through the relevant court orders (and this is valid for domestic and intercountry adoption).

Abduction

Child abduction in France, as elsewhere, very largely takes the form of unauthorised child removal by a parent, of which there are some 1,500 cases every year.[87] If the removal is from France to another country then the act is transformed from a private matter of parental removal without permission, to a public issue of criminal-

84 Ibid., at para 26.

85 See UN Committee on the Rights of the Child (51st session, 2009) when it expressed concern that a mother giving her child up for adoption, if she wished, could conceal her identity and oppose the right of the child to know his or her origins, depriving the child of a part of his or her rights. The Committee reiterated its previous recommendation that France take all appropriate measures to fully enforce the child's right to know his or her biological parents and siblings, as enshrined in Article 7 of the Convention.

86 In its 2004 report (Convention on the Rights of the Child Distr. GENERAL CRC/C/15/Add.240 30 June 2004) the Committee notes that the concerns and recommendations (CRC/C/15/Add.20) it made upon consideration of the State party's initial report (CRC/C/3/Add.15) in respect of the right to know one's origin (para 14), remained insufficiently addressed.

87 Abduction by a stranger is rare but not unheard of. In November 2022 a 14-year-old girl was abducted and murdered in Tonneins, one month after the similar fate of a 12-year-old girl in Paris.

ity. The governing legal framework, in the latter instance, is provided by: domestic law, the several provisions under the heading 'Encroachment on the exercise of parental authority' in the Penal Code with penalties imposed by Articles 227-5 and 227-7; and international law, under the Hague Convention and Brussels IIa.

RETURNING AN ABDUCTED CHILD

The *Cour de cassation* ruled in 2019[88] that the 1980 Hague Convention on International Abductions is not applicable when the child has been abducted to France from a country that is not a Contracting Party to the Convention and neither is Brussels IIa if the child's habitual residence was located, immediately prior to the abduction, in a similar such country. In those circumstances the parent seeking the return of the child must contact the local judicial and diplomatic authorities of the country in which the child has been abducted. Article 13 of the Convention allows the authorities of the country to which the child has been abducted to refuse to order the return of the child if there is a grave risk that such return would expose the child to physical or psychological harm or otherwise place the child in an intolerable situation. Although the French court must take into account the information provided by those authorities[89] it is not bound by the reasons that led to their decision regarding the risk that the child's return would entail.

CHILD'S BEST INTERESTS

The *Cour de cassation*, in several cases, has examined, in the light of the best interests of the child, the consequences that might follow if the return of the child (and therefore of the abducting parent) were ordered.[90]

In n° 18-23916,[91] after she had been granted physical custody of three children by a decision of a U.S. court, the mother then travelled with the children to France and refused to return to the U.S. The father applied, under the Hague Convention, for the return of the children and simultaneously an arrest warrant was issued for the mother, so she was liable to be arrested if she entered the U.S. When the case reached the *Cour de cassation* it agreed with the appeal judges that the return of the children would expose them to a serious risk of physical or psychological danger because of the father's alcoholism and the depressive and suicidal disorders from which he suffered, which made him "very irritable" towards his children. Moreover, if the mother returned, because of the arrest warrant issued against her by the American authorities, she risked being arrested, thus preventing her from ensuring the protection of the children, since the children risked being entrusted to

88 N°18-23849 (17 January 2019).
89 Civ. 1ère, 20 mars 2019, n°18-20850.
90 See, further, Leick & Darmois, 'International Children Abductions in France: A Review of the Caselaw (2019)' at: https://leick-darmois.com/en/international-children-abductions-in-france-a-review-of-the-caselaw-2019-2/
91 Civ. 1, 14 February 2019.

their father, who had produced "no evidence justifying his commitment to maintain the links between the mother and the children". It dismissed the father's appeal. The case is important because it expressly states that the French courts are not bound by the reasons for the decisions issued by the judicial and administrative courts of the state in which the child had his habitual residence prior to the abduction.

In n° 18-20546[92] the mother of the child, born in Tokyo, had returned to France for a supposedly temporary stay, during which she had filed a petition for divorce. The father's application for the child's return, pursuant to the Hague Convention, was granted by the French court on the grounds that the mother had failed to demonstrate that she was unable to return with the child to Japan. The *Cour de cassation* overturned the appeal judgment, ruling that:

> In so deciding, without investigating, as requested, whether, if the mother returned with the child to Japan, she would not find herself deprived of her parental rights, thus exposing her son, aged three years old and having always lived with her, to a serious risk of psychological danger, the Court of Appeal did not give a legal basis for its decision.

Again, the decision is important because it determines that it is for the French courts to ascertain that the potential consequences for the parent who removed the child were not likely to deprive the child of that parent and thus to contravene his or her best interests. Though it has to be said that, like the previous case, the *Cour de cassation* decision seemed to fuse the interests of mother and child: the welfare interests of the child were deemed to be inextricably bound up with those of the abducting parent, which arguably establishes an interesting precedent.

On the other hand, the recent case of *Bhadauria v. Côté*[93] concerned a mother who had taken her 16-month-old child to France without telling the father. The French court accepted that if she had acted due to domestic violence then she might legitimately claim that her actions – though unlawful – together with her request to remain in France, were justified by the best interests of the child. However, on the facts, the court found that she was unable to meet the burden of proof in relation to the allegations of family violence and was ordered to return the child.

Commercial surrogacy

Whether utilised by married couples – same sex or heterosexual – unmarried, or singletons, the motivation and investment – financial and other – of this means of becoming a parent must increase the probability that the welfare interests of such wanted children will be protected and promoted. Commercial surrogacy can, however, generate legal complications. Not least of these arises from the fact that returning couples with a baby are presenting the state with clear evidence that they

92 Civ. 1st, 22 November 2018.
93 2022 ONSC 2476 (CanLII).

have intentionally breached its public policy and by then seeking state recognition of their parental status – through adoption or registration – are requiring the state to be complicit in subverting that policy. Some of the legal difficulties have been evident in a series of cases brought before the ECtHR.

FILIATION RULES

In both *Mennesson v. France*[94] and *Labassee v. France*[95] the ECtHR recognised that the existence of a genetic link did not mean that the child's right to respect for his or her private life required the legal relationship with the intended father to be established specifically by means of the recording of the details of the foreign birth certificate; such a legal relationship and formal recognition of its status could be acquired by other means, such as adoption. Refusal to make such an entry in the registry of births did not preclude the applicant from otherwise legally establishing the parent-child relationship. However, it attached importance to the fact that the French authorities, despite being aware that the children had been identified in the United States as the children of Mr and Mrs Mennesson and Mr and Mrs Labassee, had nevertheless denied them that status under French law which the Court considered was not compliant with the children's welfare interests as it undermined their identity within French society. In addition, because French law completely precluded the establishment of a legal relationship between children born as a result of a lawful surrogacy arrangement – and one that included a genetic link with the father – it overstepped the wide margin of appreciation the state would otherwise have had in relation to such matters and had violated the children's Article 8 right to respect for their private life.[96] Again, in *D. v. France*,[97] where the female applicant had completed a surrogacy arrangement in Ukraine and had a genetic link with the child, the Court saw no reason to depart from its earlier reasoning in *Mennesson* and *Labassee*, regarding recognition of the legal parent-child relationship, and upheld the right of the French courts to refuse to register the child as the birth child of the applicant.

More recently, *C.E. & A.L. v. France*[98] comprised two joint applications.[99] The first concerned two women in a relationship during which one gave birth, following donor insemination, and both jointly parented until the child was aged six, when their relationship ended. For the next nine years the ex-partner enjoyed visitation and accommodation rights in respect of the child and also paid child support. In

94 Application No. 65192/11, (2014).

95 Application No. 65941/11, (2014).

96 The following cases were similarly concluded: *Foulon and Bouvet v. France*, Application No. 9063/14, (2016); *Laborie v. France*, Application No. 44024/13, (2017); *C and E v. France*, Application Nos. 1462/18 and 17348/18, (2019); and *D v. France*, Application No. 11288/18, (2020).

97 Application No. 11288/18, (2020).

98 Application Nos. 29775/18 and 29693/19, (2022).

99 See, further, at: https://strasbourgobservers.com/2022/10/07/c-e-al-v-france-legal-recognition-of-intended-parenthood-from-previous-same-sex-relationships-between-women/

2015, her adoption application – supported by the child's mother – was refused, as under French law, such an adoption would compromise the child's filiation and thus not be in their best interests.[100] The second related to two women in a civil solidarity pact who had lived together for several years. In 2008, one of them gave birth following a commercial surrogacy arrangement and both parented the child until their relationship broke down, when they established an alternating parenting pattern. The ex-partner, with the agreement of the child's mother, attempted to conclude a formal legal parent-child relationship but this was rejected by the court because, on the one hand, "French law does not allow the establishment, by recognised enjoyment of a status, of a double legal parent-child relationship for the benefit of same-sex partners" and, on the other, it was not demonstrated "in concrete terms that the best interests of [the child] make it necessary to establish a second tie of legal maternal relationship to the former partner of his or her biological mother".[101] The ECtHR acknowledged the existence of family life in both cases: there was "an effective personal link"; the ex-partners had been raising the children for several years, participating in their education, having rights of visitation and accommodation and paying child support, etc. It found that in both applications the French authorities' refusal "raises a serious question with regard to the principle of the primacy of the child's best interest".[102] Nonetheless, the Court unanimously decided that the French authorities' refusal to allow the establishment of a legal parent-child relationship between a child and a woman who is the former partner of their biological mother – also the child's legal parent – whether by full adoption or by recognised enjoyment of a status did not violate Article 8 of the Convention. It would seem that although the Court recognised the merits of the applicants' claim and considered that the decisions of the French authorities were not compliant with the best interests of the children, it felt bound to respect the French laws on filiation and their cultural significance.

DISCLOSURE OF ORIGINS INFORMATION

A.L. v. France[103] concerned the domestic courts' refusal to legally establish the applicant's paternity *vis-à-vis* his biological son – who had been born as a consequence of a surrogacy contract in France – after the surrogate mother had entrusted the child to a third couple. The ECtHR held that there had been a violation of Article 8 due to the French state's failure to honour its duty of exceptional diligence. It found that the domestic authorities had prioritised the best interests of the child, and had balanced the applicant's right to respect for his private life, on the one hand, with his son's right to respect for his private and family life, on the

100 The *Cour de cassation* had previously ruled that the Civil Code "precludes two maternal or two paternal legal parent-child relationships from being established in respect of the same child".

101 Application No. 29693/19, (2022) at para 25.

102 Ibid. at para 104.

103 Application No. 13344/20, (2022).

other. Nevertheless, the fact that the proceedings had taken more than six years was incompatible with the duty of exceptional diligence. In cases involving a relationship between a person and his or her child, the lapse of a considerable amount of time could lead to the legal issue being determined on the basis of a *fait accompli*.

IDENTITY

The right of a child to a name was established by the ECtHR in *Guillot v. France*[104] when it ruled that as it was the "means of identifying persons within their families and the community", it fell within the scope of the right to respect for private and family life as enshrined in Article 8 of the ECHR. An interest "in obtaining information necessary to discover the truth concerning important aspects of one's personal identity, such as the identity of one's parents",[105] as affiliation is a fundamental aspect of one's own identity.[106] The ECtHR has found that details of a person's identity and the interest "in obtaining information necessary to discover the truth concerning important aspects of one's personal identity, such as the identity of one's parents"[107] are relevant to personal development. This was reinforced by the CRC in its 2016 report[108] when it reiterated its recommendations that all appropriate measures should be taken to fully enforce a child's right to know his/her biological parents and siblings. It urged France to adopt the necessary measures for all information about parent(s) to be registered and filed, in order to allow the child to know, to the extent possible and at the appropriate time, his or her parents. The Committee also recommended that the State party consider removing the requirement of the biological mother's consent to reveal her identity and to increase its efforts to address the root causes leading parents to choose confidential births.

If a putative father refuses to undergo genetic testing, national courts, within their discretion, may establish paternity based on other evidence and factors, giving priority to the child's right to respect for their private life and their right to know their origins.[109] In a case where an adolescent child refused to undergo genetic testing because he wanted to keep the surname of his mother's husband, domestic courts nevertheless recognised paternity in favour of the biological father, finding that the child's best interests lay primarily in knowing the truth about his origins. The ECtHR consequently found that the domestic courts had not exceeded their margin of appreciation in recognising the biological father and setting aside the legitimisation of the child as the son of his mother's husband. There had therefore been no violation of Article 8.[110]

104 Application No. 22500/93, (1993), at para 21.
105 *Odièvre v. France* op. cit., para 29.
106 *Mennesson v. France*, Application No. 65192/11, (2014), para 96.
107 *Odièvre v. France* op. cit., para 29.
108 CRC/C/FRA/CO/5, at para 33 (see, also, earlier recommendation at CRC/C/FRA/CO/4, para 44).
109 *Canonne v. France*, Application No. 22037/13, (2015).
110 *Mandet v. France*, Application No. 30955/12, (2016).

Court orders

French family law addresses the same issues as its common law counterpart but does so with a functionality that is given effect by reference to measures in its civil law codes rather than by orders issued by the judiciary. So, the range of court orders is much shorter.

WARDSHIP

'Ward of the state' – *pupille de l'État* – is to be distinguished from 'ward of the nation', which is a civil status conferred by the state on someone whose parent was injured or killed in war, or during a terrorist incident, or while carrying out certain public services.

This public law status is governed by Article 224-4 of the Social Action and Family Code. A child of that status is either: *né sous X*; has been found abandoned or is unregistered; is judicially committed into the care of the ASE; is an orphan; or is a child who, for whatever reason, has no parent or person with parental responsibility to care for them. Wards of the state are eligible for adoption, and continue to be wards unless and until they are adopted. In practice, only a small minority of wards are adopted; the majority remain in state care until they reach 18 years of age.

GUARDIANSHIP

In special circumstances, a non-parent (e.g. a foster parent, grandparent, or other relative) can apply to the *juge et tutelles* (guardianship court) for a *tutelle* order (guardianship). While the application may have been made to secure care responsibility for a child for whom no one has parental responsibility, or in respect of the need to manage the property/finances of such a child, the order may well vest responsibility for both matters in the appointed guardian, who may be a relative or close family friend.

PROTECTION ORDER

This may be issued under Article 515-9 *et seq.* of the Civil Code and requires a judge to give a decision within six days of the hearing date.[111] It is intended to protect spouses or ex-spouses from threatened abuse by prohibiting all contact between the parties and if necessary between the violent spouse or ex-spouse and the children. The order will specify the judicially determined arrangements made in relation to the future exercise of parental authority in respect of the children. In particular, it may direct that the parent suffering the abuse is to be solely responsible for exercising parental authority and deprive the abusive parent of his or her access and accommodation rights or make the right conditional upon attendance at a particular venue.

111 Law of 28 December 2019.

Conclusion

Arguably, France shares with Great Britain an ethos that for most of the 20th century equated government with public service: social institutions, infrastructure, and the 'public good' being government business; civil society – always taking up more space in France – left to fill in the gaps; the autonomy of individuals assured of government respect unless their actions intruded on that 'public good'. By the end of that century, and increasingly so in the 21st, both countries have seen shrinkage in the state's role as 'guardian of the public good' as it sheds and transfers traditional responsibilities. Family law has not escaped this trend.

In France, however, the state/family relationship has always been somewhat different to that in the U.K. While the difference may be more apparent in the arena of public family law as it relates to children – for example, as regards the position of the *juge des enfants* in civil and criminal matters – it is also evident in private and hybrid family law where the French filiation rules are discrete but significant. The jurisdictional differences are illustrated by the characteristic features of adoption in France which is pivotal to the public/private divisions in family law. The fact that both simple and plenary forms of adoption are available allows its intra-familial use, particularly as regards stepparents and other applicants for whom ongoing contact between the parties is desired, to be diverted towards simple adoption. The retention of *accouchement sous X*, despite CRC misgivings, is a benchmark indicator of continuing private family principles, as is the resistance to non-consensual adoption from the public care system. Commercial surrogacy would appear set to become an interesting challenge for the public/private divide in French family law.

Part III

Germany

6 Policy, principles, legislation, and courts

Introduction

The Federal Republic of Germany (*Bundesrepublik Deutschland*), a civil law jurisdiction with a population of some 84.3 million in 2022,[1] is the most populous member state in the European Union. Re-unified in 1990, its 16 partly autonomous states (*Länder*), each with a legislature – with a degree of independence on specific matters – are legally bound by a federal Constitution and by the rulings of its Constitutional Court. This is a strongly federalist state, as Article 30 of the Basic Law declares: 'the exercise of state powers and the discharge of state functions is a matter for the *Länder*'. Family law is to be found largely in the Civil Code and related amendments, but many provisions in the Social Code are also relevant.

This chapter begins by examining the background social factors that have shaped the modern role of the principle that the best interests of the child – *Kindeswohl* – must apply in certain circumstances. Following a brief overview of formative policy and principles, the chapter outlines the current legal framework of legislation and courts, domestic and international. It considers the role of the child in court: legal representation; the right of the child to be heard; and the significance of the giving or withholding of their consent. Similar to Chapter 3, its objective is to provide foundations for the following two chapters.

Policy, principles, legislation, and courts

In Germany's federal constitutional system, the distribution of responsibility varies between the federal and *Länder* levels according to the policy area. This sectoral strategy results in responsibility for family law matters being the subject of federal laws while the *Länder*, but mostly the Communes (i.e. cities and boroughs), are responsible for providing the Youth Welfare System. However, the overarching provisions of the Constitution establish a basic national platform for the policy, principles, legislation, and judicial decisions relating to the family and for the related welfare interests of the child. In that respect, as Detloff and Mariny point out:[2]

1 See German Federal Statistic Office: https://www.destatis.de/

2 Detloff, N. and Mariny, D., 'National Report: Germany', p 3, at: http://ceflonline.net/wp-content/uploads/Germany-Parental-Responsibilities.pdf

DOI: 10.4324/9781003415688-10

> Art. 6 para. 1 of the German Constitution states that marriage and family shall enjoy the special protection of the State. This means that in addition to the subjective rights embodied in Art. 6 of the German Basic Law this provision also contains a constitutional 'institutional guarantee' and a 'basic norm decisive as to value.'[3] 'Family' includes the relationship between parents and their children, whether legitimate or illegitimate.[4]

According to Article 6 para 2 of the German Constitution, the education and upbringing of children is the prerogative of their birth parents. This emphatic principle was introduced to prevent any state education or indoctrination of children as had been experienced during the Nazi regime. It is, however, subject to the caveat that the state supervises the manner in which parents educate and raise their children[5] (see, further, below).

Policy

Legislative protection for children *per se* probably began, as in other countries, with industrialisation and a growing social awareness of how very young children were being drawn into exploitive work processes and dangerous work environments. The Prussian regulations on the employment of young workers in factories of 1839 established what might have been the first German threshold of state protection for child welfare. This was expanded exponentially by Chancellor Otto von Bismarck when he introduced the Insurance Act of 1883 to provide protection on a universal basis by means of what was the first social health insurance system in the world. By 1885, 10% of the population was insured and entitled to cash benefits in case of illness (50% of wages for a maximum of 13 weeks), death, or childbirth. This scheme was gradually expanded until the final step towards universal health coverage was taken in 2007. Health insurance, either statutory or private, was then mandated for all citizens and permanent residents.

Background

The modern child protection system, as we now know it, also had its beginnings in the social changes of the late 19th century. As Wolff and others have noted, its roots lay in a sense of shared responsibility between churches, nongovernmental charitable agencies, and the local government services,[6] an alliance which has continued ever since.

3 Citing: BVerfG, 17.01.1957, BVerfGE 6, 55, 71 *et seq.*; 29.07.1968, BVerfGE 24, 119, 135; 04.05.1971, BVerfGE 3 1, 58, 67 *et seq.*; 18.07.1979, BVerfGE 51, 386, 396 *et seq.*; 30.11.1982, BVerfGE 62, 323, 329.

4 Citing: BVerfG, 29.07.1959, BVerfGE 10, 59, 66 = FamRZ 1959, 416.

5 Article 6 para 2, 2nd sentence.

6 Wolff, R., Biesel, K., and Heinitz, S., 'Child Protection in an Age of Uncertainty: Germany's Response', in Gilbert, N., Parton, N., and Skivenes, M. (eds). *Child Protection Systems: International Trends and Orientations*, Oxford University Press, New York, (2011), at pp 183–203.

CHILD PROTECTION: RECOGNITION OF THE NEED

Kindeswohlgefährdung – or child endangerment – was first written into the Civil Code in 1900.[7] This term as then defined – 'the physical, mental or psychological best interests of the child or his/her property' – has been at the heart of the national child protection system ever since. The process of developing a modern legislative framework was initiated by the introduction of the Child Protection Act (*Jugendwohlfahrtsgesetz*) which came into force in 1924 and was amended in 1961. As Reinhardt explains:[8]

> In 1990 a system change took place with the introduction of the Child and Youth Welfare Act (*Kinder-und Jugendhilfegesetz*, last amended in 2021) which – implementing the principle of proportionality – defined youth welfare primarily as help and social support and only as a secondary consideration provided rules for intervention. The Child Protection Act 2012 (*Kinderschutzgesetz*) added detailed provisions for identifying and assessing children at risk as well as stating grounds for protective intervention. Additional Acts dealt with the protection of minors in public (*Jugendschutzgesetz*) and in employment relationships (*Jugendarbeitsschutzgesetz*).

It has been judicially determined that a child will be considered to be 'endangered' if it can be foreseen with a high degree of certainty that future developments will result in considerable harm to him or her.[9].As has been explained, this requires three criteria to be satisfied: weighty grounds to assume current endangerment; significant impact of the endangerment on the child's current or future health and well-being; and certainty of the prognosis of the impact.[10] There is no statutory 'checklist' of welfare components; each case is viewed and determined in accordance with its own particular set of facts.

Contemporary policy strands

One or two policy strands, discernible at an early stage, have for generations continued to form key strands in Germany's approach to safeguarding the welfare interests of children. A very basic strand has been that of respecting and supporting the family, and the role of parents, to bear care responsibility for their children. This can be seen in the many indications in family law of state deference to parents together with federal early intervention and family support programmes.

7 The Civil Code, s 1666.

8 Note to author (16 May 2023).

9 Federal Supreme Court ruling, 1956.

10 Schmid, H. and Meysen, T., 'What Is Meant by Child Endangerment?' in Kindler H. et al. (eds.), *Handbook on Child Endangerment According to § 1666 BGB and General Social Service (ASD)* German Youth Institute, Munich, (2006).

Another, and perhaps related, strand is the continued reliance upon residential care rather than on foster parents. It would seem probable that this is a forced choice due to a lack of foster parents. The legal preference for foster care, as more conducive than residential facilities for promoting the welfare interests of a child, was established by the Constitutional Court more than 50 years ago. It then ruled that the state had to look for a 'replacement family' in order to ensure bonding opportunities for children in its care.[11] Ever since, there has been no doubt that a child's developmental needs would be better served by family life in a foster placement than in residential accommodation and the fact that, nevertheless, only approximately half of the children constituting the child care population were so placed has been attributed to difficulties in recruiting foster parents. Alternatively, it is possible that this long-running problem reflects a wish to avoid placing a child in a position where they might form attachments to alternative parental figures: a residential placement being viewed as offering a more neutral setting, non-prejudicial to maintaining relationships with family of origin. The prospects of returning home a child so placed might be perceived as more favourable because of a lack of competing loyalties.

RESPECT FOR PARENTAL AUTHORITY AND BIRTH FAMILY UNITY

Although the Civil Code of 1896 used the term 'parental authority' (*Elterliche Gewalt*), in reality that authority was paternal and it was restricted to the father of a legitimate child. This was finally altered on 31 March 1953 when gender equality principles were embedded in Article 117(1) of the Basic Law. From then on, the courts struck down an increasing number of family law provisions on the ground that they were unconstitutional and many provisions of substantive family law were re-codified by the Equal Rights Act – *Gleichberechtigungsgesetz* – of 18 June 1957. The gender equality imperative affected not only marriage law but also child law as it resulted in the abolition of any difference between so-called 'legitimate' and 'illegitimate' children and the removal of those terms from family law. In 1979, the term 'parental authority' was replaced by 'parental care' but despite repeated Committee on the Rights of the Child (CRC) recommendations, has not yet transitioned to 'parental responsibility'.

INSTITUTIONALISATION

More so than most other European countries, Germany in the post-World War II (WWII) period was faced with the problem of tens of thousands of homeless orphans. Such children were often placed for adoption overseas – for example in the U.S. and Scandinavia – or accommodated domestically in orphanages and other church-run institutions. It has been estimated that between 500,000 and 800,000 children brought up in church and state institutions between 1945 and 1975 suffered

11 See BVerfG, (29.07.1968), BVerfGE 24, 119–55, at paras 67–8.

from poor living conditions and abusive treatment. This narrative was maintained in East Germany where again many children endured appalling hardship in facilities such as Torgau, a notorious closed juvenile home, one of the country's 150-odd homes for 'difficult' children. Some 4,000 youths aged 14 to 18 were locked up in these facilities during the period 1964–1989 [12].

German policy in relation to residential care for children continues to be much closer to France than to the U.K. (see, further, Chapter 8).

STATE PRE-SCHOOL PREVENTATIVE INTERVENTION

Low socioeconomic status is closely linked to poor child health and development outcomes, as well as increased risk of adverse experiences in early childhood. In Germany, studies have shown that 26.0% of children living in families of low socioeconomic status show symptoms of mental health problems, compared with 9.7% of children in families with high socioeconomic status.[13] Poverty is closely associated with issues of child health care and protection.[14]

In that context, the results of a 2007 landmark research project,[15] examining children's health and development, set the policy direction for preventative intervention, as implemented by Germany's Early Childhood Intervention programme, which has continued ever since. Indeed, it has also been the declared legislative intent underpinning such federal legislation as the Federal Child Protection Act 2012 and the Act to Strengthen Health Promotion and Prevention 2015.

Principles

Any consideration of governing principles in the many laws relating to children – or of the general applicability of other principles – would have to bear in mind the significance of the various 'culture shocks' that have impacted German society in recent years. The 'guestworkers', the reunification, Isis terrorist attacks, and the 2015 ongoing 'migrant crisis', have each brought challenges to disrupt social cohesion in this country. The traditional differences between *Länder* have been exacerbated, or just made more complicated, by these events. Consequently, there are risks in assuming that principles in family law apply with consistency in relation to the same issues across Germany.

12 See, further, 'Closed Juvenile Detention Centre', at: https://coldwarsites.net/country/germany/closed-juvenile-detention-centre-torgau/.

13 See Kuntz, B. et al.,'Social Inequalities in Health of Children and Adolescents in Germany: Results of the Cross-sectional KiGGS Wave 2 Study', *Journal of Health Monitoring*, (2018), Vol 3, pp 17–33.

14 See, further, Renner, I. et al., 'Improving Psychosocial Services for Vulnerable Families with Young Children: Strengthening Links between Health and Social Services in Germany', *BMJ*, (2018), at: https://www.bmj.com/content/363/bmj.k4786

15 See the KiGGS [Study on the health of children and adolescents in Germany] baseline study, at: https://www.kiggs-studie.de/english/results/kiggs-baseline-study.html.

The paramountcy principle

There is no unequivocal statement in the Constitution declaring that the welfare interests of the child must be treated as of paramount importance in decisions affecting his or her upbringing, though in the Civil Code the best interests of the child are declared to be of paramount importance when determining his or her adoption.[16] Moreover, as a signatory to the United Nations Convention on the Rights of the Child (UN CROC), Germany has formally acknowledged that the Article 3 reference to such interests as being 'a primary consideration' is binding on its domestic law (see, further, 'Conclusion').

BEST INTERESTS

The nearest approximation to legal recognition of paramountcy is the guarantee given in Article 6(2) of the Basic Law that the state will uphold any exercise of parental responsibility that is undertaken in the interests of welfare of the child. Other legislative references tend to be confined to 'best interests'.

The Social Code, for example, imposes an obligation on all professionals working with children to do no more than have regard for their best interests.[17] The Civil Code, s 1671(2), requires the best interests of the child to be taken into account by the Family Court in deciding whether sole parental responsibility should be assigned to one parent when both live apart, while s 1680(2) makes the same best interests test applicable in determining whether parental responsibility is to be attributed to the surviving parent should the parent holding sole parental responsibility die. Further, under s 1682, a threat to the best interests of the child can justify the latter being ordered to reside in the joint household of the parent not holding parental responsibility and their partner. Even in the relatively recent amendment to the Basic Law, which included a reference to the 'best interests of the child', the wording avoided conferring any particular weighting but instead settled for a requirement that such interests 'be taken into account in an appropriate manner'.[18] Interestingly, the welfare of a child is not defined; there is only a generalised reference to matters to be construed as contributing to 'welfare' or 'best interests'. There is no equivalent in German law to the common law 'welfare checklists' which identify specific components defined as constituting a child's welfare interests and the circumstances in which the 'welfare test' is applicable. Instead, in the absence of legislative statements of principle, German law focuses on practice requirements that place a clear child protection obligation – *Kinderschutzauftrag*[19] – on all engaged in social services, education, and health care (see, further, Chapter 8).

16 The Civil Code, s 1741.

17 Book VIII of the Social Code, s 8a.

18 See, further, Dethloff, N. and Mariny, D., 'National Report: Germany', at: http://ceflonline.net/wp-content/uploads/Germany-Parental-Responsibilities.pdf

19 See Book VIII of the Social Code, s 8a, and Child Protection Act (KKG), s. 4

In 2022, the CRC expressed concern 'that the principle of the best interests of the child is not being applied in all proceedings affecting children' and recommended that it be consistently applied 'in all policies, programmes and legislative, administrative and judicial proceedings affecting children, including in relation to trafficking and migration and asylum procedures'.[20]

PARAMOUNTCY: CHILD CONSENT

As a broad rule, parents and others are entitled and often required to take account of a child's age and maturity when permitting them to take independent responsibility for decisions,[21] though there are circumstances in which the consent of a child alone is sufficient. This is especially the case if the medical treatment is of minor importance when the validity of consent to medical treatment will depend on the maturity and understanding of the child. The courts sometimes only require a 'natural understanding' (*natürliche Einsichtsfähigkeit*). However, the conditions under which the consent of a child alone will suffice are a matter of controversy: some insist that the accompanying consent of a parent is also generally necessary.

An interesting if anomalous illustration of the legal weighting attached to a child's consent lies in their capacity – even if under seven years of age and without the maturity or discernment necessary to qualify as a legally competent minor – to request that the *Jugendamt* take him or her into care.[22] If the agency considers that there is a credible risk to the welfare interests of the child, or that the child's perception of risk is sincere if misguided, then they are bound to comply with the request.

PARAMOUNTCY: ADOPTION

The Civil Code, s 1741, declares that:

> A child may be adopted if such adoption will serve the welfare of the child and if it is to be expected that a parent-child relationship will develop between the adopter and the child.

That the welfare interests of a child – *Kindeswohl* – are to be treated as of paramount significance, is an implied requirement of the Convention on the Rights of the Child, Article 3(1), but it is not stated as such in German adoption law. This applies also in relation to recognition of foreign adoption orders: these need to be substantiated by evidence only that the child's best interests have been fully taken into account if they are to be recognised in Germany. Moreover, the s 1748

20 CRC/C/DEU/CO/5-6, at para 16.
21 The Civil Code, s 1626 II.
22 Op. cit., s 42(1).

provisions of the Civil Code[23] lend added weight to the rights of birth parents, relative to the welfare principle, by establishing a high threshold for dispensing with the need for parental consent before a child in state care can become available for adoption (see, further, Chapter 9).

The parental rights principle

Parental rights are as defined in ss 1626–1698 of the Civil Code and protected by the Constitution, leading to the relatively strong position of birth parents. Parental rights were in effect paternal rights until challenged in 1953 by the principle of gender equality forcing the Article 3(2) amendment to the Civil Code which granted spousal equality. The relative importance attached to parental rights was reinforced by a 1968 court decision which held that 'helping, supportive measures of the State aimed at establishing a responsible behaviour of the natural parents have priority',[24] an assertion clearly not wholly compliant with the paramountcy principle.

Although the legislative intent behind the recent amendment to the Basic Law was purportedly to constitutionally embed the welfare interests of the child, the government has offered the reassurance that this will not affect parental rights: that the rights and responsibility of parents will not be limited; the substance of their rights will continue to be guaranteed. The amendment specifically makes no change to the existing relationship between parents, children, and the state; the basic rights of the child are not being expanded to the detriment of others.[25] This is curious. Reinhardt explains:[26]

> This is due to the experiences during the Nazi regime when children were arbitrarily taken away from their parents to be given for adoption to party officials or celebrities. Given that in many child protection cases the welfare interests of a child and parental rights are in direct conflict, the result of children getting 'stuck' between their families of origins and applicants for adoptions (possibly their fosterparents) is obvious, but law courts – although it would be possible – are very hesitant to grant adoptions without the consent of the birthparents due to the history of forced adoptions in Germany.

PARENTAL RESPONSIBILITY AND CORPORAL PUNISHMENT

The physical chastisement of a child by a parent or anyone else is now prohibited by s 1631 of the Civil Code. Other disciplinary measures are, however, permissible.

23 The Civil Code, ss 1741–1772, deals with the legal requirements for and the effects of adoption.

24 BVerfGE 24, 119, (1968).

25 See, further, at: https://www.bundesregierung.de/breg-en/service/archive/rights-of-child-in-basic-law-1841338

26 Note to author (16 May 2023).

The justification for parental physical chastisement of children was judicially examined and rejected in *Wetjen and Others v. Germany*[27] which concerned members of the Twelve Tribes Church (*Zwölf Stämme*) who lived in a community which upheld the right of parents to apply corporal punishment. This was administered, using a cane on children between 3 and 12 years of age by whichever adult was in charge at the relevant time. On application from the local *Jugendamt* office, the court withdrew the applicant parents' rights: to decide where their children should live; to take decisions regarding the children's health, schooling, and professional training, and transferred those rights to the *Jugendamt*. Accordingly, in September 2013, all the community's children were taken into care. At that time, the child Wetjen was two years old and being breastfed but, on his mother's refusal to wean him, he was forcibly removed from maternal care and placed in a foster home. In November, the Family Court determined – in accordance with Articles 1631, 1666, and 1666a of the Civil Code – that leaving Wetjen in the community or returning him there would lead to him being subjected to corporal punishment, thus infringing his personal dignity and integrity, values protected by the German Basic Law. It found that the use of corporal punishment from such an early age would prevent the free development of his personality and instead teach unconditional obedience. On appeal in January, the court heard from the father who pleaded that a mild caning constituted neither violence nor child abuse and from the children who expressed a wish to return to parental care. Nonetheless, in March the court upheld most of the rulings made by the Family Court.

When the matter came before the European Court of Human Rights the Court found that the risk of systematic and regular caning constituted a relevant reason to withdraw parts of the parents' authority and justified the German courts' decision to take the children into care. It noted that 'member States should enforce legal provisions prohibiting corporal punishment of minors by proportionate measures in order to make such prohibitions practical and effective and not to remain theoretical'.[28] It therefore concluded that: there were 'relevant and sufficient' reasons for the withdrawal of some parts of the parents' authority; the domestic courts had struck a reasonable balance between the interests of the applicant children and those of the applicant parents; that in so doing they had aimed at protecting the best interests of the children and this did not fall outside the margin of appreciation granted to the domestic authorities. Accordingly, it held that there had been no violation of Article 8.

SHARING PARENTAL RESPONSIBILITIES

Married parents are in law recognised as being vested with joint custody or parental responsibility – *gemeinsames Sorgerecht* – for any child born to them during the course of their marriage. Being vested with joint custody entitles and requires the

27 Application Nos. 68125/14 and 72204/14, (2018).
28 Ibid., at para 78.

parents to take all major decisions affecting the welfare interests of their child – *Angelegenheiten von erheblicher Bedeutung* – jointly on an equally shared basis.

Where the parents of the child are unmarried, then the mother is vested exclusively with those rights/responsibilities unless and until they both complete the joint declaration of custody process. However, since the introduction of s 1626(a) into the Civil Code, the father has had the right to apply for joint parental custody which must be granted if this is compatible with the welfare interests of the child and the mother agrees or does not have good reason to justify its refusal. There is a legal presumption that paternal involvement is in the child's best interests. This is reflected in the Law on the Strengthening of the Rights of the Physical, not Legal Father 2013. If an unmarried father shows sustainable interest in the child, he will be granted visitation rights and the right to information concerning the child. Only if this is against the best interest of the child will those rights be refused.[29]

The permanency planning principle

This principle is imperfectly realised in Germany.[30] Mainly this is because adoption from state care – which in the U.K. has come to be viewed as virtually a synonym for permanency planning – is rarely used.[31]

The principle takes effect during the course of formulating the care plan, which is mandatory for every child entering the public care system. The provisions in the Social Code Book VIII on child and youth welfare include adoption as a permanency option for children in out-of-home-care.[32] They require permanency planning if a sustainable enhancement of parenting in the family of origin cannot be achieved in a time frame that takes the child's development into account. At that point the *Jugendamt* are required to assess whether adoption is an option before initiating a long-term placement (and may do so later in the course of such a placement).[33] However, as has been pointed out, adoption agencies and general social services mainly work independently from each other, and adoption agencies are rarely involved in care planning.[34] So, in practice, the adoption option rarely forms part of care plan considerations. Instead, the permanency planning will focus on the foster care or residential options and take into account the feasibility of rehabilitation.

29 The Civil Code, s 1686a.

30 See Maluccio, A., Fein, E. and Olmstead, K.A., *Permanency Planning for Children: Concepts and Methods*, Tavistock, London, (1986).

31 See Meysen, T. and Bovenschen, I., 'Adoption from Care in Germany: Inconclusive Policy and Poorly Coordinated Practice', in *Adoption from Care*. Policy Press, Bristol, UK, (2021).

32 Social Code Book VIII, ss 36(1) and 37 lit. c.

33 Ibid., at s 37 lit. c.

34 See Hoffmann, B., 'Adoption in the Care Planning Process – Case Workers' View', *JAmt*, Vol. 84, pp 10–16, (2011); and Bovenschen, I. et al., *Recommendations of the German Research Centre on Adoption: Future Perspectives for Adoption Practice and Adoption Legislation,* German Youth Institute, Munich, (2017).

The proportionality principle

A child is a developmental 'work in progress'. A 'one-size-fits-all' application of the law, which did not take account of where a child was on that continuum, would therefore constitute a denial of that very basic premise. This is perhaps most clearly evident in criminal law which requires a matching of *mens rea* (wilful intent) with *actus reus* (criminal act) allowing for a sliding scale of culpability. It can also be seen in the law relating to consent. Its relevance is similarly apparent in the context of rules of justice: the need for a guardian *ad litem* to elicit and advocate for a child's welfare interests; for court proceedings and processes to be made meaningful and accessible; and for decision-making which respects a child's sense of time. There are very many ways in which the law must be adjusted to fit with the evolving capacity of an individual child.

Proportionality – *Verhältnismäßgkeit* – is a key principle in German family law. Essentially, it requires that state intervention in family affairs be at the minimum level necessary to restore standards and safeguard the welfare of a child. This constitutional principle has many applications in child welfare law. For example, it results in the requirement that state intervention be preceded by counselling and practical help for families (*Hilfe vor Eingriff*) and that every effort must always be made to include the birth parents in any decision-making affecting their children, e.g. by including them in a joint care planning (*Hilfeplanung*)[35] and by giving them every opportunity to make choices (*Wunsch- und Wahlrecht*).[36] It also underpins the cardinal rule that family conservation has priority over family separation (*Familienerhaltung vor Familientrennung*).[37]

Legal system: legislation, courts, and representation

It may not be an exaggeration to say that after the ending of WWII, Germany's legal system was largely rebuilt. Thomas Mann's comment, 'but nothing is more certain than that the old society and economic system has irretrievably come to an end', was possibly more apt then than a generation earlier.[38] The new political and legal architecture, resting on fundamental democratic principles and headed by a Constitution carefully crafted to balance – among other things – the family/state relationship, was launched in 1949. In 1951 this was placed for safekeeping in the hands of the Federal Constitutional Court (*Bundesverfassungsgericht*) which has ever since ensured that German law does not stray far from its basic constitutional principles. Since then, of course, an ever-tightening framework of internationally sanctioned human rights conventions has further bound Germany and its

35 Social Code VIII, s. 36 and 37 lit. c.

36 Code VIII, s. 5.

37 Author acknowledges advice from Jörg Reinhardt on this matter (note to author, 16 May 2023).

38 See Thomas Mann diary entry for 15 April 1919 in Mann, T., *Thomas Mann Diaries 1918–1939* (Hermann Kesten, ed.), 1984, Robin Clark Ltd (publisher).

law – including that which relates to families and the welfare of children – into the mainstream of contemporary jurisprudential developments.

Legislation: international law

Germany ratified the International Covenant on Civil and Political Rights in 1973, with effect from 1976, and the Convention on the Rights of the Child in February 1992, though it only withdrew its reservations – which related in particular to the rights of foreign children – in May 2010 and has declined to incorporate the latter into its Basic Law.[39] Since 2022 Germany has adhered to Brussels II *bis* but has not ratified the International Convention on the Protection of the Rights of All Migrant Workers and Members of Their Families.

United Nations declarations and resolutions – including the United Nations Universal Declaration on Human Rights – are assumed to be binding on the basis of Article 25 of the United Nations Charter. Germany has also ratified: The Hague Convention in 2002; the Optional Protocol to the Convention on the Rights of the Child on a Communications Procedure in 2013; the Council of Europe Convention on Action against Trafficking in Human Beings in 2012; and the revised European Convention on the Adoption of Children in 2015. It has implemented The Hague Convention by way of the Adoption Intermediation Act and two separate statutes: the Adoption Convention Implementation Act which concerns intercountry adoption placements and co-operation between national Central Authorities; and the Effects of Foreign Adoption Act which regulates the recognition of foreign adoption orders.

Curiously, in 2005 the federal government response to the United Nations inquiry into Violence Against Children, included the statement that 'We have no information on cases concerning violence against children in which the country's courts or tribunals have referred to international or regional human rights standards'.[40] This, as Reinhardt explains, may be due to a technicality: the international regulations were assimilated into German law during the process of ratification, so there is no longer any need for separate information on references to the international rules as they are now all part of German law.

Legislation: domestic law

As Dethloff and Martiny have pointed out,[41] the primary source of German family law is the Fourth Book of the Civil Code (*Bürgerliches Gesetzbuch*) with its three sections: 'Civil Marriage' (ss 1297–1588), 'Family Relationships' (ss 1589–1772), and 'Guardianship' (ss 1773–1921). The statutory provisions on custody, contact,

39 See CRC/C/DEU/5-6, (2019) at para 13.

40 See Investigation by the Secretary General of the United Nations on Violence against Children, Questionnaire for Governments: Responses by the Federal Republic of Germany May 2005, at p 3.

41 See Dethloff, N. and Martiny, D., 'National Report: Germany', at: http://ceflonline.net/wp-content/uploads/Germany-Parental-Responsibilities.pdf

and parental responsibilities are set out in 'Family Relationships'. The Civil Code and these particular provisions have, however, been subject to much amendment and in addition the welfare principle as is stipulated in UN CROC has been transferred to national German laws by numerous legislative amendments.

The Constitution

Referred to as 'the Basic Law' – *Grundgesetz* – this federal Constitution came into effect in 1949; in addition, each *Länder* has its own, but subordinate, Constitution.

Article 6, which enshrines the welfare interests of the child principle, is of central concern for present purposes. It outlines the parental right to have contact with their child. Article 6(1) stipulates that 'marriage' and 'family' are under the special protection of the state while Article 6(2) establishes that it is the primary responsibility of parents to safeguard their children, their livelihoods, and protect them as well as provide for their supervision (state supervision of parents and families is thereby implied).

In 2022 the CRC recommended that the government 'strengthen efforts to incorporate children's rights explicitly into the Basic Law'.[42] The federal government's proposals on this matter are presently the subject of public consultation.[43]

The Civil Code (Bürgerliches Gesetzbuch)

This provides the basic, over-arching, federal civil law framework, within which family law provisions address matters such as child care, guardianship, and adoption. Section 2 states that the age of majority begins at 18.

Provisions relating to child care are to be found in ss 1626–1698b and address such matters as: the parental duties of care and protection; the suspension or removal of parental rights; and the appointment and duties of a guardian or curator. Provisions relating to the adoption of minors are to be found in ss 1741–1766. The role of the welfare principle has been implemented by using the term 'the best interests of the child' (*Kindeswohl*). According to the Civil Code, s 1697a, any decision of a Family Court on parental rights, contact, or child protection has to be determined in accordance with the best interests of the minor concerned.[44]

SECTION 1684 – CHILD'S RIGHT TO CONTACT

This provision explicitly recognises the separate and independent right of a child to have and to maintain contact with his or her parent/s.

42 CRC/C/DEU/CO/5-6, at para 6.

43 See, further, at: https://www.bundesregierung.de/breg-en/service/archive/rights-of-child-in-basic-law-1841338

44 The Civil Code, s 1741.

SECTION 1741 – ADMISSIBILITY OF ADOPTION

Adoption is permissible if it serves the best interests of the child and if it is expected that a parent-child relationship will arise between the adoptive parent and the child.

SECTION 1778 – PARENTAL RIGHT TO SUGGEST A GUARDIAN

This provides for a parental right to apply to the Family Court and suggests the appointment of a guardian in respect of a named child.

The Social Code (Sozialgesetzbuch)

The Social Code represents public law and Book VIII contains rules on the support and services provided to children including those involved in judicial proceedings. In public law, the term 'child welfare' (*Kinder- und Jugendhilfe*) refers to social provisions and social services provided for minors and their parents by the Youth Welfare Services (*Jugendamt*) in order to enable children and youth to grow up as self-determined, autonomous, and socially capable individuals.[45] In particular, s 81 requires the *Jugendamt* to co-operate with all bodies 'whose activity impacts on the living conditions of young people and their families' (viz. the courts, schools, health care facilities, police, and other regulatory agencies). Therefore, the law relating to Youth Welfare is part of the Social Code. There are, however, many more regulations in public law dealing with the well-being of minors or child protection (*Kinder- und Jugendschutz*) or which enforce their individual rights in various sectors of administrative and judicial proceedings.

The Criminal Code 2019 (Strafgesetzbuch)

Establishes 16 as the age of consent.

SECTION 19 – LACK OF CRIMINAL RESPONSIBILITY

This states that persons who have not attained the age of 14 at the time of the commission of an offence shall be deemed not to have committed a criminal act.

SECTION 171 – BREACH OF DUTY TO CARE OR UPBRINGING

A dereliction of duty to provide care or education for a person under the age of 16, which creates a danger that the person's physical or mental development could be seriously damaged, will be a criminal offence.

45 The Social Code, book 8, s 1.

SECTION 176 – SEXUAL ABUSE OF CHILDREN

Whosoever engages in sexual activity with a person under 14 years of age or allows the child to engage in sexual activity with himself shall be liable to imprisonment as will anyone who seriously physically abuses the child or places the child in danger of death.

SECTION 236 – CHILD TRAFFICKING

Whosoever in gross neglect of his duties of care and education leaves his child, ward, or foster child under 18 years of age with another for an indefinite period for material gain shall be liable to imprisonment.

Act on Proceedings in Family Matters and in Matters of Non-contentious Jurisdiction (Gesetz über das Verfahren in Familiensachen and in den Angelegenheiten der freiwilligen Gerichtsbarkeit) or Family Matters Act

This Act contains procedural rules including those relating to family and child welfare matters.

Youth Protection Act (Jugendschutzgesetz)

Article 1 of this legislation defines a child as someone under 14 years of age and an adolescent as over 14 but under 18. Article 8 states that if a child or young person is in a place where he or she is in imminent danger to his or her physical, mental, or psychological well-being, the competent authority or agency must take the necessary measures to avert the danger. It also gives effect to Article 12 of UN CROC by stating a child's right to be heard on matters concerning him or her and to have those views taken into account. This legislation, updated in 2021, implements the requirements of the General Comment on the Rights of Children in the Digital Environment, adopted by the UN CRC in February 2021.

The Strong Families Act 2019

Intended to provide financial assistance for families in poverty, this legislation reforms and improves the child benefit system. It targets support for school meals and transport for families in need and further increases funding for school materials.

The Federal Child Protection Act 2011 (Bundeskinderschuztgesetz)

Taking effect in 2012, this legislation seeks to ensure better cooperation between agencies involved in child protection, in particular as regards child abuse. The *Jugendamt* are required to cooperate with the Family Courts, prosecutors and prison authorities, police, schools, kindergartens, together with various bodies and agencies in the public sector with a view to improving preventative effectiveness.

Articles 4.3 to 5 impose a mandatory reporting requirement on any staff of a public service facility to inform the appropriate authorities if they become aware of a risk to the welfare of a child or young person.

The Adoption Intermediation Act 1976

This legislation, as amended in 2002 and 2020, is part of the Social Code and addresses all aspects of arrangements to be made in relation to child adoption beginning with counselling of the parties involved, examination of adoption applicants, placement decision, and post-adoptive care and counselling. The welfare principle has a central role in this legislation[46] which belongs to public law.[47] It also states the legal requirements relating to matters such as: the functions of adoption agencies, their accreditation, and the role of professional staff; prohibitions regarding advertising and solicitation; adoption support services; and notification duties.

Other

The CRC in its 2022 report welcomed the various legislative measures taken to implement the Convention, including the adoption of the Act to Strengthen Active Protection of Children and Juveniles, the Second Act Amending the Youth Protection Act, the Act to Combat Sexualised Violence against Children, the Act on Modernising Criminal Procedures, the Act to Combat Child Marriages, the Act on the Protection of Children with Variants of Sex Development, the Act on Providing All-Day Care and Education for Primary School Children, and the Act to Improve the Combating of Human Trafficking and to amend the Federal Central Register Act and Book VIII of the Social Code.[48]

The courts

Civil law in the Republic of Germany is administered through complex federal and state court systems, the latter replicated in each of the 16 *Länder*. Judicial authority, the five independent branches of law, and the differentiation of court jurisdictions are governed by Articles 20(2), 90, and 95 of the Basic Law. As Germany does not recognise the common law doctrine of precedent, no court is bound by the decision of a higher court. However, and unlike their French counterparts, the German judiciary are less inclined to apply the law in a minimalist manner – following the prescriptive rights and duties as stated in the Civil Law provisions – but are more likely to extemporise, referencing German and international academic texts, to explore issues, direct lines of inquiry, and justify decisions taken. For present purposes the following courts would seem most relevant.

46 See recommendations of the *Länder* (9th ed), 2022, Nr. I 1, at p 13 and Reinhardt, J. and Kemper, R., *Adoptionsrecht* (4th ed), Nomos Verlagsgesellschaft, (2021), at p 23.

47 See s. 68 Nr. 12 The Social Code, book 1.

48 CRC/C/DEU/CO/5-6, at: https://unfairtobacco.org/wp-content/uploads/2022/10/CRC_Germany_Concluding-Observations_Sept2022.pdf

The Federal Constitutional Court (Bundesverfassungsgericht) (BVerfG).

Established in 1951, this federal court functions as 'the guardian of the Basic Law'. Its jurisdiction is confined to ensuring that the law is stated, interpreted, and judicially applied in a manner that is constitutionally compliant and to ensure that fundamental rights are upheld. This is mainly achieved by reviewing court judgments against provisions of the Constitution.

Supreme Court of Justice (Bundesgerichtshof) (BGH)

This, the federal Supreme Court – one of five Supreme Courts that comprise the Federal Court of Justice – is the court of final appeal for all civil and criminal cases. It hears some family law cases on appeal.[49]

Courts of Appeal (Oberlandesgericht)

These are regional courts that hear appeals from decisions taken by courts of first instance. This court has a Family Division which hears appeals from Family Court decisions on cases such as divorce, child custody, maintenance, etc.

The Family Court (Familiengericht)

This is the local court of first instance (*Amtsgericht*).[50] The Family Court has to decide on disputes as defined in s 112 of the Law Concerning the Proceedings in Family Law Cases and Cases of Non-contentious Matters. In the main these concern: parental responsibilities;[51] questions regarding the child's residence, which are often framed as an issue of parental care;[52] adoption;[53] and questions of contact.[54] There are approximately 600 such courts in Germany.

Generally, in addition to the child and his or her parent/s, the following are present in Family Court proceedings: the judge; the *Jugendamt* staff; the guardian *ad litem* (*Verfahrensbeistand*); the youth office legal adviser (*Beistand*), or a supplementary curator (*Ergänzungspfleger*).

Representation for children

It is noteworthy that children aged 14 years or older can act in all matters affecting them without the participation of their legal representative.[55] This includes the right of a child of that age to bring a maintenance claim against their parent/s before the

49 Law on the System of Judicature, s 133.
50 Ibid., s 23a.
51 The Civil Code, s 1628.
52 Ibid., at s 1671.
53 Ibid., s 186.
54 Ibid., at ss 1684 and 1685.
55 Ibid., s 112.

Family Court,[56] and he or she may also file an application for interim measures (*Einstweilige Anordnung*) in all matters affecting them, without the need for a legal representative.[57]

LEGAL REPRESENTATIVE

In principle, the parental right of custody includes the right to act as the legal representative of their child. Exceptions to this principle include: procedures on the determination of parentage; in legal dispute between a close relative on the one hand and the child on the other. In such cases the Family Court appoints a supplementary curator – *Ergänzungspfleger* – to represent the child. A child does not have party status and cannot, for example, choose their own legal representative or refuse legal assistance.

GUARDIAN AD LITEM

German law provides for the mandatory appointment of a guardian *ad litem* – *Verfahrensbeistand* – in Family Court proceedings in all matters concerning the child, whenever necessary to protect their welfare interests,[58] unless those interests are adequately represented by a lawyer or another appropriate legal representative. It will be obligatory: where the decision could result in the separation of a child from his/her family or care giver;[59] or in a step-parent adoption where the court considers that the application gives rise to a conflict of interests that may jeopardise the child's welfare.[60] Such an appointment must be made in any adoption procedure if this is necessary to ensure the best interests of the child.[61]

The role of the guardian *ad litem* is crucial. It falls to this professional to: explain to the child the purpose and the stages of proceedings and the implications arising from any decisions made; elicit from the child, the family, and from such other sources as may be relevant, the information necessary to assess the welfare interests of the child for the purposes of the proceedings; and advise the court accordingly. The appointment of the guardian *ad litem* ends with the conclusion of the proceedings.

The child in court

There are no specific rules requiring a child-friendly court environment, nor are there any legal measures explicitly stipulating that a child can be examined *in camera*, behind a screen, or through a video link. However, these measures are possible.

56 The Act on Court Procedure in Family Matters and Non-litigious Matters, ss 9(1), 60 and 167(3).
57 Ibid., ss 9(1) and 167(3).
58 The Act on Court Procedure in Family Matters and Non-litigious Matters, s 50.
59 The Procedure in Family Matters Act, s 158.
60 Ibid., s 1796.
61 The Act on Court Procedure in Family Matters and Non-litigious Matters, s 191.

Also, as far as is feasible the child has to be informed in an appropriate manner about the subject matter, the issues, and the possible results of the proceedings.[62]

CONSENT OF CHILD

German law only very rarely provides any explicit right for a child to give or withhold consent although for the past 150 years it has been clear that a child under the age of 14 cannot give a valid consent to sexual acts.[63] In adoption proceedings and as regards abortion, the consent of the child concerned is required if he or she is aged 14 or older; if younger, the legal representative may consent on their behalf. As regards applying for social welfare benefits under the Social Code, a child must be aged 15 or older; if younger he or she will need parental authorisation.

While their actual consent may not be a specific requirement, he or she has a constitutional right to have their wishes considered, as far as this is judged to be compatible with their welfare interests. The older the child, the more seriously their wishes are to be treated.

CHILD'S RIGHT TO BE HEARD

In general, it is the duty of the guardian *ad litem* (*Verfahrensbeistand*), the youth office as legal adviser (*Beistand*), and the supplementary curator (*Ergänzungspfleger*), to ensure that children are heard in all matters that affect them and that they are consulted in the manner in which they wish to be heard.

A child of any age has a constitutional right to be heard in the Family Court on a matter concerning them but only if older than 14 years of age can he or she act on all matters affecting them without necessarily having a legal representative.[64] Generally this is by means of a face-to-face oral interview. The court may refrain from hearing a child only for serious reasons such as where this could be psychologically harmful.

The age and maturity of the child concerned will be influential in determining whether a proposed hearing could be harmful and on the appropriate extent to share information with him or her.[65] In the absence of any statutory rules on ages, the caselaw is contradictory as to the age it is best to hear children: some judiciary have argued that children as young as three may be heard; others have proposed a minimum of four or five years; there seems to be consensus that a child any older must generally be heard.

In adoption proceedings, unlike the position in most other countries, judges are required to hear a child in person and must do so regardless of the age of the adoptee.[66] Taking into account the child's age, development, and emotional stability, the

62 The Act on Voluntary Jurisdiction, s 50b(2).
63 The Criminal Code 1872, s 176.
64 The Act on Court Procedure in Family Matters and Non-litigious Matters, ss 9(1) and 167(3).
65 Ibid., s 50b(2).
66 The Family Matters Act, s 192.

court will decide whether to hear the child: alone, or together with birth parents, or with prospective adopters, and with or without siblings; in the court or in the family home; in the presence of experts; and on one occasion or more.

The court must hear a child personally in proceedings concerning the child's care, custody, or the administration of their assets in any case, regardless of his or her age.[67] Nonetheless, in its 2022 report the CRC urged the government to 'ensure that all children, including children under 14 years of age, can express their opinions and be heard in all decisions affecting them, including in courts and administrative and civil proceedings, and establish legal standards for ensuring that such proceedings are child-friendly'. In the light of the aforementioned s 159(1), this recommendation would seem superfluous.

Other official and regulatory bodies

Germany has agencies – some statutory, others non-governmental – that provide child-specific advice and advocacy or include such a focus within a broader, rights-oriented service provision. Arguably, they are more passive – advice-giving, awareness-raising entities – than their assertive counterparts in some other countries. The latter often have a remit that includes research on contemporary issues and leading the lobbying of government to effect change in laws relating to child welfare.

JUGENDÄMTER

These communal Child Welfare Offices, spread across Germany and located in every borough (*Landkreis*) and city (*Kreisfreie Stadt*), are responsible for family support service provision.

GERMAN INSTITUTE FOR HUMAN RIGHTS (DEUTSCHES INSTITUT FÜR MENSCHENRECHTE)

Among the functions of this body are its responsibility for monitoring the implementation of UN CROC in Germany and promoting an awareness of children's rights.

OMBUDSMAN (OMBUDSSTELLEN)

In 2019 it was reported that the German federal government has not complied with the UN Committee's recommendation 14 from 2014 'to establish an appropriate, permanent national office', although 'some states have municipal or state coordination centres that deal with sub-aspects of the UN Convention on the Rights of

67 The Act on Voluntary Jurisdiction, s 159(1).

the Child'.[68] In fact, such independent advisory offices were introduced by law in 2021 to provide free information and support for children and/or their families. They actively promote the rights of children and youths and advocate on behalf of their interests. In cases of disagreement between families and the Youth Welfare Authorities the Ombudsmen act as mediators to seek possible compromises.[69] Similar offices are being established across Germany.

INDEPENDENT COMMISSIONER ON CHILD SEXUAL ABUSE ISSUES

This permanent office was established in 2010, following earlier CRC recommendations, and is assisted by the National Council against Sexual Violence Committed against Children and Adolescents.

Other

While there is little in the way of national agencies dedicated to assertively promoting the welfare/rights of children, the mix of agencies to be found in each *Länder* – mostly in the communes – include a vast range of entities that endeavour to do so.

The German charity Children's Fund (*Deutsches Kinderhilfswerk*), established in the 1970s, provides a national service that includes alleviating the effects of poverty on children and their families and support for refugee children and young people as they integrate into German society. Also child protection services – like *Kinderschutzbund, Kindernotrufe* – or others are specifically engaged in child welfare all over Germany whilst many local services exist in the communes.

Conclusion

In Germany, even more so than in France, the state and its institutions were rebuilt in the aftermath of WWII. Most importantly, a new Constitution was inaugurated in 1949 and in 1951 this was entrusted to a newly established Federal Constitutional Court (*Bundesverfassungsgericht*) which has ever since ensured that German law does not stray far from its basic constitutional principles.

In some ways, however, the pre-WWII relationship between family and state continued or was even strengthened. The Civil Code in particular, which houses the main legal provisions relating to the family and children, dates from 1881 and continues to be revised, amended, and supplemented in response to emerging social changes.[70] Traditional deference to parental status, and respect for the relative autonomy of the family unit from unwanted state interference, became rein-

68 See *Implementation of the UN Convention on the Rights of the Child in Germany 5th/6th supplementary report to the United Nations*, at: https://umsetzung-der-kinderrechtskonvention.de/8-b-childrens-rights-policies/?lang=en

69 The Social Code, book VIII, s 9a.

70 The Civil Code, Article 6(1) places 'marriage' and 'family' under the special protection of the state; Article 6(2) establishes that children are primarily the responsibility of their parents.

forced as a reaction to the Nazi era when the state exercised direct fascist control over all its citizens. This may well militate against a whole-hearted recognition and acceptance of the welfare interests of a child as separate and perhaps in conflict with the interests of parents. The fact that Germany is a signatory state to the UN CROC does not necessarily mean that its family law has fully embraced and now applies the paramountcy principle.

7 The welfare principle in contemporary practice

Public family law – civil and criminal jurisdictions

Introduction

Germany, in recent years, has become a multicultural society.[1] This may be partially a consequence of absorbing both its citizens from the former German Democratic Republic and the influx of Muslims and other ethnic groups that comprised the migrant crisis. It is also the result of an assimilation of several million 'guest workers' particularly from Turkey. However, it may simply reflect the result of a deliberate public policy to break with the social homogeneity that led the country into its era of fascist ideology. Whatever the causes, the traditional patriarchal family model – around which so much of German family law was built – is undergoing profound challenges.

This chapter like its French counterpart (see Chapter 4), deals with the public law as it relates to children. It is similarly in two parts: first the civil law (child protection, etc.); then the criminal (juvenile delinquency, etc.).

Beginning with civil law and consensual state intervention in family affairs on child welfare grounds, the chapter considers the duty to support vulnerable families, the delivery agencies, and the services provided. It then examines the grounds for coercive intervention: the threshold of harm requiring the state to investigate standards of parental care and protection; mandatory reporting; the use of 'baby boxes'; and the role of the *Jugendamt* (Youth Welfare Offices). It explains the process whereby children transfer from parental to state care and considers the out-of-home placement options. It assesses the veracity of the state duty to plan for and ensure the rehabilitation of children to their families of origin and explores the issues associated with unaccompanied migrant minors and trafficking.

The second part of the chapter explores the legal system as it relates to child offenders. It explains the functions of the juvenile justice system, the judicial role, and the court disposal options. It identifies and considers the preventative custodial and community-based approaches to offenders. It assesses the comparative effectiveness of the system in terms of its output and incidence of recidivism.

1 See, further, Habermas, J., in Taylor, C., *Multiculturalism and the Politics of Recognition*, Princeton University Press, Princeton, NJ, USA (1994).

DOI: 10.4324/9781003415688-11

Public family law: civil jurisdiction

German society has undergone significant upheavals over the past generation or two. Reunification brought its own socioeconomic challenges accompanied by a significant jolt to cultural awareness as the nation sought to blend the cultures of both east and west Germany and find a new coherent identity. This struggle to achieve social cohesion has been further complicated by the need to absorb the very many migrants arriving in Germany and becoming permanent residents. The 'guest worker' – *Gastarbeiter* – phenomenon had been impacting German society since the 1950s–1970s, when bilateral agreements with countries such as Turkey, Greece, and Morocco resulted in many citizens from those countries arriving on temporary work permits to contribute to the labour force then much needed by Germany's rapidly expanding industrial sector. While some eventually returned to their countries of origin, most did not. It has been estimated that by 2010, some 4 million people of Turkish descent, mostly Muslims, were resident in Germany. Then came the 'migrant crisis' that began in 2015 and in that year alone saw an additional 2.14 million arrive in Germany, most of whom were young men – including many unaccompanied minors – and again mostly Muslims.

In short the prolonged culture shock that has impacted Germany over the past few decades has brought with it challenges to its social norms, its family law, and indeed to its concept of 'family life'. Arranged marriages, female genital mutilation, patriarchy, and the importance of the blood-link, 'kafala', instead of adoption have been among the many customs that German family law has had to deal with.

Parents and state

International law – particularly Articles 8 of the European Convention on Human Rights (ECHR) and 3 of the United Nations Convention on the Rights of the Child (UN CROC) – established the broad parameters for the roles of parent and state in relation to their respective responsibilities for ensuring the welfare interests and rights of children. It also set the standards, identified the circumstances, and generally clarified the rationale for when, how, and to what effect such welfare interests and rights were to be applied.

Domestic law provides that the relationship between state, parent, and child is governed by Article 6 of the Basic Law. Article 6(2) places primary responsibility for family matters – and specifically for safeguarding the welfare interests of children – with the parents. The legal duty to supervise and protect a child – *Aufsichtspflicht* – falls on the parents who must provide for their child's care and upbringing. The subsidiarity principle assigns the state a secondary role in which it is required to both respect the autonomous right of parents to manage their family affairs as they see fit, and to monitor and support them to the extent necessary to ensure the welfare interests of children are not jeopardised. The combined effect of Articles 2(1) and 6(2) of the Basic Law is to place an obligation on the state to ensure that children and adolescents receive adequate and safe parental care. Where it considers that parents are failing to provide such care, the state may legitimately intervene in the constitutionally protected parent-child relationship by employing such consensual and coercive means of intervention as are authorised by law.

Prevention: consensual intervention

The *Jugendamt* are not necessarily direct service providers to families in need of support. The non-governmental organisations (NGOs; "*Freie Träger*", i.e. private agencies, not-for-profit entities, and charities) have priority over the *Jugendamt* in service provision to those in need (the so-called subsidiarity of public youth welfare).[2] Only where no private entity is available must the *Jugendamt* then undertake service provision. In addition, the *Jugendamt* has responsibility for ensuring that all required services are provided in the relevant borough or city.[3]

State duties to support families in need

As has been said, the Child Welfare system in Germany is 'family service-oriented because families in need are entitled to request family support services'.[4]

SERVICE PROVISION

Support services such as assistance for expectant mothers and those with new-born children are mandated under the provisions of the Social Code[5] and the Act on Cooperation and Information on Child Protection.[6] So, also, are services for vulnerable families with health issues and services available either at counselling centres for children, adolescents, and parents or in the form of home-visiting services.[7] All services are preventative and non-invasive in nature, but all service providers must report any parental neglect, failure to cope, dependency issues, etc. they cannot cope with to the Youth Welfare Office, thus implementing the policy priority of keeping families together before addressing parenting deficits and triggering child protection intervention procedures. Due to the constitutional principle of proportionality, any intervention in the context of children at risk must prioritise the provision of the necessary public support – such as daycare centres and therapeutic services – required to avoid child removal.[8] Furthermore, early access to families,

2 Book VIII of the Social Code, s 4.
3 Book I of the Social Code, s 27.
4 Kindler, H., 'Developing Evidence-Based Child Protection Practice: A View from Germany', in *Research on Social Work Practice,* Vol. 18 (4), (2008), at pp 319–24.
5 Book VIII of the Social Code, s 16.
6 Section 2 (1).
7 Book VIII of the Social Code, ss 17, 18, and 52a; Act on Cooperation and Information on Child Protection, s 2.
8 Galm, B. & Derr, R., *Combating Child Abuse and Neglect: Child Protection in Germany – National Report*, Deutsches Jugendinstitut e.V. (2011), at: https://www.dji.de/fileadmin/user_upload/bibs/DAPHNEGermanReportLayoutFIN.pdf

even before birth of a child, was introduced in 2012[9] to install a primary preventative system of help and support for vulnerable families. This form of intervention may also serve as an early warning system.

SAFE HAVENS

The provision of designated safe havens – or 'baby boxes' for facilitating anonymous births – where mothers can relinquish their babies, is illegal but continues to be tolerated by the state. In 2014 the possibility of birth under 'preliminary' anonymity (*Vertrauliche Geburt*) was introduced following criticism of the earlier practice of total anonymous birth.[10] In 2022, the Committee on the Rights of the Child (CRC) noted with appreciation the adoption of the Act on the Expansion of Assistance for Pregnant Women and Confidential Birth Arrangements and the consequent decrease in the number of cases of anonymous child abandonment. The Committee recommended that Germany 'continue to strengthen measures to promote the use of confidential births and ensure that information about the biological origins of such children are preserved, with a view to eliminating the use of baby boxes'.[11]

Protection: coercive state intervention

Section 1631(2) of the Civil Code states the governing principle that:

> Children shall be entitled to a non-violent upbringing. Physical punishments, psychological injuries and other degrading acts shall be inadmissible.

Section 1666(1) defines 'harm' to children as the endangerment of the 'physical, mental or psychological best interests of the child or his/her property'. The customary categories are listed as criminal offences in the Criminal Code (*Strafgesetzbuch*): child neglect (ss 171 and 221); physical maltreatment (ss 223 and 224); physical maltreatment and neglect (s 225); and child abuse (ss 174, 176, 176a, 176b, 180, 182, 184, and 225).[12] For example, s 176 of the Code defines and prohibits sexual abuse as follows:

> (1) Whosoever engages in sexual activity with a person under fourteen years of age (child) or allows the child to engage in sexual activity with himself shall be liable to imprisonment from six months to ten years.

Further provisions elaborate on the offence and related punishments. Other laws are also relevant, such as the Federal Child Protection Act, which took effect in

9 Act on Cooperation and Information on Child Protection, s 2.
10 UN Committee on the Rights of the Child (CRC), 25 February 2014, op. cit., at para 31.
11 CRC/C/DEU/CO/5-6, at para 19.
12 See, further, Silver, H.K. and Kempe, C.H., 'Problem of Parental Criminal Neglect and Severe Physical Abuse of Children', *Journal of Diseases of Children*, (1959).

2012, and is intended to strengthen the active protection of children and young people.

Interestingly, child protection – *Kinderschutz* – has been interpreted as extending beyond the customary categories of 'endangerment' – and beyond the usual health and safety bans on alcohol and cigarettes – to include violent video games (*Killerspiele*). This was achieved by way of a 2008 amendment to the Youth Protection Act (*JuSchG*) prohibiting the sale or the advertising of video games, movies, or other forms of media depicting extreme violence.

In 2021, the Youth Welfare Authorities reported more than 59,900 cases where the best interests of a child or young person were endangered because of neglect or psychological, physical, or sexual violence and nearly 967,700 cases where help, support, or counselling was granted by the Youth Welfare Offices due to educational deficits beneath the threshold of an endangerment of child welfare.[13] As a result, child endangerment reached its second highest level since the beginning of the statistics in 2012, while the number of cases in need of help also hit a new high. The CRC in its 2022 report stated that it 'remains seriously concerned about the high prevalence of violence against children, including sexual exploitation and online violence',[14] and the Committee recommended that 'Germany strengthen measures to ensure child victims or witnesses of violence have prompt access to child-friendly and multi-sectoral interventions and support'.[15]

Duty to promptly intervene

In normal circumstances, *Jugendamt* intervention in family affairs requires Family Court authorisation. However, where the 'child endangerment'[16] is assessed as urgent and it is impractical to seek prior authorization, then the *Jugendamt* is obliged to promptly take the child into emergency custody (*Inobhutnahme*).[17] Otherwise, the *Jugendamt* have no independent right to remove a child from their family; such an invasive intrusion must be authorised by the court.

MANDATORY REPORTING AND CHILD HELPLINES

There is no mandatory public duty to report knowledge of child neglect or abuse unless severe crimes are concerned.[18] There is, however, a mandatory duty on those working with children – whether in a public agency or a *Freier Träge* – to report any evidence

13 See, further, at: https://www.destatis.de/DE/Themen/Gesellschaft-Umwelt/Soziales/Jugendarbeit/Tabellen/hilfen-erziehung-jungevolljaehrige.html

14 Ibid., at para 22.

15 See, further, at: https://www.ohchr.org/en/press-releases/2022/09/un-child-rights-committee-publishes-findings-germany-kuwait-north-macedonia

16 Under Articles 1666 and 1666a of the Civil Code (child maltreatment, child sexual abuse, and neglect of the child).

17 Book VIII of the Social Code, s 8a (2).

18 The Criminal Code, s 138.

of a child needing protection to the local *Jugendamt.*[19] The national child helpline – *Nummer gegen Kummer* – provides a free phone counselling service for children, adolescents, and parents. There are also several local child-specific – *Kinder- und Jugendtelefon* – phone helplines and the right of any minor to seek assistance from the Youth Welfare Office independently from his or her parents. So, only professionals – such as social workers, teachers, psychologists, and health care or social service staff – are obliged to act when aware of any harm to the welfare interests of a child.[20]

CHILD PROTECTION CENTRES

Germany has community-based child protection facilities – *Kinderschutzzentrum* – which are NGO service providers specifically designated to provide services for those affected or threatened by violence (including child maltreatment, child neglect, and sexual abuse), perhaps the equivalent of women's refuge centres in the U.K. There are 28 such centres where family members can receive advice and counselling.

MULTI-AGENCY CO-OPERATION

The *Jugendamt* are legally required to co-operate with all bodies 'whose activities have an impact on the living conditions of young people and their families' (viz. courts, schools, health care facilities, police, and other regulatory agencies).[21] Further, any risk assessment in respect of a child suspected of being in need of protection must be carried out by a 'collaboration of several specialists' and the decision reached must be made collectively.[22] Thus, there is mandatory legal obligation on all those who work with children to be alert to the possibility of any possible 'endangerment of minors' and to initiate child protection procedures when necessary.

Investigation

The *Jugendamt* are legally responsible for conducting investigations to establish whether there is 'grave evidence of child endangerment'[23] but some doubt has been expressed as to their effectiveness in this regard.[24] Rönsch has noted that in the period 2001–18, while total expenditure on child protection increased by 146%, the number of withdrawals of parental custody rose by 65%, and the number of children taken

19 Ibid., s 42.
20 Book VIII of the Social Code, s 8a (4); Act on Cooperation and Information on Child Protection, s 4.
21 Ibid., s 81.
22 Ibid., s 8a. According to the statistics: in about one-third of all cases immediate action is required; in another third there is generally a need for help or assistance; and the remaining third are usually irrelevant.
23 Ibid.
24 Rönsch, H., 'Effectiveness of Laws and Policies Governing Permissive Parenting in Pursuit of the Reduction of Severe Child Abuse in Germany', *Children and Youth Services Review*, Vol. 119, (2020), at: https://www.sciencedirect.com/science/article/pii/S0190740920307416

into protective care increased by 29%, the net result was not a reduction or containment in the number of children at risk. Instead, the actual number of cases of severe child abuse in Germany rose by 39%. Increased rates of expenditure may result only in increased rates of detection, with no moderating impact on rates of prevalence.[25]

There have been some cases highlighted by the media which provide insight into the consequences of state non-interventionism in family matters. In 2011, there was the much publicised case of the stepfather who had been sexually abusing his step-daughter for 20 years from when she was 13 years of age; she had borne him eight children. More recently, media reports in November 2022 revealed that an eight-year-old girl had been kept locked up in her grandparents house for almost her entire life: never attending school nor dental check-ups nor any other health/social care services; she had no friends and was never seen playing with other children; in brief, she had no social interaction of any form.[26] Such cases would seem to indicate that the protective monitoring role of the *Jugendamt* is failing some children.[27] A strong sense of family matters being private and a low tolerance for prying that might result in exposure to community wrath – which, while not specific to German society, does have particular connotations for that society – could be a contributing factor to what seems to be a reticence to make the necessary enquiries.

Care proceedings

A characteristic feature of German child protection law is the deference paid to parents at all times. The peremptory 'child rescue' approach evident in the U.K. and some other common law countries, where the paramountcy principle dictates the nature of engagement with parents, is a good deal less pronounced in Germany. However, at the point of initial intervention and risk assessment, the legal focus on parents and their 'rights'[28] is balanced to a degree by a legal requirement to elicit and take into account the views of the child.[29]

CARE PLAN

Every child admitted or committed to the public care system for six months or longer must have a care plan that states the purpose, location, and duration of

25 See Gilbert, R. et al., 'Child Maltreatment: Variation in Trends and Policies in Six Developed Countries', *Lancet,* (2011) at: https://scholar.google.com/scholar_lookup?hl=en&publication_year=2011&author=R+Gilbert&author=J+Fluke&author=M+O%27Donnell&author=A+GonzalezIzquierdo&author=M+Brownell&author=P+Gulliver&title=Child+maltreatment%3A+variation+in+trends+and+policies+in+six+developed+countries

26 See 'Eight-year-old child reportedly locked up for life in Germany', *The Brussels Times* (April 22, 2023), at: https://www.brusselstimes.com/318698/eight-year-old-child-reportedly-locked-up-for-life-in-germany

27 As required under Book VIII of the Social Code, ss 8a and 42.

28 Ibid., s 42(3).

29 Ibid., s 8a.

the out-of-home placement. The plan is formulated through cooperative negotiations between the child and his or her parents, professionals of the Youth Welfare Authorities and NGO services, and possibly other persons (e.g. siblings, birth parents without parental rights, and perhaps others) and should be updated regularly, normally every six months. The child concerned must be consulted in relation to any alteration of his or her care plan.[30]

EMERGENCY PROTECTION ORDER

Having conducted an investigation and established that a child is in urgent need of protection, the *Jugendamt* are legally responsible for then removing him or her to an emergency placement (*Inobhutnahme*).[31] As both the removal and the placement are subject to parental rights they require either parental consent or subsequent Family Court authorisation. Only strong evidence of a serious risk to the welfare of a child will justify removal or retention of that child against parental wishes.[32]

State care

State intervention in family affairs is authorised by the Child and Youth Services Act, incorporated as Book VIII in the Social Code, and by s 1666 of the Civil Code, but is exercised with extreme caution. As Schweppe has explained,[33] the law provides that infringement of parental custody should never go beyond that which is the minimum necessary to safeguard the best interests of the child – *Grundsatz der Verhältnismäßigkeit* (the principle of proportionality).[34]

In 2021, approximately 47,500 children were taken into temporary care on grounds of protection, an increase of 5% from the previous year. This is mostly due to an increase in the number of unaccompanied migrant minors (plus 49%) whereas protection due to child welfare endangerment dropped by 6%. Interestingly, 170 of those cases were responses to requests from the children concerned.[35]

Threshold for state care

Taking a child into care and the withdrawal of parental responsibility is regarded as an extreme measure to be exercised only when a child is clearly in need of protection (*Kindeswohlgefährdung*). In such circumstances the *Jugendamt* have statutory powers to remove children, as above, and detain them to the extent necessary to

30 Ibid., s 8a (1).

31 Ibid., s 42.

32 Ibid., s 42(4).

33 See Schweppe, K., 'Child Protection in Europe: Different Systems – Common Challenges', *German Law Journal,* Vol. 3(10), (2002).

34 The Civil Code, s 1666a.

35 See, further, at: https://www.destatis.de/DE/Presse/Pressemitteilungen/2022/07/PD22_315_225.html

avert danger to the child or others, pending a court ruling on whether to impose restrictions on parental rights.[36] Paradoxically, and most unusually, a German child of any age has an unconditional right to require the authorities to admit him or her to state care.[37]

In general, aside from the last mentioned anomaly, the threshold for taking children into custody would seem to be higher in Germany than in other developed nations: only if there is no other option can children be taken into residential or foster care against the wishes of a parent or guardian.[38] However, in practice the German authorities have at times been found to act precipitately in intervening on child welfare grounds. The European Court of Human Rights (ECtHR) has had the opportunity to consider threshold criteria in at least two cases. In the first, *Kutzner v. Germany*,[39] the German courts deprived parents of parental custody for their daughters because they had learning disabilities and their intellectual capacities were determined to be insufficiently developed to permit them to raise their children. This was found to be unreasonable and disproportionate by the ECtHR which ruled that the total revocation of the parents' legal custody, and the abrupt removal of the children, constituted a deprivation of parental care that violated their Article 8 rights. In the second, *Haase v. Germany*,[40] seven children were peremptorily removed into care on an emergency basis including a seven-day-old baby removed from hospital. This occurred on the same day of the court hearing, without providing the parents with an opportunity to contest the court order. The ECtHR found that the fact and manner of state action was not justified by any circumstances of urgency and held that there had been a violation of the parents' Article 8 rights. In the subsequent case of *Wetjen and Others v. Germany*,[41] the peremptory removal of a number of children – including a breastfed child – was again an issue (see, further, Chapter 6).

CURATOR

The Civil Code provides that, where the welfare of a child is at risk, the Family Court may restrict or withdraw parental responsibility if this is necessary to protect the child's welfare.[42] In such cases the court has to appoint a curator (*Ergänzungspfleger*) as specific aspects of parental responsibility are then restricted and will need to be undertaken by others: a curator may, for example, have the right

36 See *Inobhutnahme*, s 42 Social Code VIII.

37 Social Code, Book VIII, s 42(1).

38 See Higher Regional Court of Berlin-Brandenburg, OVG 6 S 8/17, (28.3.2017).

39 Application No. 46544/99, (2002).

40 Application No. 11057/02, (2004).

41 Application Nos. 68125/14 and 72204/14, (2018).

42 The Civil Code, s 1666. This provides that, where the physical, mental, or emotional welfare of a child is placed at risk by neglect or mistreatment of the child or because parents otherwise fail to comply with their parental duties, the Family Court shall order the measures necessary to protect the child when voluntary measures have been insufficient to protect the child's welfare.

to determine the child's place of residence or the necessary medical treatment. In cases where there has been a complete withdrawal of parental responsibility, the court has to appoint a guardian (*Vormund*). This will happen most obviously where the child has been abandoned or in severe cases of child neglect or abuse (see, further, Chapter 6).[43]

As a rule, an individual person should be appointed as guardian, but the court may appoint a *Verein* (private association) or the *Jugendamt* in cases where no appropriate person is available.[44] Most often guardianship is now administered by the local *Jugendamt* office. National German statistics for the year 1999 show that such authorities were appointed to be guardian or curator in 80% of the court proceedings involving the (partial) withdrawal of custodial rights. The children found by the court to have been failed by parental care are then placed in foster homes, with other relatives, or in residential care.

Foster care: partnership and rehabilitation

Foster care has been the placement of choice for children in need of an out-of-home placement since at least the 1968 decision of the Constitutional Court (see, further, Chapter 6). However, it has never become the primary resource for such children as it has in the U.K. and most other common law countries. Reinhardt makes the point that: 'although state/parent partnerships ostensibly form the basis for the planned rehabilitation of children in care, the Youth Welfare Authorities face the fact that in many cases there are no suitable fosterparents available for children in need of such placement thus forcing the authorities to leave children in residential care'.[45] Therefore, of necessity residential care continues to provide placements for a larger proportion of the child care population than is now the case in the U.K. and other countries.

FOSTER CARE

In 2021 there were approximately 87,300 children formally placed in full-time foster care with numbers slightly decreasing in the last four years after a steady rise before (e.g. in 2005 there were 50,364 children and young people in family foster care and in 2015 there were 71,501[46]). The current regulatory regime for foster care, as noted by Wolf, is unsatisfactory:[47]

> In Germany, there are no universally recognized standards for foster care services. For this reason, local agencies vary considerably in terms of their

43 The Civil Code, s 1773.

44 Ibid., s 1791a and 1791b.

45 Note to author (17 May 2023).

46 See, further, at f/n 14.

47 See Wolf, K., 'Promoting the Positive Development of Foster Children: Establishing Research in Germany', *Adoption & Fostering*, Vol. 36(1), (2012), pp 40–51, at p 41.

> principles, operation and staffing ... no government agency exists that could establish let alone implement, standards.

Reinhardt adds 'although there are recommendations by the State Youth Welfare Offices with high standards on the examination of possible fosterparents, the authorities are often forced to lower their standards in order to be able to find fosterparents at all'.[48]

In practice long-term foster care provides the legal framework for perhaps one-third of the children in the public care system due to parental absence, failure to protect, or failure to provide adequate care. Guardianship and custody orders provide alternatives to adoption for some in certain circumstances, but only very rarely. There are no legal orders, let alone a continuum of private family orders, designed specifically to offer options for vesting varying aspects of parental responsibilities in those providing an alternative to parental care. However, in 2021 the law introduced the possibility of a court order that prevents children being taken from the foster families by their birth parents ("*Dauerverbleibensanordnung*").[49] The CRC in its 2022 report recommended that Germany 'further strengthen its system of foster care, introduce uniform standards and quality criteria and prevent frequent transfers of children in foster care and other alternative care settings'.[50]

KINSHIP CARE

In Germany, the preferred foster care placement is with a relative.[51] Of the total foster care population in 2005, approximately 60% of the children were in kinship placements.[52]

PARTNERSHIP AND REHABILITATION

The local *Jugendamt* office has a duty to make appropriate efforts to reunify a family, within a reasonable period following the admission of a child into the care system,[53] while birth parents of a child in foster care have the right to request reunification services at any time.[54] Also, under Article 6(2) of the Basic Law and s 1684 of the Civil Code, birth parents enjoy a presumptive right to maintain contact with their child (in fact it is construed as a parental duty[55]), a right also vested in the

48 Note to author (17 May 2023).
49 The Civil Code, s 1632 (4).
50 CRC/C/DEU/CO/5-6, at para 27(c).
51 See Kiraly, M. and Humphreys, C., 'It's About the Whole Family: Family Contact for Children in Kinship Care', *Child & Family Social Work*, Vol. 21, (2016).
52 See Walter, M. and Blandow, J., 'Foster Care in Germany', (2004) at: https://www.uni-siegen.de/foster-care-research/network_conferences/1st_conference/files/foster_care_germany_-_kindler.pdf
53 The Social Code VIII, s 37.
54 The Civil Code, s 1632.
55 Ibid., s 1684(1).

child.[56] This applies when the child is in foster care unless a Family Court rules that contact endangers the welfare of that child.[57] Indeed, unless the court has stripped parents of their innate rights, then – under s 1673 *et seq.* of the Civil Code – those rights are merely suspended and the authorities are required to prepare the parents and child for the legal resumption of their relationship.

However, in practice, children will only be returned to the birth parents if the latter can show that they have been able to restore the standards of care expected from those with parental rights: a complete change of life and attitude is required compared to the *status quo ante*. So, for example, in *Haase v. Germany*,[58] the ECtHR found that the domestic court had been justified in deciding that the best interests of a child were served by not reuniting him with his birth parents. The court explained:[59]

> Experience shows that when children remain in the care of youth authorities for a protracted period, a process is set in motion which drives them towards an irreversible separation from their family. When a considerable period of time has passed since the children were first placed in care, the children's interest in not undergoing further de facto changes to their family situation may prevail over the parents' interest in seeing the family reunited. The possibilities for reunification will progressively diminish and eventually be destroyed if the biological parents and the children are not allowed to meet each other at all.

Generally, as Wolf has noted, 'in Germany there is substantial criticism of the practice of reuniting children with birth families'. He asserts that 'efforts to support the birth family are sparse … it is usually only after several years living in foster care that the issue of return to the birth family is raised … much more rarely than in the U.K., birth families are reunited'.[60] In practice, only in 4–5% of the cases are birth families reunited. A virtual absence of non-consensual adoption means that by far the majority of children remain in the care system until they age out.

Residential care

As has been noted 'the German child welfare system is characterized by a high proportion of placements in residential care compared to foster care'.[61] In fact this has long been the case (e.g. in 1998 82% of 'looked after' children living away from

56 Ibid., s 1626(3).

57 Ibid., s 1684.

58 Application No. 11057/02, (2004).

59 Ibid., at para 103.

60 See Wolf, K., 'Promoting the Positive Development of Foster Children: Establishing Research in Germany', *Adoption & Fostering*, Vol. 36(1), (2012), pp 40–51, at p 49.

61 See Schrödter, M., 'German Residential Care: Doing Extremely Well in Doing the Wrong Thing', conference paper presented at 'The International Social Work & Society Academy', Sofia, Bul-

home were in foster care in England in contrast with only 39% in Germany[62]). In 2005, for example, there were some 61,806 children in residential homes (50,364 in foster homes), 81,310 in 2015, and approximately 100,000 in 2017, considerably more than in foster care. Residential care has become the default placement for two-thirds of the child care population as, for them, family life in a foster home is unavailable. Residential care is almost entirely run by independent, not-for-profit social care organisations, with providers typically offering a wide range of services from social worker and family support, to foster care and children's homes. It is an expensive service that features small units (usually six to eight chidren) run by professional staff who function within an educational ethos that aims to address relationship issues and prompt reflective insight.

The CRC in its above-mentioned 2022 report expressed concern regarding 'the increasing number of children living in alternative care and, in particular, in closed institutions and without proper assessment of their best interests'.[63]

SECURE ACCOMMODATION

Given that in Germany the child protection services provide ongoing support for young adults up to the age of 21 and even 27 in certain cases, it is to be expected that there would be an occasional need for secure accommodation for some of those in out-of-home care. If such accommodation is to be compliant with the right to liberty requirement in Article 5 of the ECHR then it must meet the *Storck* test.[64] This necessitates that the deprivation of liberty be: in a specific restricted space for a not insignificant period of time; without the consent of the detainee; and be authorised by the state or other proper authority. However, there would appear to be a lack of information available on the use of such facilities.

Adoption

In Germany, while both plenary and simple adoptions are legally possible, as is the adoption of adults, the adoption of children must be by plenary proceedings.[65] However, domestic adoption, as a consensual third-party process – where the adopter is a 'stranger' to the child – and where the state or a state-approved agency facilitates the placement, has been declining for years and is now a relatively rare occurrence in Germany. Non-consensual adoption from state care and intercountry adoptions are also a rarity.

---

garia, (August 2014), at: https://www.researchgate.net/publication/265162609_German_Residential_Care_Doing_Extremely_Well_in_Doing_the_Wrong_Thing

62 See White, K.J., 'The Ideology of Residential Care and Fostering: Re-framing Children's Services', *NCVCCO Annual Review Journal* No. 3, (2002), at pp 231–42.

63 CRC/C/DEU/CO/5-6, at para 26(a).

64 *Storck v. Germany* [2006] 43 EHRR 6.

65 See Mignot, J-F., *Child Adoption in Western Europe, 1900–2015*, HAL, (2019), at: https://shs.hal.science/halshs-02008838/document

DOMESTIC VOLUNTARY ADOPTION

When a domestic adoption application is lodged the court is required to protect the anonymity of the applicant adopters,[66] investigate and examine all relevant facts *ex officio*,[67] and it must hear submissions from the adoption agency,[68] the child,[69] and all other children already living in the adopters' family (see, further, Chapter 9).

ADOPTION FROM STATE CARE

As adoption is essentially a consensual process, there are very few adoptions of children – about 5% – from the care system, even though in many cases the need for parental consent has been judicially removed. According to the German Association for Child Protection in 2010, the number of children entering the public care system increased by 81% in the previous four years[70] but in that year only 250 left it by way of non-consensual adoption. There is no policy, established practice, or seemingly any exact statistical data relating to the adoption of children from the care system in Germany. The local *Jugendamt* office is required to consider whether adoption from care placements is legally possible but this rarely leads to the necessary arrangements being made.[71] Unlike other countries such as the U.K. and the U.S. the increase in the child care population does not seem to trigger policy debates in Germany leading to law reforms that might enable the adoption option to be available to a greater proportion of that population[72] (see, further, Chapter 9).

Unaccompanied migrant minors and trafficking

A singular feature, distinguishing Germany from its western neighbours, is the scale of the influx of migrants in recent years. In 2015 alone, the *Jugendamt* took custody of over 42,300 unaccompanied refugee children.[73] It continues to be the most popular destination for refugee and migrant children, registering 37% of all child asylum applications in Europe between January and June 2020 (25,755 children).[74]

66 The Civil Code, s 1758.
67 The Procedure in Family Matters Act, s 26.
68 Ibid., s 189.
69 Ibid., s 192.
70 See, further, at: http://www.dw.de/new-child-protection-law-aims-to-strengthen-families-rather-than-divide-them/a-6329547
71 The Social Code VIII, s 36, para 1.
72 Bach, R., 'Von Kindeswohl und Kinderwunsch', *Bad Boll*, (2011). However, see Botthof, A., 'Die Annahme als Kind als Alternative zur Dauerfpflege', *FamRZ* (*Zeitschrift für das gesamte Familienrecht*) 2016, pp 768–73. Also, see, further, at: https://www.dji.de/ueber-uns/projekte/projekte/expertise-und-forschungszentrum-adoption-efza.html
73 See, further, the Federal Statistics Office of Germany.
74 See, further, at: https://www.unicef.org/eca/emergencies/latest-statistics-and-graphics-refugee-and-migrant-children

The *Jugendamt* are required to take an unaccompanied migrant minor into emergency – *Inobhutnahme* – state care[75] in the municipality in which they had their first contact with authorities or in which they were found. The normal 'taking into state care' procedure then follows. This includes the appointment of a legal guardian[76] by the competent Family Court and the so-called 'clearing procedure', which includes an examination of whether there are alternatives to an asylum application, such as family reunification in a third country or the application for a residence permit on humanitarian grounds.[77] The guardian acts as the minor's legal representative, but also as a personal counsellor with whom unaccompanied minors can develop a plan for the future. In 2020, some 17% of the total intake of 45,400 children to temporary state care were unaccompanied migrant minors.[78]

Rights and welfare interests

All children in Germany – including unaccompanied minor migrants – have legal rights to basic necessities such as health, accommodation, education, and protection. In practice this has not always been easy to arrange, given the numbers arriving in Germany and the transient nature of the migrant population. In its 2022 report, the CRC was critical of the 'lengthy stays by some asylum-seeking and refugee children in reception centres and collective accommodation facilities, including in centres that are not child-friendly, which limit their access to education' and urged that 'their best interests are given primary consideration in all asylum processes and that their views are heard, taken into account and given due weight'. In addition, measures should be taken to: 'prevent the separation of migrant children from their parents' and to 'prohibit the arrest and detention of asylum-seeking and migrant children on the basis of their own or their parents' migration status'.[79]

The considerable number of 'missing migrant children' is also a matter of concern. In 2016, nearly 9,000 children and young people were reported missing. By the beginning of 2018, that number had fallen to 5,334 and by the beginning of 2019 it had dropped to 3,192. The latest records available show that in 2021 some 1,600 unaccompanied minors were missing in Germany: nearly 1,000 were reportedly aged between 14 and 17 years; and just over 600 were aged 13 and younger.[80] The main reason for the decline is simply that it reflects the corresponding decline in the rate of asylum seekers but may also be attributable to their onward migration to countries such as Denmark and Sweden.

75 The Social Code VIII, s 42(1).

76 Ibid., s 42(3). See, further, ss 42a to 42f.

77 See, further, at: https://ejournals.bib.uni-wuppertal.de/index.php/sws/article/view/520/1021

78 See, further, at: https://www.destatis.de/EN/Press/2021/06/PE21_295_225.html

79 CRC/C/DEU/CO/5-6, at para 39.

80 See https://www.infomigrants.net/en/post/29633/hundreds-of-unaccompanied-minors-missing-in-germany

TRAFFICKING

Domestically, the Criminal Code criminalised sex trafficking and labour trafficking under ss 232, 232(a), 232(b), 233, and 233(a) while s 236 specifically prohibits child trafficking.[81]

Of the two main types of child trafficking – for purposes of cheap labour and prostitution – the latter is the more significant. In 2020 Germany recorded 406 victims of sex trafficking (427 in 2019) and 88 victims of labour trafficking (67 in 2019). Almost all sex trafficking victims were female (94%), and of those whose age was known, 42% were younger than 21. In 2020, the majority of labour trafficking victims were from Romania and Zimbabwe; 8 were younger than 21. The U.S. report on child trafficking in Germany[82] states that traffickers exploit victims of forced labour primarily at construction sites but also in hotels, seasonal industries like agriculture, entertainment, and restaurants, and in private homes, with reported increases in the number of child victims. It notes that traffickers subject Roma and foreign unaccompanied children to sex trafficking, forced begging, and other coerced criminal behaviour and that 'Romani families sometimes force their children, both boys and girls, into commercial sex on the streets'.

Government policy to deal with trafficking in children for the purpose of sexual exploitation is addressed in the 'Plan of Action II of the Federal Government for the Protection of Children and Young People from Sexual Exploitation', published in June 2011. This Action Plan has set up a multidisciplinary monitoring body which established a subworking group on the issue of trafficking in children. As part of its policy for coping with child trafficking, the government funds an NGO that is responsible for implementing the cooperation strategy for children. This has established a total of eight networks in six states and provides training for government officials and practitioners to form anti-trafficking and anti-exploitation programmes. In addition the government has introduced a Youth Protection Act, which became effective in May 2021, to increase preventative protections for children against cyber grooming and potential sex trafficking.

In its above-mentioned 2022 report, the CRC expressed concern regarding the authorities' treatment of child victims of trafficking and urged that 'their best interests are taken as a primary consideration in decisions regarding their place of stay'.[83]

Public family law: criminal jurisdiction

Since the introduction of the first Juvenile Justice Act in 1923, the law relating to children who commit offences has cultivated an approach that blends justice and welfare. This was maintained through a series of major law reforms in 1953,

81 See, further, at: https://www.lewik.org/term/15750/child-trafficking-section-236-german-criminal-code/

82 U.S. Government, *2022 Trafficking in Persons Report: Germany*, at: https://www.state.gov/reports/2022-trafficking-in-persons-report/germany/

83 CRC/C/DEU/CO/5-6, at para 41.

1990, and 2008. The present approach – embodied in the German Criminal Code (*Strafgesetzbuch*) and the Juvenile Justice Act (*Jugendgerichtsgesetz*) 1953[84] – continues to emphasise the welfare dimension with its diversion, educational, and restorative justice measures.

A federal initiative resulted in the 2021 introduction of legislation to focus inter-agency collaboration on combating sexualised violence against children and to significantly increase the sentencing range for child sexual abuse and child pornography offences in the German Criminal Code. In this context, Germany was praised by the CRC in its 2022 Concluding Observation to the joint 5th and 6th Periodic Report, for measures taken to prosecute international perpetrators of sexual abuse against children.[85]

The system

The German legal system as it relates to children in trouble with the law has been praised for being 'particularly instructive' because it 'responds to crimes committed by young people in ways that are age appropriate, centre on rehabilitation, and resort to incarceration only in limited circumstances and when absolutely necessary'.[86]

Age of criminal responsibility

Children aged 13 years of age or younger cannot be held criminally liable and none younger than 18 can be prosecuted as adults.[87] Further, for purposes of differentiating between degrees of venality in youths and adults, since 1953 the former have been treated as juveniles until they reach 21 years of age. In 2021 German police recorded almost 155,000 juvenile crime suspects, a fall of almost 10,000 from the previous year.[88]

CHILDREN IN COURT

According to the above-mentioned *Fair and Just* report the focus in a German court is:[89]

84 Amended in 1974 and most recently in 2008.

85 See 'Experts of the Committee on the Rights of the Child Praise Germany for Prosecuting International Perpetrators of Sexual Abuse against Children, Ask About the Rise of Child Pornography Cases and Children in Armed Conflict', at: https://www.ohchr.org/en/press-releases/2022/09/experts-committee-rights-child-praise-germany-prosecuting-international

86 See Fair and Just Prosecution report, *Lessons Learned from Germany: Promoting Developmentally Appropriate and Rehabilitative Youth and Young Adult Justice*, (2022), at: https://fairandjustprosecution.org/wp-content/uploads/2022/06/FJP-Germany-Youth-Justice-Brief.pdf

87 Note – under s 828 of the Civil Code – a child aged seven or older can be held civilly liable for damage he or she has caused.

88 See, further, at: https://www.statista.com/statistics/1101460/juvenile-crime-suspect-number-police-record-germany

89 Op. cit. See, further, at: https://imprintnews.org/justice/juvenile-justice-2/progressive-prosecutors-look-to-germany-for-juvenile-justice-reform/65753

> less on the seriousness of the offense and more on the young person's 'moral and psychological development' at the time the crime was committed. Judges consider a child's maturity and educational background, whether the offense was peer-influenced or impulsive. The country's juvenile justice system is also limited to those who have committed the most serious offenses, such as homicide, rape and assault.

This approach is reflected in the conduct of court proceedings. These tend to be much less formal and adversarial than in common law countries: they are exploratory in nature; judge and prosecutor sitting alongside; usually no legal representatives; witnesses summoned by the judge rather than the parties; child offender and victim encouraged to engage; no cross-examinations; the outcome designed primarily to promote an offender's social rehabilitation.

ROLE OF THE WELFARE PRINCIPLE

The ameliorative role of this principle can be seen at work in several different ways. One very significant function it serves is that of stretching the age group of those entitled to a more rehabilitative than punitive outcome in criminal proceedings. If between 18 and 20 years of age, an offender will fall within the remit of the juvenile justice rather than the adult justice system. Another is in the manner in which court proceedings, as described above, are conducted. As with any process, however, it is best judged by its outcomes. The German juvenile justice system has attracted international acclaim for prioritising rehabilitation, the success of which is evident in its relatively low rate of recidivism.

Preventative services

Children (under 14 years), juveniles (14–17) and young adults (18–20) all have the right to support and education and to be protected in their personal development by the child and youth welfare agencies. Youth services are established at the local community level, where priority is given to private non-profit organisations which must – not necessarily, depending on the services they provide – be accredited by the state Youth Welfare Departments of the *Länder*. The CRC, in its above-mentioned 2022 report, recommends that the federal government 'continues to actively promote, in all *Länder*, the application of non-judicial measures, such as diversion, mediation and counselling, and, wherever possible, the use of non-custodial measures for children, such as probation or community service'.[90]

90 CRC/C/DEU/CO/5-6, at para 42. See, also, the CRC general comment No. 24 (2019) on children's rights in the child justice system.

Community sentences

The lower end of the sanctions tariff for juvenile offenders is firmly focused on the educative and disciplinary measures necessary to effect successful social rehabilitation.[91]

The educative measures include the issuing of instructions and the requirement that the offender accept certain forms of educative assistance – socio-educational input – or residential accommodation with back-up support from social workers. These measures are not really intended to punish, but to promote the juvenile's upbringing in an educative manner. For example, the instructions may refer to the place of residence, participation in a course of social training, work, or attempts to achieve offender-victim mediation.

The disciplinary measures are also intended as a sanction. The juvenile is to be made aware of the injustice of his action, without this requiring youth imprisonment. Disciplinary measures include cautions, the imposition of conditions (reparations for the injury, apologies to the injured party, payment of money to charitable organisations or the state, community service), and detention, which can range from a weekend to four weeks. Educative and disciplinary measures can be imposed simultaneously.

Custodial sentences

These are used sparingly; in the vast majority of cases (85%) they are for a two-year period or less and the majority of those in youth custody tend to be young adults aged 18–20. It is claimed that the incarceration rate in Germany is nine times less than in the U.S. (76 per 100,000 vs. 693 per 100,000).[92]

The conditions in custodial facilities are set by the Federal Prison Act 1976 (*Strafvollzugsgesetz*), the main provisions of which have been transposed into the various Youth Prison Acts. These include principles such as: that life in penal institutions should approximate as far as possible to general living conditions; any detrimental effects of imprisonment should be counteracted; and that imprisonment should be so designed as to help the prisoner to reintegrate himself into life when liberated.

Recidivism

Research indicates that only about 30% of those serving custodial sentences re-present within three years[93] (compared, for example, with an estimated 75% in the

91 See Jehle, J-M., *Criminal Justice in Germany* (7th ed), The Federal Ministry of Justice and Consumer Protection, (2019) at p 41.

92 See *The Crime Report*, (2018), at: https://thecrimereport.org/2018/04/10/in-germany-its-hard-to-find-a-young-adult-in-prison/

93 See Dünkel, F., 'Criminology and Criminal Justice, Juvenile Justice and Juvenile Delinquency', *International and Comparative Criminology*, (2016), at: 10.1093/oxfordhb/9780199935383.013.68

U.S.). It was noted in 2016 that: 'for the last 15 years, juvenile crime rates, particularly violent offences, and the youth population in prisons have decreased (–20 percent since 2005). The practice of diversion (70 percent of all cases) has proved to be effective in preventing reoffending'.[94]

Child victims

Child victims of violence are entitled to compensation within the scope of civil law proceedings against the perpetrator.[95] If there is no compensation available there, the state provides financial support but also medical and therapeutical help under the Victims of Violence Act (*Opferentschädigungsgesetz*). The CRC, in its 2022 report, urged the strengthening of 'measures for ensuring that children who are victims or witnesses of violence have prompt access to child-friendly, multi-sectoral and comprehensive interventions, services and support, including forensic interviews and psychological therapy … with the aim of preventing the secondary victimization of those children'.[96]

Conclusion

The law relating to children in this civil law country does so in a manner not unlike that in France, but in many ways quite different from its equivalent in the common law world.

Crucially, the state/family relationship is governed by the subsidiarity principle. This is embodied in Articles 2(1) and 6(2) of the Basic Law, the combined effect of which is to respect the primary responsibility of parents to care for their children but to also place an obligation on the state to assure children and adolescents that state monitoring will ensure they receive adequate and safe parental care. However, while failing standards of such care authorises state intervention on a consensual or coercive basis, there are reasonable grounds for concluding that state deference towards parental status and family autonomy – possibly an over-reaction to state dominance of citizens and family during the Nazi era – may now result in a hesitancy, leading to raised thresholds of state intervention which could jeopardise the welfare interests of many children. Once in state care, less than half of all children are placed with foster parents, most of whom are relatives of the children, and very few of the latter – perhaps only 5% – exit the care system by being rehabilitated with their birth families, which is roughly the same proportion as those who exit by means of non-consensual adoption.

94 Ibid.

95 See the Code of Criminal Procedure, Article 403ff and Compensation for the Victims of Acts of Violence Act.

96 CRC/C/DEU/CO/5-6, at para 23(c).

The juvenile justice system has been commended for its focus on social rehabilitation rather than punishment, its limited use of incarceration, and its success in maintaining consistently low rates of recidivism.[97] Also worthy of praise is Germany's remarkable record of benign response to the needs of so many unaccompanied migrant minors.

97 See Dünkel, F., 'Criminology and Criminal Justice, Juvenile Justice and Juvenile Delinquency', *International and Comparative Criminology*, (2016), at: 10.1093/oxfordhb/9780199935383.013.68

8 The welfare principle in contemporary practice

Private family law and hybrid proceedings

Introduction

Kindschaftsrecht – or legislation on the legal status of children – is part of German private family law but there is no express mention of their rights in that law nor in the German Constitution. This results in 'children's rights' being an imperfectly realised concept and one which, as of 2023, has yet to be given much functional effect. *Kindeswohl* – or the welfare interests of a child – on the other hand, is a more relevant concept and a basic principle of German family law,[1] even if not explicitly defined. Nonetheless, there is a consensus in legal and administrational proceedings that children's welfare interests are endangered when they suffer from physical, psychical, emotional, or sexual violence or when they are physically or emotionally neglected. The role and functions of the welfare principle – in contemporary private family law and administrative proceedings – is the subject of this chapter.

Beginning with private family law, the chapter first considers the law relating to founding a family and to the resulting 'family life'. It then examines the law as it relates to family breakdown and the functionality of the principle in that context. This is followed by a broad consideration of how the state deploys public services to safeguard the welfare interests of children from disadvantaged backgrounds and minority cultures. The chapter concludes with a review of hybrid proceedings – such as adoption from state care, commercial surrogacy, and child abduction – identifying and assessing the role of the welfare principle in transcending the public/private divide in family law.

Founding a family

Demographic trends in Germany point inexorably towards a shrinking population: the death rate has been higher than the birth rate since the 1970s.[2] With a steadily increasing proportion of elderly citizens and a declining fertility rate, children are becoming ever more precious, a much-needed resource to fulfil family life and fuel

1 See the Civil Code, s 1697a.

2 Notwithstanding the fact that, as Jörg Reinhardt points out, the population increased by 1.1 million in 2021–22 (note to author, 24 May 2023).

DOI: 10.4324/9781003415688-12

investment in a secure economic future. In this context, the government's ongoing non-interventionist policy seems incongruous. A more facilitative approach towards assisted reproductive technology (ART), surrogacy, and other methods of founding a family might be prudent, if only to avert serious taxation issues burdening future generations, and would certainly be welcomed by the growing numbers of those now hoping to become parents.

Family life

In Germany, as in almost all modern developed nations, the range of relationships now recognised as constituting 'family life' has broadened in ways that previous generations would have found hard to imagine. However, the traditional patriarchal model of the family and the roles of those within it have endured rather longer in Germany, and in its family law, than elsewhere.

Socially, this is apparent, perhaps, in the continuing primacy of marital status. Marital family units are the most common form of family (70%). Although the number of cohabiting parents is continuing to increase, accounting for 11% of all families by 2018, as a proportion of all families they have remained at a fairly constant 19% for some years. Consequently, of the 13.2 million total child population in 2018, 74% were growing up with married parents which, in turn, means that children in Germany grow up in the traditional marital family – three-quarters with genetic siblings – more often than the European average (68%).[3] As has been noted 'in Germany, people still wish to marry, and marriages last longer in comparison to other countries, as is shown by the further increase in the number of marriages and the increasing lengths of time until divorce'.[4] This must provide more German children with a stable framework of relationships within which to form attachments, than is available to those in many other countries.

In family law, vestiges of the traditional model family were apparent in a slew of similar cases culminating in *Zaunegger v. Germany*[5] which concerned an unmarried father's claim to joint custody rights with his separated partner in respect of their daughter. In German family law this was a right derived from the status of marriage and reserved to former spouses: the right of an unmarried father to joint custody was entirely subject to the mother's consent, which in this case she refused. The European Court of Human Rights (ECtHR) found that to be discriminatory and in breach of the father's Article 8 right to family life. That decision and others[6] led to the law being changed in 2013 so as to place married and unmarried parents in the same position as regards rights to joint custody (see, further, below).

3 See, further, Federal Ministry for Family Affairs, Senior Citizens, Women and Youth, *Family Today: Data, Facts, Trends – Family Report 2020*, at: https://www.bmfsfj.de/resource/blob/190146/7313bd244bf3b7d05b334afc70ce7e1c/family-today-data-facts-trends-family-report-2020-data.pdf

4 Ibid., at p 5.

5 Application No. 22028/04, (2010).

6 *Sommerfeld v. Germany*, Application No. 31871/96, (2001), *Hoffmann v. Germany*, Application No. 34045/96, (2002), and *Sahin v. Germany*, Application No. 30943/96, (2004).

Preserving family life

Germany – more like France than the U.K. – places a high premium on maintaining the relationships conducive to preserving the legal integrity of birth families. This is evident for example in the commitment in principle – if less so in practice – to return a child in care back to their family of origin and in the widely spread reluctance of Family Courts to resort to non-consensual adoption. Arguably, it is also apparent in the requirement that parents continue to individually bear equal responsibility for their children after family breakdown and perhaps also in the facilitative approach to step-parent adoption.

Adoption

The most obvious distinguishing characteristic of the adoption process in Germany is that it is rapidly fading in significance: most adoptees are the stepchildren of their adopters.

Adoption remains very much part of private family law: it is essentially used to redraw legal boundaries for reforming family units; and in so doing it accommodates both child and adult adoptees in 'full' and 'simple' forms, respectively. The adoption of children (under 18) is now regulated by ss 1741–1766 of the Civil Code (*Bürgerliches Gesetzbuch*) as updated by the family law reform 1998. This, supplemented by the Adoption Intermediation Act 1976 (amended in 2002 and 2020), provides the main legal framework, the governing principles of which are essentially those underpinning family law and are drawn from the Constitution and the Civil Code, as updated in the reforms of 1976 and 1998.

In recent years, the usual factors – including rates of non-marital births, marriage breakdown, abortion, and child care admissions – have influenced the domestic availability of children. In Germany, though to a markedly lesser extent than other countries in Western Europe, domestic sources have been augmented by recourse to other countries, but this has been decreasing. The annual statistics show a steady decrease in annual adoption orders: from 8,687 in 1993, to 5,909 in 2001, 4,060 in 2011, 3,812 in 2015, down to 3,733 in 2018, but increasing slightly to 3,774 in 2020 and to 3,843 in 2021. Domestic adoptions predominate with Germany being one of the three highest in Europe (accompanied by the U.K. and Poland)[7] but adoption by non-relatives continues to fall.[8] According to the official statistics there are about 66% stepchildren adoptions and 3% kinship adoptions per year. Only about 30% are 'out-of-family' adopters.[9]

7 http://www.europarl.europa.eu/RegData/etudes/BRIE/2016/583860/EPRS_BRI(2016)583860_EN.pdf

8 See, further, at: https://www.destatis.de/EN/FactsFigures/SocietyState/SocialStatistics/SocialBenefits/PublicChildrenYouthWelfare/Adoptions.html.

9 German Federal Statistic Office, https://www.destatis.de/DE/Themen/Gesellschaft-Umwelt/Soziales/Adoptionen/Publikationen/_publikationen-adoptionen.html#_8rvxt84xp.

Welfare interests

The basic principle that adoption should serve the interests of the child is stated in the Civil Code, s 1741, para 1, which declares that 'a child may be adopted if such adoption will serve the welfare of the child and if it is to be expected that a parent-child relationship will develop between the adopter and the child'. This is generally interpreted, not as giving welfare interests any particular priority, only that the child's circumstances will improve and that this is predictable in psycho-social terms and/or by the legal safeguards that will then protect their welfare. The Committee on the Rights of the Child (CRC) has noted with concern that the principle had not been fully incorporated into federal legislation and the prioritisation of the child's best interests was not yet integrated into all areas of the legislative, executive, and judicial branches of government.[10]

In 2014 the Federal Constitutional Court delivered a judgment that triggered legislation to facilitate same-sex adoptions. While acknowledging that the constitutional provision – "marriage and the family shall enjoy the special protection of the state" – could be used to justify ruling out same sex partners adopting the other partner's adopted child, Kirchhof J nevertheless held that "in marriage as in a civil partnership, adoption provides the child in the same way with legal security and material advantages in terms of care, support and inheritance law".[11] Subsequently the government introduced legislation to rectify the law with effect from July 2014 (adoption of stepchildren) and October 2017 (out-of-family adoptions).

In keeping with its essentially consensual nature, an adoption placement will only be made after all parties have given their consent, even if a court has terminated the birth parent/s custody rights.[12] Authority to then make an adoption placement is as stated in the Adoption Intermediation Act, which requires that it be made by professionals only.[13] In this, the most crucial step in the adoption process, considerable protection is provided for the child's welfare interests by the requirement that it can only occur after a rigorous matching assessment by the professionals involved,[14] with the prospective adopters having had sight of the child and, following agreement in principle, with a full disclosure having been made of all information regarding the child's background. Placements by birth mothers are prohibited.

There have been judicial rulings that an adoption carried out without taking the interests of the child into account violates German public policy and cannot therefore be recognised.[15] Foreign adoption orders, however, can (since the introduction of 2020 legislation) be recognised even if legally flawed, as long as they serve the

10 UN Committee on the Rights of the Child (CRC), *Concluding Observations on the Combined Third and Fourth Periodic Reports of Germany*, 25 February 2014, CRC/C/DEU/CO/3-4, at para 26, available at: http://www.refworld.org/docid/52f8a2074.html [accessed 19 August 2017].

11 See, further, 'German Court Declines to Rule on Joint Adoption by Gay Couples' at: https://www.thepinknews.com/2014/02/21/german-court-rules-gay-couples-adopting-children/.

12 The Civil Code, s 1666.

13 Ibid., s 2(1).

14 The Recommendations, No. 4.

15 See *KG Berlin*, 4 April 2006 – 1 W 369/05.

best interests of the child on a life-long basis and are consistent with the essential principles of German law.[16] Interestingly, in the above phrasing of s 1741 of the Civil Code, the welfare test is interpreted – as in equivalent U.K. legislation – to require a probability that the proposed adoption will ensure the child's best interests on a life-long basis.

Consents for adoption

Both birth parents must consent to the adoption of their child, regardless of their marital status and whether or not they live together with the child.

The consent of both parents is required even if they have had their parental rights removed by court order. Interestingly, if the applicants already have children they must show that the proposed adoption will not be to the detriment of the latter nor to the welfare interests of the prospective adoptee.[17] Even where the unmarried mother has sole custody then the consent of the father to the adoption of their child must still be sought. The ECtHR, in *Zaunegger v. Germany*,[18] ruled that the legal right of an unmarried mother to refuse the father the possibility of his obtaining, with her, joint custody of their child was discriminatory, in relation to their equal right to private and family life, and constituted a breach of Article 14 taken together with Article 8 of the European Convention on Human Rights (ECHR). Consequently, the law was amended.[19]

The consent of the child is a prerequisite for his or her adoption[20] but the rules governing how it is given are unusually meticulous. So, for example: a child is not actually entitled to give autonomous consent, it must be accompanied by that of their guardian;[21] if the child is less than 14 years of age or legally incompetent, then it is the consent of their guardian that must be given.[22] The fact that a child aged 14 or more, the subject of adoption proceedings, is entitled to give consent but only if this is endorsed by a guardian seems anomalous and may well be discriminatory. Interestingly, and in contrast with other countries, there is provision for a child aged 14 or older to withdraw their consent at any time prior to the making of an adoption order – with or without the permission of their guardian.[23] No other party may do so.[24]

Although by far the majority of all adoptions proceed on a consensual basis, German law also provides for circumstances when parental consent is either unavailable, if the child has been born anonymously (*Vertrauliche Geburt*), or the right

16 See Act on the legal effects of foreign adoptions, s 4.
17 The Civil Code, s 1745.
18 Application No. 22028/04, IHRL 3698 (ECHR 2009).
19 The Civil Code, s 1626a.
20 Ibid., s 1746(1) 1.
21 Ibid., s 1746(1) 3.
22 Ibid., s 1746(1) 2.
23 Ibid., s 1746(2).
24 Ibid., s 1750(2) 2.

to exercise it has been forfeited due to parental conduct. Where a birth parent is dead, incapacitated by mental illness, or their whereabouts are unknown, then the court may dispense with the need for their consent.[25]

'Open' adoption

In theory, German adoptions are far from 'open'. The traditional approach of secrecy and anonymity for all parties is provided by the Civil Code: no information regarding the identity of the adoptee, the fact of their being subject to an adoption process, or of an eventual adoption order may be disclosed; any breach may result in judicial penalties.[26] Indeed, barring certain exceptional circumstances, enquiries from official or private sources to a family seeking confirmation that a child has been adopted are explicitly prohibited and it has been established that it is permissible for the parties concerned to deny the fact of adoption.[27]

In practice, however, open adoption is accommodated. Indeed, where all parties are in favour, then the adoption agency may facilitate a placement direct from hospital after the baby's birth, even though the birth parents are unable to give a valid consent until the child is at least eight weeks old.[28] The adoption agencies – subject to the consent of all parties – are also obliged by law (Adoption Intermediation Act, ss 8a and 8b) to establish a post-adoption exchange of information and personal contact in any form. Additionally, they have to facilitate any level of contact between the biological parent and the child throughout the latter's life. Moreover, adoption agencies are obliged to encourage adopters to advise adoptees from an early age about the fact of their adoption and of their right to access adoption files.[29] So, a considerable degree of openness and transparency is permissible.

Step-parent adoption

Step-parent adoption is by far the single largest category of German adoption and since 1977 such adoptions in respect of children are always plenary in form. In 2009, for example, of the almost 4,000 adoption orders made, about half were in favour of step-parents, by 2013 the proportion had risen to almost 60%, in 2018 of the 3,733 adoptions 61% were granted to step-parents, and by 2021 two-thirds of the 3,843 were step-adoptions. This proportion can only rise after the 2020 legislation – adding s 1766a to the German Civil Code – allowing stepchild adoption in non-marital families where there is evidence of family stability (usually interpreted as meaning the relationship has been sustained for at least 4 years). This was introduced in order to rectify an anomaly revealed by a 2019 decision of the German

25 Ibid., s 1747(4).

26 Civil Code, s 1758.

27 See *Munchener Kommentar zum Burgerlichen Gesetzburch, Band 8, Familienrecht* II, § 1758, No. 6.

28 Civil Code, s 1747, para 3.

29 Adoption Intermediation Act, ss 8a, 8b, and 9.

Federal Constitutional Court which had ruled the exclusion of stepchild adoption in non-marital families to be unconstitutional.

The consent of the other birth parent – as well as that of the spouse or registered partner – must also be available.[30] Stepchildren may be adopted by the new partner of one of the biological parents even if the adopter and the parent are not married[31] provided the other biological parent is unknown/absent or gives consent to the adoption.

In other countries there has been some controversy as to whether step-parent adoptions are wholly compliant with the long-term welfare interests of the children involved and in France they are restricted to the lesser form of 'simple' adoptions. There would seem to be no such ambiguity in Germany. In fact the scope for possible complications regarding a child's family relationships is further compounded by the fact that a considerable proportion of annual German adoptions are in favour of relatives.

Post-adoption contact

German law does not allow for an adoption order to be compromised. Aside from the distinctions between 'full' and 'simple' forms of adoption and between the restrictions imposed upon adoption by relatives, there is no possibility of using an accompanying order – for example, as to possible arrangements for post-adoption contact between an adoptee and their birth parents or siblings – that could customise the legal effects of adoption to accommodate the particular welfare interests of an adoptee.

This issue was examined in *I.S. v. Germany*[32] where the applicant complained of not being able to have regular contact with, and receive information about, her biological children who had been adopted by another couple. She submitted that the German courts' decisions on contact and information with regard to her children had breached her human rights. She alleged that she had been promised contact with and information about the children, which had not been respected. The ECtHR held that there had been no violation of Article 8. It found that, by consenting to the adoption, the applicant had knowingly given up all rights as regards her biological children. The arrangements concerning information about them had in particular been based on a mere declaration of intent by the adoptive parents. It found that the German courts' decision, to favour the children's interest in developing in their adoptive family without disruption over the mother's right to respect for her private life, had therefore been proportionate.

The 2020 amendment of the Adoption Intermediation Act stipulates that adoption agencies must try to make consensual arrangements for ongoing contact or, at least, for exchanges of information on the development of the adopted child. In practice, informal arrangements for post-adoption contact had been well established before, if only by means of an annual exchange of letters and photographs.

30 Ibid., s 1749(1).
31 Civil Code, s 1766a.
32 Application No. 31021/08, (2014).

Revocation is usually not possible in respect of adoption orders. In Germany, however, if the order was legally flawed from the outset then it may be repealed: for example, if the declaration of consent was made by mistake, under duress, or because of the legal non-competence of one of the parties;[33] unless the flaw is rectified.[34] Any revocation is subject to this not being seriously damaging to the welfare interests of the child.[35] A singular characteristic of a German adoption order, which lends considerable weight to the welfare principle, is that it may be revoked by the Family Court, at its discretion, without the need for a motion initiated by any of the parties involved, if satisfied that not to do so would seriously imperil the welfare of the child concerned.[36]

Intercountry adoption

There is now virtually no reliance on intercountry adoption. In 2004, for example, there were a total of 475: 163 from Hague-compliant countries and 312 from non-Hague (of which almost half were from Russia).[37] By 2015 they had fallen to 201, to 129 in 2018, and by 2021 they were down even further to 64.[38] It is noticeable that comparable rates in other European countries such as France, Spain, and Italy are consistently much higher.

Until 2020 privately pursued adoptions were not explicitly prohibited by law, and it would seem probable that every year a number of private prospective adopters pursued intercountry adoption in respect of children in non-Hague-compliant countries, thereby bypassing central authority oversight. Arguably, such practices amounted to 'trafficking' which is illegal and violates Article 35 of the United Nations Convention on the Rights of the Child (UN CROC). However, since the 2021 amendment to the Adoption Intermediation Act, it has been mandatory to use public or private agencies to prepare, facilitate, and monitor any placement, domestic or intercountry, which has considerably tightened the safeguards for the welfare interests of children.

Cultural/religious affinity

If a child already has adherence to a particular religion,[39] this has to be respected by an adoption agency and choice of placement should ensure religious compatibility. Birth parents have the right to stipulate the preferred religious upbringing of their child. In Germany by far the majority of all children entering the adoption process

33 Ibid., s 1759.
34 Ibid., s 1760(1) and (2).
35 Ibid., s 1761(2).
36 Ibid., s 1763(1).
37 See Annual Adoption Statistics for Receiving States: Germany, 2005, at: http://www.hcch.net/upload/adostats_de.pdf
38 See Selman, P., at: https://assets.hcch.net/docs/a8fe9f19-23e6-40c2-855e-388e112bf1f5.pdf
39 Federal Law on the Religious Education of Children (15 July 1921; 12 September 1990).

are known to, if not related to, their adopters and are remaining within their home, their culture, and framework of relationships. The customary queries regarding the tendency of this use of adoption to distort family relationships therefore apply with greater force than usual. The risk of an adoptee not having an opportunity to develop a fully informed independent identity is similarly accentuated with correspondingly adverse implications for their welfare interests.

While there are no legal constraints regarding religious upbringing, nor any legal reference to the paramountcy principle, the Guidelines do require that the child's religion be taken into account. In effect, a guarantee must be given that the child will be free to practise his or her religion.[40] On the other hand the birth parents may decide to consent to an adoption by adopters of a different religion to their own.

Reproductive rights: abortion, surrogacy, IVF, etc.

In 2022 the population of Germany was estimated at 84.3 million. Although currently the most populous country in the European Union (EU), its birth rate is one of the lowest in the world.[41] Indeed, Germany currently has the lowest percentage of family households with children in the entire EU. That being the case, it might be thought that government policy would be firmly focused on reinforcing reproductive rights but the evidence is to the contrary.

Abortion

Under s 218 of the Criminal Code, abortion is illegal except in certain circumstances: if the mandatory counselling has been received; or, if the pregnancy is the result of rape it is permissible for the first 12 weeks; or, if the pregnancy creates health risks then it is legally permissible even after the first 12 weeks. Furthermore, s 219a prohibited advertisements for abortion services. The fact that in 2022 the EU Parliament voted in favour of a resolution to make abortion a fundamental right prompted the *Bundestag* later that year to repeal s 219a.

The legal constraints may well explain why Germany has one of the lowest abortion rates in the western world (about one-third that of the U.S.). In 2020, the German abortion rate was 5.9 abortions per 10,000 women aged 15–44 years.[42]

IVF

Despite its demographic challenges, German ART services are regulated by some of the most restrictive legislation in the western world.[43] It is probable that, as Robertson has suggested, 'Germany's history of science and human rights abuse,

40 The Guidelines, (2022), No. 8.4.4.

41 The birth rate in 2022 was 1.607 births per woman, a slight increase from 2021.

42 See National Library of Medicine, at: https://www.ncbi.nlm.nih.gov/pmc/articles/PMC9275520/

43 See, further, Robertson, J.A., 'Reproductive Technology in Germany and the United States: An Essay in Comparative Law and Bioethics', *Columbia Journal of Transnational Law*, 2004, pp 189–227.

however, has made it hostile to technological and genetic control of reproduction'.[44] Consequently, the position now in Germany is that children are a scarce and much sought-after resource which must augur well for their welfare interests.

Surrogacy

Surrogacy, as defined in s 13(a) of the Adoption Mediation Act, is not only illegal but it is a criminal offence for health professionals to assist someone in need of such a service. The Embryo Protection Act 1991, s 1(1)(7), prohibits egg-donation and other forms of embryo manipulation or transfer. It provides that no medical practitioner should perform artificial insemination or embryo donation on a woman who is willing to hand the child over to commissioning parents upon birth in accordance with a surrogacy agreement. Non-compliance is a criminal offence. Moreover, s 13(b) of the amended Adoption Intermediation Act states that no person should bring together a surrogate with prospective commissioning parents or vice versa and s 13(d) prohibits commercials or announcements which seek to bring together such persons. Such complications have not deterred many German couples from availing themselves of commercial surrogacy overseas (see, further, below).

Surrogacy and the welfare interests of the child

In Germany, the very restrictive laws governing surrogacy must compromise the welfare interests of children born elsewhere to a surrogate mother and brought back to Germany by their 'parent/s' (see, further, below).

Sexual orientation and gender transitioning

Since 1980, trans gender matters in West Germany have been subject to – if not regulated by – the 'Transsexual law' (*Transsexuellengesetz*) and indirectly affected by others such as the 'Law of Descent' (*Abstammungsrecht*) and the Equality law (*Antidiskriminierungsgesetz – AGG*)[45] Since 1990, throughout Germany, if a person wished to change either their name or gender, two independent medical court experts, commissioned by a judge, had to determine whether: the person 'does not identify with the birth-assigned sex/gender, but with the other one', and 'feels a compulsion to live according to his/her ideas for at least three years'; and 'it is to be assumed with high probability, that the feeling of belonging to the other sex/gender is not going to change'. This process proved to be lengthy, expensive, and intrusive with a number of court rulings confirming that it was also unconstitutional. For example, in January 2011, the Federal Constitutional

44 Ibid., at p 192.

45 The Equal Treatment Act 2006 prohibits discrimination based on sexual orientation, gender identity, and sex characteristics in employment and the provision of goods and services.

Court (*Bundesverfassungsgericht*) declared the criteria for gender change requiring gender-affirming surgery and sterilisation or infertility to be unconstitutional.[46]

As a consequence, in June 2023, draft legislation proposals were introduced in parliament (*Bundestag*) to provide a right to gender self-identification: that is, without any need for medical involvement.

Child's consent

Children aged 14 to 17 will have the right to change their gender marker on their birth certificate and their first name(s) in the civil registration office with the support of their parents or guardians. The fact that a 16-year-old child is debarred from taking an independent decision on this matter – but not on other matters such as accessing contraceptives – is likely to attract controversy. Children, 13 years of age or less, will be entitled to do so only if they have a signed declaration of approval from their parents or guardians. This raises questions as to where the child's consent or withholding of consent fits in the process.[47] Changes only take effect after a three-month waiting period and once made the gender and name cannot be changed for one year, but thereafter may be changed annually, if necessary, which will greatly alleviate the stress formerly associated with having to make lifelong either/or decisions.

Welfare interests

The fact that children will no longer be required to undergo irreversible, life-changing, medical intervention – gender-affirming surgery, hormone therapy, or psychological consultation – in order to legally change their name and gender must be viewed as the least detrimental way of addressing their gender identity issues.

Children and reconstituted families

Because of the high incidence of family breakdown, a growing proportion of German children in each generation are now exposed to a flux of care relationships in which their welfare interests are vulnerable to being overlooked, misinterpreted, or treated inconsistently.

Family disputes

Judicial navigation of a conflict of interests between family members, following the breakdown of relationships between parents, seldom engages those of any children involved. Unless the parents disclose disagreement – which for reasons of costs

46 1 BvR 3295-07, Federal Constitutional Court, Germany (11 January 2011), at: https://www.icj.org/sogicasebook/1-bvr-3295-07-federal-constitutional-court-germany-11-january-2011/

47 Jörg Reinhardt comments 'this will be the same as in s 1746 of the Civil Code in terms of a minor's consent to his or her adoption' (note to author, 4 August 2023).

and time they are unlikely to do – the future care arrangements for their children will be determined privately. Most often it is not at the point of family breakdown but later, after each parent has become separately assimilated into a quite different nexus of relationships, that disputes arise regarding shared parental contact, visitation rights, religious upbringing, education, health care, etc.

Matrimonial proceedings

The marriage rate in Germany is in decline. In 2020, marriages were 10% lower than the previous year and they fell by a further 4.2% in 2021. As marriage rates fall, divorce rates have risen.[48] Divorce rates increased from 2.5 (per 1,000 of the population aged 15–64 years) in 1990 to 5.4 in the period 2014–20. Since the mid-1990s, the proportion of adults opting for non-marital partnerships has grown rapidly. However, the Organisation for Economic Co-operation and Development (OECD) statistics indicate a greater level of family stability in Germany than in many of the 30 countries it surveyed.[49]

Conciliation, or an attempt to resolve issues, is offered by the local Youth Welfare Offices but is not a mandatory precursor for the parties before they commence proceedings.[50]

DIVORCE, NULLITY, AND RELOCATION

The law relating to marriage (including same-sex marriage), divorce, and family breakdown generally – and associated parental responsibility proceedings – are regulated by the Civil Code, ss 1297–1921, the Law Concerning the Proceedings in Family Matters, ss 111–270, and the Law on Same-Sex Partnerships (*Lebenspartnerschaftsgesetz*).

Before the introduction of the Child Law Reform Act 1998 in proceedings for divorce (there are no judicial separations) the court had to satisfy itself that arrangements made for the children were compatible with their welfare interests. Since then the Family Court will only hear and determine issues relating to the future care of children if one of the parties files a motion accordingly. Nullity proceedings are rarely initiated and seldom successful.[51]

PARENTAL RESPONSIBILITY DISPUTES

Married parents are equally vested with joint parental responsibility and usually continue to be so vested even after a divorce (s 1687 of the Civil Code). The legal

48 See, further, at: https://ec.europa.eu/eurostat/statistics-explained/index.php?title=Marriage_and_divorce_statistics

49 See, further, at: http://www.huffingtonpost.co.uk/2012/12/29/uk-family-breakdown-rate-_n_2379845.html?view=print

50 The Code of Civil Procedure, s 278.

51 The Civil Code (BGB), s 1313.

presumption that both parents share joint custody can only be challenged if there is evidence that one of them presents a risk to the welfare of their child. In that event and in response to an application – whether or not the applicant parents are married to each other – the court will exercise its powers under s 1628 of the Civil Code to make such order regarding the distribution of parental responsibility as it deems appropriate, including ruling that custody be exercised exclusively by the blameless parent. In fact the court has discretion – under s 1666 – to make such a ruling even if there has not been an application. Further, the court may withdraw parental responsibility: in part from both parents and appoint a curator; or in whole from both parents and appoint a guardian for the child. The ECtHR has examined German judicial determinations regarding custody in a number of cases.[52] It has expressed its disquiet regarding the practice of German courts 'concerning complaints about violations of the right to respect for family life and the issue of ineffective, and in particular delayed, conduct of custody proceedings'.[53]

If a parent has sole custody then he or she may unilaterally determine their place of residence. Where both parents share joint custody then determination of habitual residence, like all other significant decisions affecting the child, must be made jointly. In cases of parental dispute then either mediation services will be engaged or the court will adjudicate on the matter. If there is a cohabiting father, he may either acquire joint custody if both parents so agree and this is officially registered in the Youth Welfare Office (*Jugendamt*) or he may be granted that status by order of the Family Court.

COURT ORDERS

As Dethloff and Mariny have explained:[54]

> The basic concept in German family law is still parental custody (*elterliche Sorge*), which includes the care of the child (*Personensorge*) and the care for the property of the child (*Vermögenssorge*), § 1626 para. 1 German CC. All other issues (legal representation, determination of residence, etc.) are either consequences of this parental custody or – as the right of contact – additional legal positions.

The Family Court may make a variety of function-specific orders in respect of children (e.g. for maintenance, regarding education, etc.) but most usually the orders are either for custody – *Sorgerecht* – or for visitation or contact rights – *Umgang* – and, again most usually, are not made in the course of divorce proceedings. When an application for such an order is lodged, the court will request a 'welfare report'

52 For example, *Moog v. Germany*, Application Nos. 23280/08 and 2334/10, (2016).

53 See *Wetjen and Others v. Germany*, Application Nos. 68125/14 and 72204/14, (2018) at para 53.

54 Dethloff, N. and Mariny, D., 'National Report: Germany', at: http://ceflonline.net/wp-content/uploads/Germany-Parental-Responsibilities.pdf

from the local *Jugendamt*. In addition, a guardian *ad litem* will be appointed to advise the court on matters relevant to the child's welfare interests. Furthermore, it is a mandatory requirement that the child be given the opportunity to express his or her views directly to the judge.

CONTACT

Contact can be direct – by means of face-to-face meetings, visits, and stays (weekend-visits, holidays, day-visits, etc.) – or indirect – by phone, letters, e-mail, etc. – and is a right vested in both parent and child. In principle, every person vested with parental responsibilities, and all others with a close relationship (like siblings, grandparents, foster parents, or any other) have a right of contact with the child.[55]

Contact has long been recognised in German law as a parental right and as such is protected under Article 6(2) of the Basic Law and in fact is best understood as a parental duty.[56] Under s 1626(3) of the Civil Code it is held to be in the interests of the child to have contact with both parents and under s 1684 he or she has a right of contact with a parent not holding parental responsibilities. The Family Court can determine the frequency, duration, and location of contact. It may also provide protection for the welfare interests of the child by appointing a special curator – *Ergänzungspfleger* – to supervise contact arrangements[57] but usually the Youth Welfare Offices provide professional 'accompanied contacts' (*Begleiteter Umgang*). The wishes of the child regarding contact must be taken into account but the judiciary have ruled that such wishes are not determinative and may be discounted.

In a trio of successive cases,[58] the ECtHR examined German law as it then related to the parental access/contact rights of unmarried fathers with their daughters. All cases were factually very similar: a father being denied in German courts a right of access/contact with his daughter now assimilated into a marital family unit following their mother's marriage; daughters having been alienated against their fathers by maternal pressure, which prevented ongoing contact, and expressing no wish for a paternal relationship. The courts in all cases ruled that: under the Civil Code, the unmarried mother was fully and exclusively vested with custody and entitled to determine the daughter's relations with third persons; unmarried fathers, as such, had little legal status and no inherent rights in relation to their children; and that the best interests of the child compelled the court not to make an order against her wishes as to do so might endanger her mental and psychological well-being. The fact that in all cases, the father had been blameless as he had been prevented from contacting his daughter, despite his best efforts,

55 The Civil Code, ss 1684 and 1685.

56 Ibid., s 1684(1).

57 Ibid., s 1666 or a so-called *verfahrensbeistand* under s 158 of the Law Concerning the Proceedings in Family Law Cases and Cases of Non-contentious Matters.

58 *Sommerfeld v. Germany*, Application No. 31871/96, (2001), *Hoffmann v. Germany*, Application No. 34045/96, (2002), and *Sahin v. Germany*, Application No. 30943/96, (2004).

was irrelevant. The court was obliged to treat the lack of consent of a discerning daughter, alienated from her father by maternal prejudice, as crucial to her welfare interests which it had to regard as the primary consideration. Ultimately, in all cases – albeit with some variation – the ECtHR found that the German courts by dismissing a father's request for contact with his daughter, born out of wedlock, amounted to a breach of his right to respect for his family life and was discriminatory. These ECtHR rulings prompted a change in German law to the extent of removing the discriminatory effects of the difference in the legal status of marital and non-marital fathers.

In Germany as in France there is a scarcity of caselaw on private family law matters – nothing to compare with the volume of recorded judgments in the common law jurisdictions – which forensically dissect the rationale for resolving parental disputes, identifying governing principles and weighing the welfare interests of a child, relative to other matters, in a wide variety of circumstances.

The welfare principle in contemporary practice: public/private family law

The welfare principle is the transcending mechanism that has done much to bridge the private and public sectors of family law in all developed nations. Arguably, however, the principle has been less effective in doing so in Germany where vestiges of parental rights – and deference to associated traditional family values – can be in conflict with the welfare interests of a child. Children's rights have not been expressly included in the German Constitution (instead they are held to be included, by implication, in the constitutionally granted human rights).[59] But the welfare interests principle is embedded as a primary reference point in the Youth Welfare Act thus integrating the United Nations Convention on the Rights of the Child into German law. As of 2023, there are ongoing political discussions regarding a possible constitutional amendment to establish concise rights for minors.

Public service matters

The German public service infrastructure – in particular its standards of health and social care services – long held to be a model for other European nations, is currently under considerable strain. Its mandatory national health insurance scheme, the oldest of its kind, continues to provide access to high-quality health care for approximately 86% of the population, the remainder opting into private health care. In recent years, however, like other developed nations, the public services have suffered from the increased health care costs of an ageing population and a lack of specialist social workers in Youth Welfare Offices and other child welfare settings.

59 See Kelsen, H., *The Pure Theory of Law*, The Lawbook Exchange, Ltd, 2009.

Poverty

The CRC in its 2014 report expressed regret regarding Germany's 'insufficient efforts to tackle the root causes which place children at risk of becoming victims to the offences under the Optional Protocol such as child poverty and discrimination against children belonging to minority groups as well as against migrant and asylum seeking unaccompanied children' and urged it to 'take every necessary effort to tackle child poverty and discrimination towards children belonging to vulnerable groups'.[60] This problem has persisted for some years, notwithstanding federal government initiatives such as the National Action Plan 'For a Germany Fit for Children 2005–2010' ('*Der Nationale Aktionsplan Für ein kindergerechtes Deutschland 2005–2010*') and the final report on the implementation of the National Action Plan aimed at the improvement of equal opportunities through education, ensuring a non-violent upbringing and preventing child neglect. It was exacerbated by the 2015 migrant 'crisis' and the general socioeconomic dislocation caused by the Covid pandemic and is not improving.[61] In 2021 some 2.88 million children under the age of 18, or more than one in five children, were considered poor or 'at risk of poverty',[62] rates which are higher than the OECD average. In 2022, despite universal child benefits of 250 euros per month per child, the CRC reiterated its concern regarding 'the large number of children still living in poverty or at risk of poverty' and the need for a 'national strategy, with the participation of children, to address the root causes of child poverty'.[63]

There are indications that the government now recognises the problem and is intent on addressing it. Building on the European Child Guarantee policy statement issued by the Council of Europe in 2021, the government has launched a National Action Plan – 'New Opportunities for Children in Germany' – which states its aim as being to improve the infrastructure for supporting vulnerable families. Additionally, in its 2022 report to the CRC it mentioned improvements to welfare benefits such as the child supplement and the support payment advance to provide targeted support to single parents. To support working parents and reduce the risk of child poverty, the government had increased the number of child care places, improved the quality of child care, and would introduce a legal right to full-day care for primary school children from 2026. Acknowledging that 'the existing financial support system for families did not reach many children and adolescents in need of support' the government representatives announced an intention to merge child benefit payments, basic income support for jobseekers, and other social assistance into a single benefit to be paid on a sliding scale based on the parents' income.

60 CRC/C/OPSC/DEU/CO/, (2014), at paras 19 and 20.

61 See, for example, Corak, M., Fertig, M. and Tamm, M., 'A Portrait of Child Poverty in Germany', *Innocenti Research Centre* (UNICEF), 2005.

62 See the Bertelsmann Foundation report on child and youth poverty in Germany, at: https://www.wsws.org/en/articles/2023/03/01/fd97-m01.html

63 CRC/C/DEU/CO/5-6, at para 34.

Employment

The *Jugendarbeitsschutzgesetz* (Youth Labour Protection Laws) prohibits children of compulsory school age (younger than 14 years of age) from being employed and regulates the conditions of employment for those aged 15–18. This is reinforced by the *Kinderarbeitsschutzverordnung* (Ordinance on Protection Against Child Labour). The protection provided by both is compliant with such international law as the International Labour Organization Convention 138 of 1973. In practice, of course, a large proportion of young teenagers are in part-time employment – at weekends, during school holidays, and/or doing seasonal work – and this does not appear to give rise to any significant issues specific to Germany. Instead the welfare interests of young children are more likely to be impaired by the employment regime of their parents. It has been estimated that in 2020: in 3.2 million German families with children under 11 years, both parents were in employment; and 548,000 lone parents with children under 11 years were in employment, just under 43% of them full time.[64]

Sub-contracting production to countries where child labour is utilised is a less tangible and more difficult problem to address. A 2020 review of Germany's National Action Plan for Business and Human Rights (NAP) revealed that there had been non-compliance with at least 50% of the targets set for companies to reduce their dependency on overseas child labour.[65] In January 2023 the federal government introduced the Supply Chain Act which sets minimum human rights standards in the supply chains of major companies and while it should help protect many children it suffers from serious limitations. As Human Rights Watch point out: it is only applicable to large companies with 1,000 or more employees; and it is only binding on immediate suppliers, not those further down the supply chain, where the most serious child labour violations often occur. [66]

MIGRANT MINORS

EU Directive 96/71/EC requires Member States to ensure that their own national protective measures with regard to the terms and conditions of employment of children and young people also apply to young migrant workers. In addition, s 233 of the German Criminal Code criminalises trafficking of migrants into Germany for labour purposes, with particularly heavy penalties when the migrants are children.

The *Jugendmigrationsdienste* (Youth Migration Services) are required to assist migrants aged 12–27 to settle in Germany. This is an onerous task. UNICEF estimated that before the 2015 migrant 'crisis': more than 1 million children 0–17 years of age were of foreign origin; there were nearly 6 million children of migrant origin under the age of 25; and of all persons of migrant origin, nearly 30% were

64 See, further, at: https://www.destatis.de/EN/Press/2022/01/PE22_N003_122.html
65 See, further, at: https://www.auswaertiges-amt.de/en/aussenpolitik/themen/monitoring-nap/2131054
66 See, further, at: https://www.hrw.org/news/2021/06/08/germany-child-labor-rising-covid-19-supply-chain-law-even-more-urgent

in the 0–20 age group.[67] Subsequently, the pressures increased. In one year (from 2015 to 2016), more than half a million minors applied for asylum in Germany.

Health

Infant mortality rates are significant national health indicators. They reflect the access of children and communities to basic health interventions such as vaccination, medical treatment of infectious diseases, and adequate nutrition. The German under-five mortality rate in 2022 was 2.3 per 1,000 live births[68] which reflects a slightly above-average national performance among the OECD nations.[69]

Routine health screening is obviously an effective health and safety strategy for the early detection of health issues and Germany has an efficient screening programme: Hamburg, for example, provides 11 preventative medical check-ups free of charge for all children between birth and the age of 18; similar free early detection and prevention programmes are provided in respect of dental hygiene. A compulsory but free national vaccination programme against measles was introduced in 2020: thereafter, any child entering day care or school facilities must produce a vaccination certificate. Germany's mandatory health insurance scheme ensures that inpatient, outpatient, mental health, and prescription drugs are available to the some 86% of the population – including children – who are currently enrolled.

Education

This prosperous developed nation provides one of the three best child education systems in the world.[70] Moreover, it also provides a better than most headstart programme for children before they enter that system: it has more children enrolled in pre-school services than the average OECD country; 39% of children under age three and 94% of children aged 3–5 were attending such facilities in 2019, compared to 25% of children under age three and 83% of children aged 3–5 in other OECD countries. Interestingly, homeschooling is prohibited – unlike in most other western countries – unless requested by the authorities.

Free compulsory education starts at age 6 and a higher proportion of the nation's children then go on to receive their education in the state system than is the case in other OECD countries: in 2018, private sources accounted for 15% of total expenditure in pre-primary institutions, slightly lower than the OECD average of 17%. Socioeconomic status is a well-established influential factor in determining outcomes of all educational systems and is also influential in Germany where a 2023 report from the Institute for Economic Research found that the academic success of

67 See, further, at: https://www.unicef-irc.org/publications/575-the-situation-among-children-of-migrant-origin-in-germany.html

68 See, further, at: https://www.macrotrends.net/countries/DEU/germany/infant-mortality-rate

69 See, further, at: https://data.unicef.org/country/deu/

70 See, further, at: https://worldpopulationreview.com/country-rankings/education-rankings-by-country

German children is influenced considerably by their parents' education and income, and by single-parent status.[71] Interestingly, and reinforcing that point, the outcomes gap between immigrants and non-immigrants is wider in Germany than in other OECD countries: the proportion of immigrant pupils achieving at least PISA level 2 in reading was 25% lower than the proportion of non-immigrants.[72] Concerns regarding such matters prompted the CRC in its 2022 report to recommend that the federal government 'strengthen measures to ensure the equal access of children in disadvantaged groups, including asylum-seeking, refugee and migrant children, children with disabilities and children from socioeconomically disadvantaged families, to comprehensive schools, higher education and vocational training'.[73]

Discrimination

Discrimination in Germany is prohibited under: constitutional provisions, Article 3, para 2; federal legislation such as the Equal Rights Act and the General Act on Equal Treatment; and under international law such as the ECHR. Nonetheless, both the CRC in its Concluding Observation to the joint 3rd and 4th Periodic Report[74] and reports from the federal government[75] express concern regarding current discriminatory practices against children. Again, in 2022, the CRC recommended that the root causes of discrimination be addressed 'with a view to eliminating discrimination against children in disadvantaged situations including asylum-seeking, refugee and migrant children, Sinti, Roma and other children of minority groups, children with disabilities, LGBTI children and socioeconomically disadvantaged children'.[76]

Most often discrimination is practised and experienced directly and purposefully but it may often also be indirect. Reinhardt comments 'that every day racism – meaning unintended but nonetheless discriminating attitudes or prejudices are an issue' and very probably adversely impact the welfare interests of many children from minority groups, particuarly in school settings.[77]

Migrants

In educational or employment contexts, a hidden effect of discrimination may be to constrain aspirations. In the former case the consequences were evident in the 2010 Ministry of Education report[78] which noted that children with a migration background

71 See, further, at: https://www.ifo.de/en/publications/2023/article-journal/der-ifo-ein-herz-fuer-kinder-chancenmonitor
72 https://www.oecd-ilibrary.org/sites/e4292276en/index.html?itemId=/content/component/e4292276-en
73 CRC/C/DEU/CO/5-6, at para 36(a).
74 CRC/C/DEU/CO/3-4.
75 See, for example, the 15th Child and Youth Report, 'Between freedom, family, all-day school and virtual worlds – Personality development and education for young people', (2017), at: https://www.dji.de/ueber-uns/projekte/projekte/15-kinder-und-jugendbericht.html
76 CRC/C/DEU/CO/5-6, at para 15(a).
77 Note to author (24 May 2023).
78 See, further, at: https://www.bildungsbericht.de/daten2010/summary10.pdf

were twice as likely to attend a vocational secondary school (*Hauptschule*) as children without a migration background – even in the same socioeconomic class – implying that discriminatory pressures were in play. It suggested that 'many school administrators and parents remain wedded to practices that effectively consign the majority of students with a migrant background to a second-class education'. It also pointed out that 'parents' choices of religious instruction, second foreign language or "social preference" have allowed the creation of distinct classes with a disproportionate majority of students from a migrant background, effectively creating a segregated stream'. More recently, the CRC in its 2022 report expressed concern regarding 'asylum-seeking and migrant children and children without regular residence status only having access to limited health services' and recommended expanding service provision for them.[79]

CHILDREN WITH DISABILITIES

In its above-mentioned 2022 report, the CRC recommended that Germany 'streamline all support for children with disabilities into one body, such as child and youth support services, with a view to ensuring that all children with disabilities have equal access to benefits under Book VIII of the Social Code'.[80] In response, the recently reformed Protection of Young Persons Act now includes further provisions that will end the practice of segregation by introducing a rule that children with and without disabilities are to be cared for together in child day care and other Youth Welfare facilities. Also, special consultants for parents and/or handicapped children have been introduced.[81] Moreover, Book VIII of the Social Code sketches the way to a fully inclusive Youth Welfare System that has to be implemented by 2028.

RELIGION AND SCHOOLS

Again, in the above-mentioned 2022 report, the CRC noted that the wearing of face coverings was prohibited in certain areas and questioned whether this prohibition was compliant with the state's obligation to protect children's right to religion and education. It recommended that an assessment be made of 'the potential impacts of such proposed bans on the rights of the child as contained in the Convention and its Optional Protocols'.[82]

Legal proceedings, processes, and court orders

Hybrid public/private proceedings are becoming a feature of German family law, as they are in other developed nations, though perhaps at a slower pace due to the retention of traditional family values in relation to parenting.

79 CRC/C/DEU/CO/5-6, at para 30.
80 Ibid., at para 29(a).
81 See Book VIII of the Social Code, s 10a
82 Ibid., at para 20.

Adoption from state care

The high number of children in the public child care system has not challenged the consensual nature of Germany's adoption process. There would appear to be a reluctance to re-examine policies that for some decades have resulted in a population of not less than 50,000 children who are left to age-out in state care, some 80% being offered only the protective umbrella of guardianship. While the rhetoric claims that every effort should be made to reunite children with birth families, little in fact is being done – or, perhaps, can be legally done – and an unusually high proportion are left in long-term residential care.

CONSENT

The court may dispense with the need for consent where the birth parent/s' custody rights have been terminated following their convictions for particularly serious and persistent violation of parental duties.[83] Also, where the birth parents are indifferent towards the welfare of their child, but not culpable of abuse or neglect, then the need for their consent may be dispensed with three months after they have received counselling as to their rights and duties in respect of their child.[84] These criteria are considered to establish a high threshold for removal of parental rights[85] which might explain why they are so seldom used. Moreover, dispensing with consent is a matter which the court is required to rule upon even when parental custody has previously been judicially removed. Consent to adoption in Germany is a function of innate parental rights and is quite distinct from any parental care responsibilities.

POST-ADOPTION STATE SUPPORT

Consensual adoption is viewed in Germany as deserving of public support services. Adoption from state care would seem to be viewed differently. Unlike the U.K. and the U.S., such adoptions do not attract ongoing financial support from the state: there is no continuation of foster care rates of payment, supplemented where a child is viewed as having any degree of health or social care needs.

The Adoption Intermediation Act (*Adoptionsvermittlungsgesetz*), last amended in 2021, has underlined the role of support services for adopters, adoptees, and their families of origin. Post-adoption services, as a public service entitlement, are provided to consensual domestic and intercountry adopters: counselling and support services are available to the adopters, the child, and the birth parents from the relevant adoption agency and/or from the local Youth Welfare Office. All adoption agencies are either Youth Welfare Offices or Central Adoption Authorities of the

83 Op. cit., at s 1748(1) 1 and 2.

84 Op. cit., at s 1748(2) 1 and Book VIII of the Social Code, s 51(1).

85 See Meysen, T. and Bovenschen, I., 'Adoption from Care: International Perspectives on Children's Rights, Family Preservation and State Intervention', in *Adoption from Care*, Policy Press, Bristol, UK, pp 121–38, (2021).

states (*Länder*), or nonprofit adoption agencies which are accredited by the federal states and regulated by the Adoption Intermediation Act,[86] many being affiliated with churches. The role and functions of adoption agencies, as defined by the Adoption Intermediation Act, include: the provision of counselling – as well as medical, psychological, psychiatric, and legal expertise and experience in placement and post-adoptive care. Since ratification of Hague, as *Terres des Hommes* points out, 'the placement of children is usually carried out by specialists, thus improving its quality' and it also noted 'a decrease in child trafficking in the area of adoption, as well as in the number of private adoptions'.[87]

There is official recognition that adopters and adoptees may require ongoing support.[88] Their entitlement to access the full range of normal family and community services must be explained and facilitated.[89] Support may include the provision of contact information for, and liaison with, local and national adoption networks and support groups. In general, the German authorities also encourage agencies to facilitate contact between adopting families and birth parents and assist with the provision of updates on the child's development, exchange of photographs, etc.[90] Since 2021 they have been obliged to regularly investigate whether any contact is possible and – if so – in what form. Also, adoption agencies are obliged to support and accompany contacts if requested.

POST-ADOPTION INFORMATION ACCESS

The German Constitution is guarded on the subject of information rights. It asserts that individuals have a fundamental right to develop their own personality, but it also warns that this is conditional upon no infringement of the rights of others or of public morals.[91] The protection provided by German law for adopters is explicitly intended to prevent information disclosure: it is prohibited to reveal the identity of an adopter, neither their name nor their address may be disclosed.[92] This prohibition, clearly prioritising the adopters' needs, is difficult to square with the welfare principle.

Article 2(1) of the Basic Law establishes the right of an adopted person to access the information necessary to discover their heritage and this has been reinforced by the German Federal Constitutional Court ruling upholding the constitutional right of every person to know his or her biological origins.[93] Adoptees aged 16 or older may access their adoption files (if under 16, the adoptive parents can claim access to the files as

86 The Adoption Intermediation Act, s 2(2).

87 See Lammerant, I. and Hofsetter, M. (eds) *Adoption: At What Cost?*, *Terre des Hommes*, Lausanne, Switzerland, 2007, at p 23.

88 The Adoption Intermediation Act, s 9.

89 The Social Code, VIII, ss 27–41.

90 Adoption Intermediation Act, ss 8a, 8b, and 9.

91 The Federal Constitution, Basic Law, Article 2.

92 The Civil Code, ss 1747(2) and 1758.

93 Decision of the German Constitutional Court, BVerfGE 79, 256; FamRZ 1989, 255.

the adoptee's legal representative)[94] and the public register, which records the facts relating to their origins.[95] Moreover, agencies are obliged to explore the potential for openness before and after the adoption order is issued (Adoption Intermediation Act, ss 8a, 8b, and 9). Although there has never been a maternal right to relinquish a child anonymously – leaving no information whatsoever – anonymous births have been tolerated. Since 1 May 2014, there is an explicit right to 'preliminary' anonymity when giving birth (*Vertrauliche Geburt*), but a child now has the right to access identifying information (*Herkunftsnachweis*) regarding the mother on attaining 16 years of age.[96]

Whether the adoption order granted is in respect of a domestic or intercountry adoption, the adopted child's details must be recorded by the Registrar for the district in which the adopters reside.[97] There is no official adoption-specific mechanism – such as an adopted children's register – that would enable members of an adoptee's birth family to identify, locate, and/or contact the adoptee. However, the Federal Central Authority – *Bundeszentralstelle für Auslandsadroption* – has information relating to all cases of intercountry adoptions with the exception of independent, private adoptions (which were common and legal until 2021) from member states of The Hague Convention and since 2021 from all other sending states. The Federal Central Authority is therefore able to trace the cases dealt with by each adoption agency and thus locate the relevant adoption files.

An adoptee's access to personal identifying information – including facts about his or her personal history – is guaranteed by law;[98] further context information on the life of the adoptee´s parents or siblings after the adoption, however, can only be permitted subject to the informed voluntary consent of the relevant birth parent and/or sibling. Facilitating adoptees in a search for information relevant to establishing their identity is acknowledged to be a public service duty and related counselling services are available, even mandatory, before access to the adoption files is given. In the event of the necessary consents being given, then the relevant adoption agency is obliged to mediate between the parties and assist in an exchange of information and/or facilitate personal contact.

Abduction

The wrongful retention of a child by one parent against the wishes of the other is prohibited under s 1632(1) of the Civil Code and may constitute the criminal offence of child abduction under s 235. Nonetheless, 5,489 children suffered that ordeal in 2018, a fraction of the some 60,000 reported missing every year. The associated legal proceedings are grounded not on the welfare intersts of the abducted child, but on the violation of parental rights.

94 The Adoption Intermediation Act, s 9b(2).
95 Personal Status Act (*Personenstandsgesetz*), s 61(2) 1.
96 Pregnancy Conflict Act, s 31.
97 *Personenstandsgesetz*, s 15, para 1, No. 3.
98 Adoption Intermediation Act, s 9b.

International abductions are governed by The Hague Convention on the Civil Aspects of International Child Abduction 1980 to which Germany has been a signatory state since 1990. The European Convention on Recognition and Enforcement of Decisions concerning Custody of Children and on Restoration of Custody of Children 1980 and the EC Regulation No. 1347 (Brussels II) are also relevant. The latter, now Brussels IIb (having been recast in 2022), requires that judgments issued and enforcible in any EU state – on matters of parental responsibility of spouses (custody, access, etc.) – be recognised and enforced in all other EU states. Both Brussels II and the European Convention are subordinate to The Hague Convention and are applied subject to any conflict with it, in which event the Hague will take precedence.[99] Germany's alleged non-compliance with the latter has been a repeated cause for complaint from the U.S.[100] These complaints have centred on: the inappropriate use by German courts of certain provisions of The Hague Convention to justify retaining abducted children in Germany; the length of time it has taken to adjudicate cases; and the failure to enforce left-behind parents' visitation rights.

RETURNING AN ABDUCTED CHILD

Criticism of the slowness of the German judicial process, its prejudicial effect on the claims of a wronged parent, and its capacity to compromise the welfare interests of an abducted child were illustrated in a recently concluded case which had begun with the abduction in 2014 of a one-year-old child by his unmarried mother from the family home in Spain and ended with the 2022 decision of the *Bundesverfassungsgericht* (BVerfG) in respect of the now nine-year-old German child. The father's initial court proceedings in Madrid in 2015 had resulted in him being granted custody of his son and the right to decide on his residence. In 2016 a German court rejected his Hague application for an order directing the immediate return of the child to Spain on the grounds that – while the child had indeed been wrongfully removed – more than a year had passed and the child was now settled in his new environment. An appeal later that year was dismissed on the ground that taking the child out of his social environment would not be in his best interest. Following subsequent proceedings initiated by each of the parties – during which both the Spanish and German courts claimed a lack of civil jurisdiction for different reasons – a Spanish criminal court convicted the mother of abduction and sentenced her to a three-year prison sentence as well as the loss of custody rights for seven years. In 2019, the mother applied successfully to a German court for sole custody. The father's counter application in 2020 to a German family court demanding the (immediate) return of his child was refused as evaluation of the child's situation showed that transferring him to Spain into the custody of a father he hardly knew (and with whom he did not even share a common language)

99 According to s 12 of the German Law of 5 April 1990, The Hague Convention has primacy.
100 See, further, at: https://www.gao.gov/products/gao-01-423

was likely to result in severe trauma. As would: removal from the parent who had provided exclusive care for most of his life; the loss of his *de facto* father (the mother having married) and his family; uprooting from school and friends; and being immersed in a foreign language and culture. Not to be deterred, the father then applied to a Madrid court for return of the child. While the mother participated in the proceedings by way of a written statement, the child was apparently neither heard nor represented. In September 2021, the Madrid court ordered the child's return to Spain and to his father – not taking into consideration that the child had no relationship with the father and spoke no Spanish – and a warrant was issued for the mother's arrest. Further proceedings led to the BVerfG granting temporary stays of enforcement in order to conserve the status quo and prevent a precipitate removal of the child. A guardian *ad litem* was also appointed. Currently, the matter remains unresolved, subject to the interim measures imposed by the BVerfG. Throughout this prolonged muddle, in which the provisions of Hague and Brussels II *bis* were not always compatible, there is no evidence that the child's welfare interests – nor indeed his fundamental rights – were given independent legal representation.[101]

CHILD'S BEST INTERESTS

The European Commission has received official complaints that Germany 'takes a highly questionable view of the best interests of "its" children in its territory following an abduction' and 'that Germany was the most reluctant of the European countries to apply the terms of the Convention'.[102] If the tardiness that characterised the above proceedings is representative then the Commission should indeed be concerned.

Commercial surrogacy

To make a human being the subject of a contract is impermissible under German law: surrogacy is therefore illegal in Germany,[103] the mother of a child is the woman who gave birth to that child.[104] A commissioning male may be recognised in law as the father only if he either: is genetically linked and initiates court proceedings to obtain legal recognition; or obtains the consent of the surrogate who acknowledges that he is the father.[105] Although, interestingly, a German court has ruled that paying a surrogate is not an illegal action and a child born by a surrogate mother can be adopted by the genetic mother.[106]

101 See, further, the editors of the EAPIL blog at: https://eapil.org/2022/11/24/german-constitutional-court-stays-enforcement-of-a-spanish-child-return-order/

102 See 'Child Abductions in Germany', Parliamentary question – E-006436/2020, at: https://www.europarl.europa.eu/doceo/document/E-9-2020-006436_EN.html

103 The Embryo Protection Act 1991, s 1(1)(7).

104 Civil Code, s 1591.

105 The Civil Code, s 1595 1.

106 See *Decision OLG Frankfurt/Main 28 February 2019 – 1 UF 71/18.*

In 2012, when a German court upheld the decision of its embassy in Kyiv to refuse a German passport to a child born as a result of a surrogate arrangement made by a German couple with a surrogate in Ukraine, it was merely confirming the traditional grounds for determining parentage. In German law, the mother was the Ukrainian surrogate and the father was considered to be her husband.[107] Because German laws are so restrictive, denying many access to their only means of attaining parenthood, some are diverted overseas to countries where such services are commercially available. As Reinhardt points out, 'statistics show a steady decrease in applicants for adoption which leads to the assumption that people in general prefer "own" children created by use of the increasing medical methods, or at least "genetically part-identical" children by using possibilities of surrogacy abroad'.[108]

One such case, which illustrates the resulting problems for the welfare interests of children born overseas through such arrangements and returning with their 'parents' to the latter's habitual residence in Germany, was brought before the German Federal Court of Justice – *Bundesgerichtshof* (BGH) – in 2014.[109] It concerned a same-sex couple in a registered partnership who concluded a surrogacy contract with a woman in California. The resulting child was genetically linked to one of the commissioning parties. Prior to the child's birth, that individual acknowledged paternity at the German Consulate General in San Francisco with the surrogate mother's consent, and by judgment of the Superior Court of the State of California, legal parenthood was assigned to the couple jointly. However, on return to Berlin, the civil registry office refused to register them as the joint legal parents, a decision upheld by the courts of first instance. On appeal to the BGH, that court held that recognition of the Californian judgment could not be refused on the grounds of violation of public policy and ordered the civil registry office to register the child's birth and state the appellants as the joint legal parents. The BGH found that German public policy was not violated by the mere fact that legal parenthood in a case of surrogacy treatment was assigned to the intended parents, if one intended parent was also the child's biological father while the surrogate mother had no genetic relation to the child. The BGH took the view that the right of the child to an identity must also be taken into account: any consideration of whether a foreign court decision is contrary to German public policy (*orde public*) must take into account the child's right to respect for his or her private and family life under Article 8 of the ECHR, citing the ECtHR decisions in *Mennesson* and *Labassee*.[110]

However, in 2019, the BGH seemed to revert to the traditional approach when it ruled that German law must be used to determine the parentage of a child born to

107 See decision of the Administrative Court of Berlin, 10 September 2012, at: http://www.ukrainian-surrogates.com/surrogacy-ban-in-germany

108 Note to author (15 April 2020).

109 Case XII ZB 463/13.

110 See *Mennesson and Others v. France and Labassee v. France*, Application Nos. 65192/11 and 65941/11, (2014).

a surrogate in Ukraine and brought 'home' to Germany immediately after birth.[111] The Court concluded that the surrogate must be registered as the mother of the child because only the woman who bears the child is considered the mother under German law. The difference between the two decisions being that while in the first there was a court order in existence that had to be recognised in Germany, in the second there was no recognition issue so only the applicable German laws had to be observed.

IDENTITY AND ORIGINS INFORMATION

Article 8 of UN CROC states that 'every child has a right to preserve her or his identity, including nationality, name, and family relations'. In Germany, as in most other countries, this is achieved through the mandatory registration of births in the local municipal registry of births, marriages, and deaths. At a most basic level, this process provides the official route for every person born in Germany to acquire an individualised legal identity.

For children born as the result of a surrogacy arrangement there are two areas of difficulty in using this process. Firstly, as surrogacy is illegal in Germany it therefore follows that it would violate public policy to knowingly use an official public process, or allow it to be used, to achieve legal status for something specifically declared to be illegal. Adoption is the only means whereby a person who is not the birth mother of a child can acquire official recognition of their legal status as parent of that child, but using adoption as a means to bypass the constraints on surrogacy and acquire that status is by no means straightforward. For one thing, evidence that the birth parent's consent was influenced by financial reward (which, by definition, is an inherent part of the surrogacy transaction) constitutes well-established legal grounds for rejecting an adoption application. For another, the courts have not always been readily convinced that the best interests test for adoption is satisfied by the long-term implications for an adopted child discovering that their origins lie not in 'being chosen' but in a financial contract. Nonetheless, in 2015 a court determined that a child of a sperm donor had the right to discover their father's name, if no-one had been registered as such. Secondly, identity is a fraught matter in a surrogacy context. This most often devolves from parent to child but determining parentage can be difficult if not impossible when: in very many cases conception has been achieved through the contribution of a donor or donors (of eggs, sperm) for which there is an international competitive market with banks of premium genetic material, often donated on conditions of anonymity; the surrogate mother, who may be married, wishes to remain anonymous and her name is not on the birth certificate; and when the commissioning couple separate, as many do, after some years of joint parenting. Given that up to five 'parents' may have been involved in each case, is not surprising that some children born of surrogacy arrangements have a compromised sense of identity.[112]

111 BGH, Mar. 20, 2019, Docket No. XII ZB 530/17, ECLI:DE:BGH:2019:200319BXIIZB530.17.0,

112 There is some evidence to the contrary. The results of a Cambridge University research project comparing the quality of life of children (from birth to age 20) born by means of surrogacy with

Court orders

This civil law country shares with its neighbour France, a need to rely on a much reduced selection of the court orders available to common law judiciary.

CUSTODY/ACCESS

Most family breakdowns, whether marital or not, are resolved through private family law proceedings. Only where a public policy issue arises – such as the dangers presented by a violent or alcoholic ex-partner, possible child abduction, or a risk of child abuse/neglect – is the court called upon to exercise public family law orders. It may then do so, for example, by utilising the powers available under s 1684(4) of the Civil Code which authorise the court to 'restrict or exclude the right of contact' on the grounds that otherwise the 'best interests of the child would be endangered'.

GUARDIANSHIP

Wardship (*Staatsmündel*) is not available for the protection of children in Germany. Guardianship – *Vormundschaft* – however, is. This has its origins in ss 1773–1888 of the Civil Code, and was reformed in 2023. A guardianship appointment in respect of a child can be made by a testator or by the Family Court, and the subject is known as a 'ward'. The appointment is most frequently made in favour of a single guardian, but the *Jugendamt* or even an association can be, and often is, appointed as guardian.

Under s 1773 of the Civil Code, the minor is entrusted to a guardian only if no one else is vested with parental responsibility for him or her. This will be the case, for example, if both parents die, if parental responsibility has been suspended, or if it has been entirely withdrawn from the parents in accordance with s 1666 Civil Code. A guardian may be appointed even before the birth of the child, the appointment to take effect at birth.[113] Once appointed, the guardian undertakes full responsibility for the child's person and property and is authorised to represent the child legally.[114]

CURATORSHIP

Curatorship – *Pflegschaft* – means the holding of parental responsibility for a limited number of matters. It is not dissimilar to guardianship, though is more limited

that of other children, found no difference. The project concluded that 'wanting children is what really matters' rather than how they were conceived. See, further, Golombok, S., et al., 'A Longitudinal Study of Families Formed through Third-Party Assisted Reproduction: Mother-Child Relationships and Child Adjustment from Infancy to Adulthood', *Developmental Psychology*, (2023), at: https://doi.org/10.1037/dev0001526

113 The Civil Code, s 1773.

114 See, further, Dethloff, N. and Mariny, D., 'National Report: Germany', at: http://ceflonline.net/wp-content/uploads/Germany-Parental-Responsibilities.pdf

in scope, and is subject to much the same rules. As explained in s 1809 of the Civil Code, it is intended to supplement rather than replace parental responsibility if and to the extent that the parents or guardian are unable to undertake specific duties in respect of their child. This court appointment is one that can be made without being bound by parental wishes.[115]

OTHER

The Civil Code allows for a range of orders on specific issues, adjustments to custody arrangements, placing the child under institutional or foster care, to other orders relating to maintenance payments or protecting children from an abusive or alcoholic parent.[116]

Providing protection for the welfare interests of a child traversed the public/private divide in the above-mentioned unusual case of *Kutzner v. Germany*,[117] in which children were abruptly removed from blameless, if perhaps inadequate parental care, where there was no evidence of significant harm and without the parents being given an opportunity to appeal (see, further, Chapter 7).

Conclusion

Federal government has a broadly non-interventionist approach to family matters. In relation to private family law, this approach is apparent in the continuing deference to 'parental authority', in the obstacles that currently prevent adoption being available for children in care, the constraints on accessing ART services and surrogacy, and in the lack of government support services for those who choose to create family life by availing themselves of international adoption and surrogacy. As mentioned in the previous chapter, this might well be an over-reaction to the control that fascist governments exercised in relation to family matters during the Nazi era.

Consequently, the law would seem relatively restrained in the opportunities it provides for recognition and protection of a child's welfare interests, let alone the assertion of his or her rights. Indeed, it might be fair to add that private family law in Germany has not strayed far from its traditional roots, as is also apparent from the relatively under-developed hybrid sector.

115 Ibid.
116 The Civil Code, s 1666.
117 Application No. 46544/99, (2002).

Part IV

Themes of commonality and difference

9 Themes and a comparative jurisdictional analysis

Introduction

France and Germany are federal republics – the former a unitary state, the latter a federation – with overarching constitutions and a shared history in the civil law tradition. They are signatory member states of all leading international instruments, including the European Convention on Human Rights (ECHR) and the United Nations Convention on the Rights of the Child (UN CROC). They have much in common despite strong cultural differences: one with egalitarian democratic political credentials; the other irredeemably associated with its relatively recent dalliance with fascism. Shared areas of commonality are particularly apparent in their contemporary domestic laws and practice – also their international exposure to many decades of European Court of Human Rights (ECtHR) rulings – relating to the welfare interests and rights of children.

This chapter, like its counterpart in the previous three books in this series, undertakes a comparative analysis of the welfare of the child principle and its role and functions in two jurisdictions – in this case, France and Germany – as profiled in earlier chapters. It does so by following the structure of the jurisdiction chapters, trawling through the material they present to identify emerging themes. It focuses on key aspects of the principle, identifying significant differentiating national characteristics and tracing some broad contemporary patterns/trends of commonality and difference.

It begins, therefore, by dealing consecutively with jurisdictional differences in matters of policy and principle, then in relation to the respective legislative and judicial regimes: giving consideration, in the latter instance, to both domestic and international law. It identifies and examines differences in public family law as it relates to the welfare/rights of children in France and Germany, first in the civil law, then in the criminal, and then in relation to private family law. Finally, it considers the extent of a convergence in the similar and increasing use of hybrid proceedings and court orders – applicable across both the public and private sectors of family law – and assesses the significance of this development.

Policy, principles, and the legal framework

Family law in France and Germany is to be found largely in their respective Civil Codes, supplemented by statutes and subject to constitutional principles.

DOI: 10.4324/9781003415688-14

Policy

Both countries are characterised by a similar strong policy of state support for the family which, in the case of Germany – as in Ireland – is entrenched in their Constitutions.

Policy: public family law relating to children – civil jurisdiction

Maintaining the parent-child relationship has been and continues to be a prominent feature of the policy governing state intervention in the family affairs of both countries. Whether its intervention is on a consensual or coercive basis, the state objective as constitutionally stated is to restore parental ability to provide a safe home for their children.

CONSENSUAL STATE INTERVENTION

Provision of preventative and early intervention services to mothers, before and after the birth of children and in the early years of childhood, is often a key strategy if vulnerable families are to be helped to avoid problems arising later. This is clearly particularly important for poorer families. State investment in support services for families with pre-school children, while high in both countries, would seem more so in France, a perception reinforced by the fact that the judiciary have discretionary authority to order the relevant authorities to provide family support services.[1]

France also has a long-standing and distinctive policy of facilitating the anonymous maternal relinquishment of infants. This policy is, of course, open to criticism: it deprives the infant of any opportunity to later acquire personal identity information; and it also very often deprives the father of any opportunitity to exercise parental rights. In Germany, a recent legislative initiative to greatly restrict this area of maternal discretion has set the two nations on divergent policy paths.[2]

COERCIVE STATE INTERVENTION

There is no equivalent in France and Germany to the U.K. policy of requiring local authorities to promptly investigate and take appropriate action on receiving information of actual or suspected child abuse. The reporting of actual or suspected harm to a child is mandatory in France but is restricted to knowledge of a 'crime' and in Germany it is also mandatory but restricted to those who work with children. France has been criticised by the ECtHR[3] for its cautious policy in relation to state

1 Civil Code, Article 375.

2 See the Act on the Expansion of Assistance for Pregnant Women and Confidential Birth Arrangements 2022.

3 *Association Innocence en Danger v. France* and *Association Enfance et Partage v. France*, Application Nos. 15343/15 and 16806/15 (2020) and *Affaire A.L. v. France*, Application No. 13344/20, (2022).

intervention in family affairs on child welfare grounds while Germany has attracted similar criticism from the Committee on the Rights of the Child (CRC).[4]

STATE CARE

The firm policy in both countries, of keeping state intervention to the minimal level compatible with maintaining parental responsibility and family unity, may well correlate with their well-established relatively low use of foster care. This reliance on institutions in preference to foster families – particularly in Germany – for a large proportion of children in state care, is unusual for such developed nations and is out of step with well-established research findings that stress the importance of consistent family life for children.[5] It may be explained by a lack of foster parents,[6] but such recruitment issues have been overcome in other countries. Whatever the reason, the continued deficit in foster care has attracted adverse comment from the CRC directed towards both countries.[7]

An interesting point of difference between the countries is their respective use of kinship placements: while this is a strong feature of child care policy in Germany, there is comparatively little reliance on the extended family for such purposes in France.

The Civil Codes of both countries require the authorities to prioritise the safe rehabilitation of a child in state care to their family of origin.[8] In France, this is reinforced by statutes that require planning for family reunification, wherever feasible, for every child taken into state care and in practice there is considerable investment in 'the ideology of maintaining the parent–infant relationship at all costs'.[9] While in Germany there is no explicit equivalent legal obligation, the Constitutional Court has stated that the proportionality principle requires that every possible attempt be made to reunite families.[10] Nonetheless, almost all children remain in state care until old enough to be discharged because, as Reinhardt explains, 'the threshold of separating children from their families is so high that in cases of separation there is hardly ever a prospect of reunification as the level of parental misconduct is so severe that the child's welfare would usually be endangered by a return'.[11]

4 See UN Child Rights Committee findings on Germany, Kuwait, North Macedonia, Philippines, South Sudan, Ukraine, Uzbekistan, and Viet Nam (2022), at: https://www.destatis.de/EN/Themes/Society-Environment/Social-Statistics/Public-Children-Youth-Welfare/_node.html

5 See, for example, Bowlby, J., *Attachment and Loss*, Basic Books, New York, (1969).

6 Jörg Reinhardt explains that the continued use of residential care is not a policy but a default forced choice due to a serious lack of foster parents (note to author, 9 June 2023).

7 See, for France, at: CRC/C/FRA/CO/5, at paras 53 and 54. For Germany, see, further, at: CRC/C/DEU/CO/5-6, at para 27(c).

8 For France, see Civil Code, Article 3750-2. For Germany, see the Civil Code, s 1673 et seq.

9 See Berger, M., *The Failure of Child Protection Services*, Dunod, Paris, (2003).

10 See BVerfG, 13.07.2022, 1 BvR 580/22 and 15.11.2022, 1 BvR 1667/22.

11 Note to author, 9 June 2023.

Policy: public family law relating to children – criminal jurisdiction

For both France and Germany, the modern legal system as it relates to children can probably be safely dated to the aftermath of World War II (WWII). It is probably fair to say that systems then formed, around a central policy commitment to education and rehabilitation, set the trajectory for their child offender laws on a similar welfare-oriented path.

THE WELFARE/JUSTICE BALANCE

In France, the dual civil/criminal jurisdiction administered by the *juge des enfants* represents an approach that now seems quite singular and somewhat out of step with contemporary policy elsewhere which has long since abandoned it in favour of keeping a legal focus on welfare interests quite separate from that on criminal activity. The Civil Code directive that the *juge des enfants* should 'always strive to obtain family's consent to the measure envisaged' highlights the weighting given to considerations of welfare rather than justice and is indicative of underlying state deference to family integrity. In practice, however, this approach is not dissimilar to that adopted in Germany where the emphasis is also less on accountability and more on the needs of the offending child.

Policy: private family law relating to children

Increasingly, the primary trend in family law is the developing cross-sectoral capacity of the welfare principle: whether the proceedings are public or private in nature, a policy thrust that requires the law to follow the needs of the child. Arguably, the more rigid distinction between public and civil law in Germany results in the welfare principle having a more diffuse definition and a weaker capacity for cross-sectoral application.

FOUNDING AND PRESERVING FAMILIES

The ECtHR has ruled that Article 8 in itself does not confer a right to 'found a family':[12] 'family life' must exist before the protection of Article 8 can be applied.[13] Nonetheless, in both France and Germany, as in many other developed nations, the same wide range of family forms exists and this most basic of human rights – defended by Article 12 – remains unquestioned (see, further, Chapter 2).

Germany differs from France in that the right to found a family is recognised by the Constitutional Court and finds protection under Article 6 of the Constitution.[14] The laws of both, however, are guarded in relation to the terms on which prospec-

12 *E.B. v. France*, Application No. 43546/02, (2008).

13 *V.D. and Others v. Russia*, Application No. 72931/10, (2019).

14 See BVerfG 31, 67 or 36, 161; Antoni, in: Hömig/Wolff, Grundgesetz für die Bundesrepublik Deutschland, 12th ed. 2018, p 131.

tive parents can access relevant family forming services. In contrast, the right not to legalise parenting arrangements, and the right to dissolve arrangements that have been legalised by the acquisition of marital status, are matters that in both counties have been left to the discretion of the parties concerned.

France and Germany are alike in that they have policies which place a high premium on maintaining the relationships conducive to preserving the legal integrity of birth families. In that respect they differ, arguably, from the U.K. and the U.S. This shared approach is evident in their equally committed policy – at least in theory – of working towards the return to parental care of children admitted to the public care system and in the reluctance to facilitate the termination of birth family relationships by resorting to the non-consensual adoption of such children.

ADOPTION

In both countries, public policy has ensured that adoption remains very largely a private family law process, most often used to legally secure intra-family arrangements. It shares the same distinctive jurisdictional characteristics and these differentiate it from adoption in the U.K. and the U.S. In France and Germany this domestic legal process: is available in plenary and simple forms in respect of both children and adults (though simple adoption has not been available for children in Germany since 1977);[15] provides for a degree of maternal annonymity; is used primarily and without constraint by step-parents; does not permit the paramountcy principle to have a role in determining a child's eligibility; and is subject to legal restrictions as regards 'openness' and information disclosure. As an intercountry process, it shares in the same steep downward trend that has now come to characterise this process in many countries.

FAMILY PLANNING, ABORTION, SURROGACY, IVF, ETC.

The policy towards abortion as a public service is similar in both countries, but availability is much more restricted than in others, such as the U.K. IVF is similarly available but constrained. Surrogacy, a rapidly growing form of medical tourism, remains firmly contrary to public policy in both France and Germany (see, further, below).

FAMILY BREAKDOWN: ARRANGEMENTS FOR CHILDREN, ETC.

In no area of family law is the general policy of state retreat more evident than in the aftermath of family breakdown. Whether or not the parents are married, the law now leaves it to the parties to sort out their affairs. Only if they choose to go to court to contest some aspect of their previously shared assets and parental

15 See Mignot, J-F., *Child Adoption in Western Europe, 1900–2015*, HAL, (2019), at: https://shs.hal.science/halshs-02008838/document

responsibilities will the law have anything to say about how the parties resolve their differences. Formerly, the law would have stepped in and required parents to present proposed arrangements for the future care of their children. The legal dissolution of their marriage – or a judicial separation (not available in Germany) – would then have been conditional upon those arrangements satisfying the court that they were compatible with the children's welfare interests. Now in France as in Germany, and in many other developed nations, it has become standard public policy to regard such arrangements as being among the family remnants to be treated as private: proposed arrangements for children, post-family breakdown, will be a matter of concern to the state only if a parent makes it an issue. Although by far the majority of breakdowns escape initial judicial scrutiny, an increasing proportion of court time is later absorbed by such disputes and with determining what sort of arrangements do or do not satisfy the welfare interests of the children involved.

Principles

Germany and France are among the initial signatory states of the ECHR, UN CROC, and other foundational international instruments. They are also both strong supporters of the ECtHR. Unsurprisingly, therefore, their family law – including that which relates to the welfare interests and rights of children – is governed by much the same set of principles.

The paramountcy principle

In neither country is there an unequivocal statement in any area of law to the effect that the welfare interests of the child must be treated as of paramount importance in determining any particular issue, though in both judicial notice has been taken of the fact that Article 3 of UN CROC applies to domestic law. It seems probable that in both countries the paramountcy principle would conflict with traditional presumptions – constitutionally protected in Germany – favouring family unity, parental status, and maintenance of the parent-child bond.

PARAMOUNTCY: CHILD CONSENT

Any interpretation of 'paramountcy' would be deficient if it failed to: accommodate the right of the child concerned to contribute to any decision-making process affecting his or her welfare interests; establish when and why a child may independently determine such decisions; and define the grounds for differentiating between the two. While both countries have no difficulty in acknowledging the first, neither has any firm rules governing the identification of the few instances when the second might be possible nor does either have any clear rules regarding the third.

The fact that in France the adoption of a child aged 13 or older is wholly conditional upon the consent of that child does give meaningful effect to the principle but it remains unrepresentative of the legal weighting generally given to a child's views in French family law proceedings. Indeed, continuation of the '*accouchement sous*

X' practice would seem a total refutation of the principle. In Germany, the anomalous right of a young child – even if younger than seven years of age – to require the authorities to take him or her into state care, is open to a capricious rather than paramount interpretation of welfare interests. Arguably, the weighting given to parental status in both Germany's Civil Code and the Constitution would nullify efforts to give legal precedence to the paramountcy principle.

The parental responsibility principle

The law in both France and Germany continues to bear vestiges of the traditional respect given to parental rights; in neither has this been wholly eclipsed by the concept of parental responsibilities. Again, in France the perpetuation of the '*accouchement sous X*' practice, allowing for an absolute and permanent renunciation of all parental rights and responsibilities, is indicative of state reluctance to radically intervene in matters integral to parental status. However, both countries now prohibit the physical chastisement of a child by a parent or anyone else and both have embraced and applied the concept of 'joint parental custody'.

State deference towards parental status is most clearly visible in the comparative – compared, for example, with the U.K. and the U.S. – lack of policy and legislative initiatives to facilitate the non-consensul adoption of children, failed and abused by their parents, who must by default remain in long-term state care (see, further, below).

The permanency planning principle

The purpose of permanency planning is to assess and prepare a child requiring out-of-home care for a placement – such as adoption, kinship, or foster care – on a long-term basis. The permanence option should promote the child's links with their racial, cultural, and religious heritage. In both countries the question as to whether a child requires permanency planning will arise on entry to the care system when the professionals concerned formulate – with the child and his or her parents, as far as is feasible – a 'care plan'. Although the law in both countries allows for the removal of parental rights/responsibilities from those who have most grievously failed or abused their children and permits the non-consensual adoption of the children concerned, in fact this rarely happens.

Permanency planning in France and Germany is probably largely a misnomer as the law in both requires short-term placements while the authorities concentrate their efforts in giving effect to their legal duty to prepare the family home for the safe return of the child. In practice the reasons requiring admission tend to persist and the child remains in care. Although, again in both countries, there is a presumption that the placement should be in a foster home rather than in residential care (i.e. a children's home or some such facility), a surprisingly large proportion of the child care population is not accommodated in foster families; certainly a much larger proportion are in residential care than would be the case in the U.K. and in many other developed countries. It might be speculated that this is at least partially due – like the avoidance of non-consensual adoption – to a legal assumption that return to parental care is the objective, and state authorities therefore choose placement options that will not be viewed as compromising that legally required outcome.

The proportionality principle

The principle of proportionality requires the means used to achieve a given objective to be limited to what is necessary and sufficient (see, also, Chapter 1). A measure is considered to be compatible with the principle of proportionality if it pursues a legitimate aim and if the means employed are both necessary and as non-restrictive as possible; they must be the minimum necessary to achieve the objective.

While the principle is prominent in the law relating to children in both countries – and both have been equally subject to ECtHR rulings on the matter – it would seem to have a more structured presence in German law. This may well be a consequence of Germany's mid-20th-century history of involvement with fascism and the resulting emphasis given to the principle in the Constitution.

The subsidiarity principle

The principle of subsidiarity is predicated on an understanding that the exercise of authority will be exercised at the lowest level necessary to achieve commonly agreed objectives and that entities exercising that authority will be guaranteed functional independence at that level (see, also, Chapter 1). In Germany it is probable that subsidiarity, like the proportionality principle, has been embedded in the Constitution in order to counter any possible assumption of centralised control of authority at the highest level. In both countries this principle can be seen in the laws governing the state-family relationship which very much place primary responsibility for safeguarding the welfare of children on their parents while requiring the state to provide such resources as may be necessary to ensure that parents can continue to care.

The legal system and the public sector: legislation, courts, welfare/rights, and representation

France and Germany, adjoining parliamentary democratic republics in the heart of Europe, have had a troubled history but since the ending of WWII have led the building of a new international legal architecture for human rights, equality, and non-discrimination. Both have also largely rebuilt their domestic family law frameworks.

Legislative framework

The fact that France is a unitary state while Germany is federated naturally results in a much more complex legislative framework for the latter and gives rise to complications when comparing the two.

INTERNATIONAL LAW

Both France and Germany have ratified the United Nations Convention on the Rights of the Child, the Hague Convention on Protection of Children and Co-operation in Respect of Intercountry Adoption, and many more international instruments (see, further, Chapters 4 and 7, respectively).

DOMESTIC LEGISLATION

As both countries belong to the civil law tradition, the main body of domestic law lies in their respective Civil Codes and, also in both cases, the Codes together with other legislation and regulations shelter under constitutional umbrellas. While amendments to the Civil Codes of both countries have provided a modernised body of law relating to children, it should be noted that the CRC in 2022 found the German Code to be weighted in favour of parents and recommended that the government 'strengthen efforts to incorporate children's rights explicitly into the Basic Law'[16] (see, further, Chapters 4 and 7).

Courts and regulatory framework

Both France and Germany are subject to the ECtHR appeal process and to CRC monitoring in respect of children's welfare interests and rights. They both have a similar hierarchy of national courts and ancillary regulatory bodies, commissions, etc. but the federated governance structure of Germany means that the federal hierarchy (excluding a constitutional court) is virtually replicated in each of the 16 *Länder*. While they each have Family Courts (*juge aux affaires familiales* and *Familiengericht*, in France and Germany, respectively), France unlike Germany has a unified legal system – led by the *juges des enfants* – with a combined civil and criminal jurisdiction dedicated exclusively to the needs and deeds of children and youths.

The absence of any national Ombudsman for children, or similar body, in Germany is a characteristic that differentiates that country from France.

Representation for children

The court hearings in both countries strive to be child-friendly. This is most obvious in France where, in sharp contrast to standard common law practice, the parties and the child are all encouraged to speak directly to the judge without the customary procedural stages and without lawyers, expert witnesses, cross-examination, etc. There a child has party status in proceedings regarding their welfare – unlike a similar child in Germany – and may, therefore, elect to be legally represented. In Germany, unlike France, the child subject of proceedings will mostly be supported by a guardian who will elicit their views, ascertain their welfare interests,

16 CRC/C/DEU/CO/5-6, at para 6.

and advocate on their behalf before the judge. Nonetheless any child has the right to be heard personally by the judge in any family court proceedings.[17] If aged 14 or older the child may, if they so wish, represent himself or herself in all matters affecting them without the need of a legal representative.

CHILD IN COURT

In both countries a child of any age has the right to directly address the judge on a matter that concerns his or her welfare interests.

CONSENT OF CHILD

In France a child's legal right to give or withhold their consent is restricted to proceedings for his or her adoption (whether plenary or simple but is conditional upon their being 13 years of age or older).[18] A similar right is available to a German child aged 14 or older[19] and a much younger child – perhaps below the age of 7 – can unilaterally consent to be removed from their family home and be taken into state care.[20]

Public bodies

Much the same range of public bodies, exercising much the same child protection functions, are operational in both countries and in both, these functions are shared with or franchised out to state-registered non-governmental organisations (NGOs) and to some services provided by religious organisations.

GOVERNMENT DEPARTMENTS FOR CHILDREN

In 2022, UNICEF expressed concern regarding the lack of a national 'Ministry for Children' in France – able to co-ordinate existing government and voluntary bodies and plan and execute national child welfare/rights strategies – and its call for such a body to be established has recently been answered.[21] Arguably, the same deficit continues to exist in Germany where the federated distribution of duties for child welfare/rights leads to greater desiccation – within the aggregated policy and service provision responsibilities of the Ministry for Family, Senior Citizens, Women, and Youth – and where, consequently, the need for such a national 'Ministry for Children' may be greater.

17 See Family Proceedings Act, s 159.
18 The Civil Code, Articles 345 and 361.
19 The Civil Code, ss 1746 and 1747.
20 The Social Code, s 42(1).
21 See *Droits des Enfants en France* (2022), at: https://unicef.hosting.augure.com/Augure_UNICEF/r/ContenuEnLigne/Download?id=480588C0-E8CD-4A6A-B8D8-80AAA060B4C4&filename=SynthDroitsEnfantsFrance2022_final_pages.pdf

CHILDREN'S COMMISSIONER/OMBUDSMAN/RAPPORTEUR

Both countries have bodies with functions equivalent to an 'ombudsman for children'. In France the office of *Défenseur des Enfants* is an independent but government-funded body, which functions as a subsidiary of a national human rights agency, is located within it, and shares its regional offices. Its effectiveness, at least in terms of 'narrowing the gap between stated rights and actual rights and to tackling the phenomenon of rights not being accessed' and influencing government policies, is open to question.[22] In Germany, while there is no national office there are mandatory locally based *Ombudsstellen* agencies across Germany which provide services that perhaps accentuate information giving and mediation/conciliation rather than assertive rights advocacy.[23]

The welfare principle in contemporary practice: public family law – civil jurisdiction

State intervention in family matters is most visible, contentious, and morally troubling in the civil jurisdiction of public family law as it relates to the welfare interests and rights of children. Whether that intervention is consensual or coercive, it will be accompanied by accusations in the media that it was too precipitate or too late, too heavy-handed, or too superficial. In recent years, as society becomes more pluralistic and rights aware – and is constantly exposed to 'real-time' media scrutiny – state intervention has also had to develop a correspondingly more culturally sensitive approach when balancing the rights/welfare interests of children against parental values.

Prevention: consensual intervention

While the law in both France and Germany requires service provision appropriate to prevent vulnerable families from failing to provide for the care and protection of their children, the former differs from the latter – and from the U.K. and other countries – by empowering the court (the *juge des enfants*) to order support for parents in the form of specific services. Placing such authority in the hands of the judiciary, rather than leaving it to the discretion of local health and social service authorities, is a singular and indicative characteristic of the special French state-family relationship.

State duties to support families in need

The principle of subsidiarity requires the state in both France and Germany to respect and support parents in the upbringing of their children, which is their

22 See *Défenseur des Droits*, 'Report of the Defender of Rights to the United Nations Committee on the Rights of the Child', (2020), at: https://www.defenseurdesdroits.fr/sites/default/files/atoms/files/report_of_the_defender_of_rights_to_the_united_nations_committee.pdf

23 The Social Code, s 9a.

prerogative right and duty.[24] In Germany, this is accompanied by a stronger implication of state supervision of parents to ensure that the standards of care owed to their children are not breached.

SERVICE PROVISION

The law requiring the state to support families in need would appear to be more explicit in France, more specific as to the range of appropriate services, and – by empowering the *juges des enfants* to direct service provision – has a more authoritarian approach to ensuring effective service delivery.

In France, there would seem to be an array of professional services – social workers, psychiatrists, psychologists, etc. – in addition to the normal social care services – financial assistance, day-care for children, home help, etc. – that the judiciary can direct to reinforce weak or failing parental care. Moreover, in France unlike in Germany, the judge may appoint a *tuteur* to take over the administration of family welfare benefits and to take such steps as may be necessary to safeguard and improve the welfare interests of children.

SAFE HAVENS

Insofar as a process that permits a parent to safely and anonymously abandon their child is compatible with the latter's welfare interests, then it can be said that both countries make available much the same preventative provision. While 'safe havens' are illegal in Germany, they are in use there as in France. However, both now have in place procedures – *accouchement sous X* and *Vertrauliche Geburt* – which in effect supersede the need for 'safe havens'.

Protection: coercive state intervention

Both countries – in common with all other developed nations – have laws providing for the protection of children from abuse or neglect, stating the grounds for removing child victims into state care and for instigating criminal prosecutions against parents or others who have caused a child to be harmed.[25]

MANDATORY REPORTING

In France, unlike Germany, the law imposes a universal mandatory requirement on anyone who has information regarding child neglect or abuse to notify the appropriate authorities. In Germany a similar but not universal mandatory duty

24 See: for France, the Civil Code, Article 371-2; and for Germany, the Basic Law, Article 6(2).

25 See: for France, Article 371-2 of the Civil Code and Article 222-17 of the Criminal Code; for Germany, 1666 of the Civil Code and ss 171-84 of the Criminal Code.

is imposed on all those working with children – whether in a public agency or an NGO (*Freier Träger*) – to make such a report to the authorities.

Duty to promptly intervene

In both countries, intervention by the authorities in a family for the purposes of investigating suspected child abuse/neglect normally requires prior court authorisation but in urgent situations this can be dispensed with. Again, in both countries, there have been cases where delayed intervention has clearly compromised the welfare interests of the children concerned.[26] Moreover, the CRC has expressed deep concern about levels of domestic violence against children in France and the lack of relevant data collection systems.[27]

MULTI-AGENCY COLLABORATION

While both countries require inter-agency collaboration in cases of actual or suspected child abuse/neglect, this is a mandatory legal requirement in Germany where decision-making must be on a collective basis. There is good reason to believe that official deference to family privacy – compounded by an unwillingness to pry into and be suspected of reporting on a neighbour's affairs – is inhibiting the ability of German authorities to detect and effect early intervention in such cases.

The fact that in France the *juge des enfants* assumes and retains direct responsibility of a case, once investigations confirm there is cause for concern regarding the welfare of a child, very probably provides a more effective basis for case management than in Germany; though much turns on the expertise of the judge. Judicial authority, applied by the same judge throughout the course of state intervention in a family, provides consistent management with a capacity to direct professional engagement, service provision, and inter-agency co-operation. If, as Eglin claims the role of the judge 'makes the French system close to a defence of the birth family and parents' rights ideology' this would constitute a singular feature of the French child protection system and one that differentiates it from its German counterpart.

Care proceedings

In both countries – but more so in France – proceedings are conducted in a much more child-friendly setting and manner than would normally be the case in the U.K. and most other common law jurisdictions. Again, in both, a child of any age has the right to directly address the judge on a matter that concerns his or her welfare interests. In Germany, unlike France, such a child will nearly always be

26 See: for France, *Association Innocence en Danger v. France* and *Association Enfance et Partage v. France*, Application Nos. 15343/15 and 16806/15 (2020); and for Germany, see 'Eight-year-old child reportedly locked up for life in Germany', *The Brussels Times* (22 April 2023), at: https://www.brusselstimes.com/318698/eight-year-old-child-reportedly-locked-up-for-life-in-germany

27 CRC/C/FRA/CO/5, at paras 27, 42, and 43.

supported by a guardian *ad litem* which provides a significant guarantee that their welfare interests will be ascertained and brought to the attention of the judge.

CARE PLAN

A care plan is a mandatory requirement in respect of every child admitted or committed to the public care system in France and Germany. While the prescribed contents are much the same, a significant jurisdictional difference is that in France the plan is finalised by the judge which must, presumably, make agency discretionary deviations from their agreed role and objectives a little more difficult. In both countries, the child and parents are expected and encouraged to contribute.

State care

The amount of children entering the public care system in both countries has been steadily increasing for some years. In France, in 2013, more than 318,000 child welfare cases were opened; by 2020, that number had grown to more than 370,000.[28] In Germany, 50,364 children and young people were in foster care in 2005, and in 2015 there were 71,501, but by 2021 the foster care population had increased to 87,300,[29] an increase of 5% from the previous year.

The threshold for removing children from parental care would seem high in both countries, relative to the U.K. for example, but more so in Germany where children can only be removed from parental care if there is no other option. In this context, France has carved out a middle ground: the *service d'adaptation progressive en milieu naturel*, allows a child to return home on condition that parents accept and fully participate in an intensive programme designed to improve parenting skills. This expensive and invasive programme will involve teams of professionals working in the family home and in specialist units which parents must attend, it may last years, but it maintains the child in their home, in parental care, and in their community: able to continue school attendance and local friendships.

Foster care and residential care

Both countries share a characteristic that distinguishes them from the U.K. and other countries: although both prioritise foster care as offering the best form of out-of-home placement; they continue to place a relatively high level of reliance on residential care.

FOSTER CARE

The fact that a high proportion of out-of-home placements are consistently made in favour of residential facilities is often explained as a default response due to a lack

28 See https://www.statista.com/statistics/468238/numbers-child-protection-benefit-recipients-france/
29 See, further, at: https://www.destatis.de/EN/Press/2022/10/PE22_454_225.html

of foster parents. However, it seems at least possible that it may correlate with both a strong state deference to parental status/family unity and to the, at best, marginal relevance of the paramountcy principle. In those countries where child protection laws have unequivocally assimilated this principle, the right of a child to have their developmental needs – of which emotional attachments and psychological security are crucial – met by a consistent and caring family framework, simply takes precedence over the possibility of return to the risks inherent in a failed birth family structure. Unless, at point of admission to state care, there is persuasive evidence that a child's family of origin is amenable to sufficient change to enable it to offer safe 'good enough' parenting, then the paramountcy principle dictates that the child's short-term development needs be given priority. The practice, if not the law, in both France and Germany would seem equivocal as regards whether the objective is restoration of parental status/family unity or protecting the right of the child to have their developmental needs safely and appropriately catered for.

KINSHIP CARE

A curious point of difference between the two countries is their respective use of kinship foster placements. While in Germany the majority of children in foster care are placed with a relative (60% in 2005), this is true for only a small minority in France (7% in 2007).

RESIDENTIAL CARE

Both countries have a continued and consistently high level of recourse to residential care, though both accept that foster care caters more appropriately for a child's developmental needs. It is not altogether clear why this is.

Secure accommodation is provided in both countries for children and youths – who are most often offenders – assessed as presenting a risk to themselves or others and requiring supervised health care.

Rehabilitation and concurrent planning

Rehabilitation of a child in state care with their family of origin is firmly mandated in the laws of France[30] and Germany.[31] This is reinforced in France by legal requirements for parent-child contact to be maintained and by judicial rulings to the effect that out-of-home placements must not continue unless justified in accordance with Article 375 of the Code. Similarly in Germany, s 1684 of the Civil Code establishes the right – and indeed the duty – of birth parents to maintain contact with their child.

30 The Civil Code, Article 375-2.

31 The Civil Code, s 1684, and Art. 6(2) of the Basic Law.

PARTNERSHIP AND REHABILITATION

The fact that out-of-home placements in France are time limited to two years, after which they must be reviewed and renewed – unless steps are taken to legally remove all parental rights – together with the above-mentioned parent-child contact rights, should focus the attention of the authorities on preparatory arrangements for family reunification. This is emphasised by Article 375-2 of the French Civil Code which requires the *juge des enfants* – rather than the *Aide sociale à l'enfance* (ASE) – to directly supervise the *assistance éducative* procedure to correct the functioning of the family so that it is better able to protect the child on his or her return. Broadly similar legal requirements apply in Germany where s 37 of the Social Code and s 1673 *et seq.* of the Civil Code, respectively, direct the *Jugendamt* to make appropriate efforts to reunify a family and to prepare parents and child for the legal resumption of family life.

Whether the above legal rights and duties imposed upon parents and the authorities actually constitute a genuine partnership, binding both parties in a working relationship purposefully dedicated to family reunification, is perhaps best assessed by the outcomes. In Germany, it has been estimated that family reunification is achieved for no more than 4–5% of the child care population. In France, judging from the CRC recommendation to the authorities that they should 'facilitate the rehabilitation and social reintegration of children' it would seem that much the same problems exist there.[32] In both countries, instead of being reunited with their families of origin, or being absorbed into adoptive families, most children remain in state care until discharged when they reach 18 years of age.

Adoption

The laws of France and Germany provide simple and plenary forms of adoption, as mentioned earlier, but while adults and children may be adopted, the latter in Germany are restricted to plenary adoptions. In both countries, the adoption of children has been in decline for several years.

DOMESTIC VOLUNTARY ADOPTION

In France as in Germany, the role of the authorities in domestic adoptions is largely restricted to placing – or regulating the placing – of children abandoned, voluntarily relinquished, acquired overseas, or freed by the courts. They are also responsible for regulating the approval of prospective adopters, supporting adopting families, and managing information disclosure enquiries from adoptees (see, further, below). In both countries, adoptions by step-parents are most common.

32 CRC/C/FRA/CO/5, at para 54.

NON-CONSENSUAL ADOPTION FROM STATE CARE

Conceptually this is problematic in France where parental ties have been regarded as legally inviolable, except in the most extreme circumstances. However, as in Germany, where children are in state care following their abandonment, anonymous relinquishment, or where the courts have removed parental rights/responsibilities, then, as parental consent is unavailable or unnecessary, the authorities can proceed to place such children for adoption (see, further, below).

Unaccompanied migrant minors and trafficking

In recent years – peaking in 2015/16 – both countries, but particularly Germany, have experienced an unprecedented influx of migrants, including unaccompanied minors. A large proportion of the latter have been male Muslim youths, many of whom have had difficulty adjusting to a social context very different to their country of origin. While the scale of the problems associated with unaccompanied migrant minors is greatest in Germany, the conditions of those living in transit camps on the coast in northern France probably give rise to most concern in terms of the threat to their welfare interests.

Rights and welfare interests

Unaccompanied migrant minors have presented logistical problems for the authorities, resulting in the minors having difficulty – or encountering discrimination – in accessing the same health, education, housing, welfare benefits, and general social facilities that are available to others. To a large extent these problems have probably been due to the volume of such minors entering France and Germany within such a short time. The Asylum Procedures Directive, Article 25(6), explicitly requires a host nation to have regard for the welfare interests of the child when taking any decision as to granting or withdrawing asylum.[33] However, the CRC has been critical both of French non-compliance with this Directive[34] and with Germany regarding its treatment of unaccompanied child migrants and has recommended that the latter takes all the necessary measures to improve the situation of children seeking asylum and child migrants.[35]

FAMILY UNITY

It is clear that Article 9 of UN CROC establishes the right of a child not to be separated from their parents unless staying with them could be harmful to the child or if it is otherwise impossible. The ECtHR, at the turn of the century, confirmed that states are obliged to facilitate the family reunification of unaccompanied minors

33 Directive 2013/32/EU.
34 CRC/C/FRA/CO/5, at para 73.
35 CRC/C/DEU/CO/3-4.

and to always apply the best interests principle when doing so.[36] It is also clear, however, that in the intervening years the volume of migrating children – with or without parents – has greatly increased and separation has become a frequent consequence of the migrant processing system in both countries. This has repeatedly been the subject of court cases and protests by human rights organisations. In 2021, the ECtHR, in response to a request for advice from the Federal Administrative Court regarding the 'retention of family unity' in the context of migrants seeking refugee status, reaffirmed the importance of this principle.[37] In 2022, the UN CRC expressed its concern regarding the German authorities' treatment of migrant minors and urged that measures should be taken to: 'prevent the separation of migrant children from their parents'.[38] In 2023, the Court of Justice of the European Union found that the strict requirement to submit an application for family reunification in person meant that, for some people, family reunification was impossible, and ruled that such an obstacle, preventing family unity, was impermissible.[39] It would seem probable that this ruling indicates that the courts are now taking a firmer stand on this issue and in future both countries – and others – will be required to comply with Article 9.

TRAFFICKING

The 2022 extension to the Framework Resolution of the Council of the European Union on Combating Human Trafficking is intended to accommodate criminal offences for human trafficking for the purposes of exploitation in the labour force and to supplement the Palermo and Warsaw protocols. In particular, the Optional Protocol on the Sale of children – specifically Article 2(a) – prohibits this form of child abuse. This provides the current framework for combating trafficking in France and Germany. While the crime of trafficking is most usually associated with the purposes of the sex and labour trades it is particularly pernicious due to its close involvement with such other forms of organised crime as migrant smuggling, drug trafficking, extortion, money laundering, and document fraud. The European Commission estimates that one in every four persons trafficked is a child.[40] There is little in the way of statistical data to gauge the trends in the rates and purposes of trafficking in both countries nor any hard evidence to differentiate between them in terms of their response to the welfare interests of the children involved.

36 *Mubilanzila Mayeka and Kaniki Mitunga v. Belgium*, Application No. 13178/03, (2006) and *Johansen v. Norway*, Application No. 17383/90, (1996).

37 See Case C-91/20, ECLI:EU:C:2021:898, at: https://eur-lex.europa.eu/legal content/EN/TXT/PDF/?uri=CELEX:62020CJ0091&from=IT

38 CRC/C/DEU/CO/5-6, at para 39.

39 See Case C-1/23 PPU, at: https://www.infomigrants.net/en/post/48305/no-requirement-to-apply-in-person-for-family-reunification-eu-court-rules

40 See, further, at: https://home-affairs.ec.europa.eu/policies/internal-security/organised-crime-and-human-trafficking/together-against-trafficking-human-beings_en

The welfare principle in contemporary practice: public family law – criminal jurisdiction

As with so much else, the criminal justice systems of France and Germany – including the manner in which they relate to children – were essentially rebuilt in the aftermath of WWII. In both countries the system then initiated had a strong leaning towards welfare considerations, an approach that survived a succession of youth justice reforms and continues to shape their criminal jurisdictions as they relate to child offenders in the 21st century.

The justice system and children

The singular defining characteristic of French juvenile justice that differentiates it from its German counterpart – and from that of other countries such as the U.K. – is that it is presided over by a judge who manages the criminal and civil proceedings as part of a unified system; though in recent years new laws have tended to emphasise the criminal track. Both countries have been similarly influenced by Directive (EU) 2016/800, on procedural safeguards for children who are suspects or accused persons in criminal proceedings, and have drafted the safeguards into their domestic law.

AGE OF CRIMINAL RESPONSIBILITY

The age of criminal responsibility is an aspect of the law relating to children which differentiates France from Germany. While children in the latter – aged 13 years of age or younger – cannot be held criminally liable and cannot be prosecuted as adults if younger than 18, in France a child aged 10 may be tried in a criminal court and from the age of 13 will be treated in law as an adult and as such is eligible for a prison sentence. In France the age of criminal responsibility is somewhat nebulous as it is determined in accordance with a child's 'capacity for discernment' which can be below 10 years of age but is otherwise presumed to be at age 13. In Germany youth offenders will be treated as juveniles until they reach 21 years of age. Clearly this difference in age parameters must allow a significantly larger proportion of child offenders in Germany than in France to benefit from not having their conduct criminalised, though the Perben Law of 2002 and more recent developments in France – fast-track procedures, etc. – are narrowing the gap.

Children in court

In France, the *juge des enfants* conducts informal hearings in his office with the child concerned, his or her parents, and the victim, together with the social worker and such other professionals who may be relevant in attendance. The judge arrives at a conclusion as acceptable as possible to all parties and thereafter in effect manages the local team of ASE staff, psychologists, etc. to ensure that agreed objectives are efficiently pursued. In contrast, the German system centres around an orthodox juvenile court criminal proceedings but these are conducted in a child-friendly manner, with every child supported by a guardian *ad litem*, and with a focus on the offender's state of mind, social and family background, and on an outcome that will aid his or her social rehabilitation.

ROLE OF THE WELFARE PRINCIPLE

The most telling indicator of how the welfare/justice considerations are balanced lies in the nature of the tariff of sanctions and in their use by the judiciary. In both countries the influence of the welfare principle can be seen most starkly in the fact that community measures are imposed far more frequently than custodial sentences. A significant jurisdictional difference lies in the respective age parameters allowing German youths to avail themselves of juvenile rather than adult proceedings together with the associated sentencing tariff. Counterintuitively, perhaps, given France's reputation for a welfare-oriented approach, it is surprising to learn that French juveniles aged 16 and over can find themselves tried as an adult in a criminal court, whereas in Germany an offender aged between 18 and 20 will fall within the remit of the juvenile justice rather than the adult justice system.

COURT ORDERS: COMMUNITY AND CUSTODIAL SENTENCES

While France and Germany are both proponents of a more welfare than punitive approach to child offenders, it would seem that France is developing a tougher policy by introducing non-custodial sanctions such as fines, restitution, curfews, etc. There is now a new emphasis on accountability and consequences for deviant behaviour: children as young as 13 years of age may be sentenced to a term of imprisonment. In Germany, a notable feature is the low recourse to custodial sentencing: it has been estimated that the incarceration rate in Germany is 9 times less than in the U.S. (76 per 100,000 vs. 693 per 100,000).[41] It should also be borne in mind that both countries have been warned by the CRC to be attentive to the needs of children who are victims or witnesses of violence.[42]

RECIDIVISM

As with all systems, however, the best measure of their efficiency lies in the quality of their output. The fact that in Germany only about 30% of those serving custodial sentences re-present within 3 years[43] (compared, for example, with an estimated 75% in the U.S.), coupled with consistently declining crime rates, would seem to

41 See *The Crime Report*, (2018), at: https://thecrimereport.org/2018/04/10/in-germany-its-hard-to-find-a-young-adult-in-prison/

42 For France and Germany, see, CRC/C/FRA/CO/5, paras 83–6 and CRC/C/DEU/CO/5-6, at para 23(c), respectively.

43 See Dünkel, F., 'Criminology and Criminal Justice, Juvenile Justice and Juvenile Delinquency', *International and Comparative Criminology*, (2016), at: 10.1093/oxfordhb/9780199935383.013.68

offer convincing testimony to the effectiveness of the German juvenile justice system. That Germany has one of the lowest rates of child-offender recidivism in the world is an important differentiating factor and one that must work to the benefit of the welfare interests of many more German than French juveniles.

The welfare principle in contemporary practice: private family law

In retrospect, it would seem that in general, private family law was initially just that – private. State intervention was restricted to laying down a framework of eligibility rules for citizens to enter and exit marital status and conduct rules which identified the reciprocal rights and duties that its members owed to each other for the duration of that legal entity, their marital family. As the social status of marriage has faded so, it would seem, has the shell of associated legality. Private family law has shifted its focus from aggregating to disaggregating legal relationships; from a concern for the integrity of the spousal relationship to that of parenting. State intervention has defaulted to policing the most basic strand in the web of family relationships: parental responsibilities; whether parents are married or not, whether the child is a birth child or not, private family law is now mostly about navigating the variables in the parent-child relationship.

Founding a family

In recent years the law has been a good deal more concerned with the beginnings than the endings of family life. The restrictions on access to abortion, the use and misuse of embryos, genetic editing, intercountry adoption, and commercial surrogacy are among the issues to founding a family that have attracted regulatory controls. The law in France and Germany now accommodates a wide range of different family forms and yet, in both, traditional values impose legal constraints on the means available to found a family: accessing assisted reproductive technology (ART) services is problematic, commercial surrogacy is prohibited, and adoption from state care is seldom possible. However, it should be remembered that despite the variation in contemporary family forms, in both countries the heterosexual marital family with 2.4 children remains the ubiquitous norm.

Adoption

As mentioned earlier, adoption in France and Germany remains firmly centred in private family law. It is essentially consensual in nature and caters for simple and plenary adoption orders and for the adoption of both children and adults (in Germany, the adoption of children is restricted to the plenary form). In both countries it is fading in significance: traditional third-party adoptions (by an unrelated 'stranger') are rare; it is now mostly used to shore-up step families, though in France – unlike Germany – step-parents are confined to 'simple' adoptions.

The maternal right to anonymity, when a mother relinquishes her child for adoption, is a distinguishing jurisdictional characteristic. Such a right has never been recognised in German law, though the practice has been tolerated (since 2014 the mother has an explicit right to 'preliminary' anonymity but the adoptee on reaching 16 years of age has the right to know her identity).[44] The continuing right of a French mother to avail herself of the *accouchement sous X* procedure is particularly contentious. It has been confirmed as perfectly legal by the ECtHR[45] but is viewed as regrettable by the CRC.[46]

The fact that the paramountcy principle has no legal bearing on the adoption process in either country is a shared characteristic that restricts the use of adoption – practically prohibiting entry to those children in most need – as a public service. In theory, adoptions in both countries are far from 'open'. The traditional approach of secrecy and anonymity for all parties continues to be provided by law. In practice, most adoptions are intra-family or by foster parents so there is usually ongoing contact and information disclosure between all parties. Also, in Germany, since 2021, adoption agencies and other intermediaries have been obliged to promote openness between the adoptive and the birth family. A differentiating jurisdictional characteristic is the variation in reliance on intercountry adoption: in Germany, this has declined from what was always a low level to its current virtual cessation; in France, while there has also been a steep decline, the fall is from a much higher level and French adopters continue to rely on foreign sources but very often they look to non-Hague-compliant countries.[47]

Reproductive rights: abortion, surrogacy, IVF, etc.

In France and Germany, as in most developed nations, access to improved methods of contraception and the availability of legal abortion, together with better techniques for assisting conception, more relevant welfare benefits, and pre- and post-birth support services, have combined to radically reduce the number of unwanted births and to correspondingly increase the proportion of those that are wanted. Nevertheless, there are significant jurisdictional differences in the law governing conception and births.

It is apparent, for example, that access to ART services in Germany is restricted and tightly regulated – most probably a reaction to the inhuman eugenic experimentation that occurred during the Nazi period – whereas in France, IVF and other reproductive medical services are relatively readily accessed. Germany can also be distinguished from France in terms of abortion law, as in Germany, abortion is in fact illegal (except in special circumstances) during the first 12 weeks of pregnancy;[48] and in terms of rates of abortion as these are considerably higher in

44 Pregnancy Conflict Act, s 31.
45 See *Odièvre v. France*, [2003] 1 FCR 621.
46 CRC/C/FRA/CO/5, at para 55.
47 Op. cit., at para 55.
48 The Criminal Code, s 218.

France.[49] The caselaw emanating from the ECtHR[50] would seem to indicate that abortion is set to become a polarising socio-political issue in Europe as it has in the U.S.[51] though judging from recent political initiatives in France and Germany and elsewhere in Europe – with the exception of countries such as Poland – it is probable that developments are likely to lean more towards relaxing than restricting access to abortion services.

Both countries share the same approach to surrogacy: it is illegal in both; and domestic law presents similar issues for commissioning parents returning home with 'their child'[52] (for 'commercial surrogacy' see, further, below).

Sexual orientation and gender transitioning

'Gender dysphoria', the medical term used to describe the distress associated with any incongruity between the experienced gender and the gender assigned at birth, was initially the standard diagnosis which indicated the resulting equally standard psychiatric treatment programme for children who claimed they needed to change their gender identity. However, as has been pointed out, there is no test to distinguish between persisting gender dysphoria and transient adolescent dysphoria.[53] This realisation, that a child's perceived gender identity issues are not amenable to medical analysis, together with the rapidly escalating numbers of children with such perceptions and the trauma caused to those who later regret having committed to irreversible medical interventions, has led to the present situation where, in Europe alone, some 11 nations have removed the medical dimension and substituted gender self-identification. This has been the case with both France and Germany and, of course, it has brought its own set of problems for which there are no simple solutions.

Child's consent

In France, accessing gender-transitional treatment – such as puberty blockers and hormone replacement treatment – is the right of a child and one that may be exercised at any age though surgical procedures will require parental consent until the child concerned is at least 14 years of age. In Germany, the age requirement for access to any form of medical treatment without the consent of a public authority

49 In 2021, France had an abortion rate of 15.5 per 1,000 women aged 15–49. In Germany it was 5.4, but because of the low time threshold, many German women are known to have travelled abroad for abortions.

50 See *A.M. and Others v. Poland*, Application No. 4188/21, (2023).

51 As represented by the decision in *Dobbs v. Jackson Women's Health Organization*, No. 19-1392, 597 U.S. ___ (2022) overturning *Roe v. Wade*, 410 U.S. 113 (1973).

52 See: for France, *Mennesson v. France*, Application No. 65192/11, (2014); and for Germany, Case XII ZB 463/13.

53 The National Academy of Medicine report, 'Medicine and gender transidentity in children and adolescents', (2022), at: https://www.academie-medecine.fr/la-medecine-face-a-la-transidentite-de-genre-chez-les-enfants-et-les-adolescents/?lang=en

and/or parents is not firmly established in law but is dependent upon the maturity and discernment of the child concerned. Should they wish to change their gender identity by means of altering their birth certificate, they will only be entitled to do so if aged 14 years of age or more, otherwise they will need a signed declaration of approval from their parents or guardians.

Welfare interests

This is a very difficult issue surrounded by a great deal of uncertainty as to what exactly can be construed as serving the welfare interests of the child concerned. It would seem only fair to note that at either end of the spectrum the outcomes speak for themselves: for many children the transition is a positive benefit, they are happier and more confident; for some, the transition has been felt to be a mistake, they are a good deal worse off, probably irretrievably. Perhaps the point made in the 2022 report by the National Academy of Medicine regarding – is fair comment.[54]

> the addictive role of excessive engagement with social media, which is both harmful to the psychological development of young people and is responsible for a very significant part of the growing sense of gender incongruence.

Family breakdown

Family breakdown and reconfiguration are much more common than previously. Consequently, serial parenting – bringing with it complications for children in terms of attachments, trust, and relationship boundaries – has become an accepted feature of contemporary social life in France and Germany as in all other developed nations.

Matrimonial and separation proceedings

As elsewhere in Europe and among the developed nations more generally, the marriage rate in France and Germany is in decline, divorces are increasing, and there is a steady growth in the proportion of children who are not living with both birth parents, some sharing home life with others to whom they are not genetically related. Germany differs from France, however, in that its family life is generally more stable which, presumably, increases the probability of more German children growing up in a secure framework of consistent relationships.[55]

France and Germany – along with many other developed nations – share the fact that judicial proceedings following family breakdown entail no more than a cursory check that the parties are satisfied with the arrangements for sharing the future

54 Ibid.
55 See, further, at: http://www.huffingtonpost.co.uk/2012/12/29/uk-family-breakdown-rate-_n_2379845.html?view=print

care of their children; judicial scrutiny of those arrangements will only occur in the very small minority of cases where the parties are in dispute and raise the matter before the judge. In that event, the law in both countries starts with the presumption that both parents retain joint parental responsibility in respect of their children until they reach maturity. There is no statutory 'welfare checklist' in the law of either country to assist the judiciary in resolving disputed care arrangements. Instead, based on the history of each parent's direct care of their child, the relative merits of their proposed future care arrangements, and the wishes of the child, the judge will make such rulings in relation to custody and visitation rights as seem most conducive to furthering a child's welfare interests. Unlike the law in other countries such as the U.K., the courts in France and Germany do not have available to them a menu of statutory orders each specifying a particular function that can be explicitly permitted or denied to one or both of the parties.[56] In this respect Germany differs from France in that it can make specific private family orders such as for custody and contact. While both countries share the common legal characteristic that the child concerned must be able to exercise their right to advise the court as to their views regarding proposed arrangements for their care, in neither country is this right determinative.

The welfare principle in contemporary practice: public/private family law

The welfare principle would seem to have less capacity to transcend the private and public divisions in family law, and create a middle ground of hybrid public/private proceedings, in Germany than in France. That capacity is necessarily closely linked to whether or not the principle is given a paramountcy weighting and, if so, whether this applies to a significant theme in family law – such as child protection and/or custody – which is not the case in Germany. Nonetheless, in both countries there is evidence that the principle is to a varying extent bridging the public/private divide and facilitating a flow of matters traditionally regarded as belonging to private family law (e.g. adoption and surrogacy) or to its public counterpart (e.g. foster care and parental abduction) into a new hybrid arena where the previous concern of the law to balance the interests of the parties has been displaced by the welfare principle as the governing standard.

Public service matters

These are two of the most prosperous of the 28 EU countries and are among the most advanced economies in the G7. They – particularly Germany – are also recovering from a series of socioeconomic shocks. Whether their public service

56 As mentioned elsewhere, the absence of 'a menu of statutory orders' may simply reflect a fundamental difference between the common law – founded on the 'no writ, no remedy' approach – and the more accommodating flexibility of the civil law.

infrastructure is sufficiently resourced to maintain a focus on the current welfare interests of children is open to question.

Poverty

The CRC has expressed concern regarding the level of poverty and its effect on the welfare of both French and German children. In relation to France, it regretted 'the situation of 20% of children living in poverty and the large numbers of homeless children'.[57] It expressed similar regret about Germany's 'insufficient efforts to tackle the root causes which place children at risk of becoming victims to the offences under the Optional Protocol such as child poverty and discrimination against children belonging to minority groups as well as against migrant and asylum seeking unaccompanied children.'[58] There would seem little room for equivocation here: France and Germany are among the world's richest countries – in 2022, Germany was ranked 4th – and yet poverty continues to adversely impact the living conditions and life opportunities of so many of their children. Though, to be fair, the levels of child poverty are worse in comparable countries such as the U.K. where 4.2 million children, or nearly one in three, were estimated as living in poverty in 2021–22.[59]

EMPLOYMENT

Given the above-mentioned levels of poverty, and the ongoing cost-of-living crisis causing hardship for many lower- and middle-income families, it would be surprising if there were not a number of underage workers engaged in part-time or seasonal employment in France and Germany, as elsewhere, but there would not appear to be any reports of this currently giving rise to exploitation concerns in either country.

However, child labour is undoubtedly a factor present in the global supply chains of French and German companies, as it is for those of many other nationalities: child labour is in effect franchised out, impairing the welfare interests of children in underdeveloped countries, in order to improve profit margins for companies in those that are more developed; a well-established form of competitive colonisation. There are indications that steps are now being taken in both countries to address this form of child exploitation by proxy, but it remains to be seen just how rigorous the promised overseas child protection measures will be if they begin to erode the competitive edge of leading companies. The practice in less developed countries tends towards leaving the market to dictate workforce terms and conditions, enticing foreign companies to follow the profit trail by relocating or reassigning production lines to locations where supply chain issues involving child labour are more obscure.

57 CRC/C/FRA/CO/5, (2016), at para 69.

58 CRC/C/OPSC/DEU/CO/, (2014), at para 19.

59 See, for example, https://www.actionforchildren.org.uk/blog/where-is-child-poverty-increasing-in-the-uk/

MIGRANT MINORS

The sizeable domestic diaspora of transient unaccompanied migrant minors gives rise to a high probability that many are engaged in unlawful employment. A large proportion of recent migrants are young men, of whom some – including children – are enduced into forced labour and employed in unregulated and unskilled sectors and a minority will be drawn into child prostitution and drug trafficking.[60]

HEALTH

One of the more blunt measures of effective state preventative intervention on health grounds, to protect the welfare interests of children, is the infant mortality rate. This key indicator for child health and well-being also serves more broadly as a measure of a nation's social and economic development. While almost routinely utilised in order to evidence the need for more resources in underdeveloped countries, it has also been applied to France and Germany with results that have generated concern.

This health indicator reveals a significant jurisdictional disparity: France's infant mortality rate is a good deal higher than that of Germany, causing the CRC to express alarm at the persistent excessively high level of infant mortality in France.[61]

EDUCATION

Like infant mortality rates, educational attainment also owes a good deal to parental socioeconomic status. In both respects, that factor largely accounts for Germany's performance being considerably and consistently better than that of France, with correspondingly greater benefits for the welfare interests of German children. However, the corollary is likely also true: the disparity in educational achievement is accentuated to the detriment of children from families of more vulnerable socioeconomic status; those who underachieve in Germany's excellent education system are more likely to continue that underachievement in the job market. School attainment, being most often a reliable predictor of future employment success, suggests that in Germany many children from single-parent, impoverished, and/or immigrant families are destined to be less successful in that respect than those from other backgrounds.

Discrimination

Discriminatory conduct is clearly illegal and a public law matter, but because it is proscribed in relation to personal aspects of private life – age, disability, gender reassignment, race, religion or belief, sex, or sexual orientation – it often has a hybrid nature.

60 See, for example, the Global Slavery Index at: https://www.walkfree.org/global-slavery-index/2018/findings/country-studies/germany/

61 CRC/C/FRA/CO/5, (2016).

The continuance of discrimination and its negative effect on children is a shared jurisdictional characteristic of France and Germany and one that has attracted comment from the CRC. In relation to France, it expressed concern in 2016 regarding the ongoing discrimination against children in many areas including the continuing racial discrimination and stigmatisation suffered by Roma children.[62] In relation to Germany, it recommended in 2022 that steps be taken to eliminate 'discrimination against children in disadvantaged situations including asylum-seeking, refugee and migrant children, Sinti, Roma and other children of minority groups, children with disabilities, LGBTI children and socioeconomically disadvantaged children'.[63]

CHILDREN WITH DISABILITIES

Again, the negative effect of discrimination on children with disabilities is a characteristic shared by France and Germany and one that has attracted critical comment from the CRC, though directed more forcefully and repeatedly towards France.

In relation to France, the CRC in 2016 drew attention to 'the persistent discrimination against children with disabilities, especially children with multiple disabilities, in their access to education, regarding equality with others, including during recreation, extracurricular activities, in school facilities, and vocational training'. In relation to Germany, it recommended in 2022 that the federal government 'streamline all support for children with disabilities into one body, such as child and youth support services, with a view to ensuring that all children with disabilities have equal access to benefits under Book VIII of the Social Code'.[64] It would seem that Germany has since complied with this suggestion which would differentiate its policy from France in terms of providing an inclusive education for children with disabilities.

Legal proceedings

In both France and Germany, the spectrum of matters which span the public/private divide – from abortion, IVF, and surrogacy to non-consensual adoption – would seem to lean more towards the conservative and private end than is the case in countries such as the U.K. Another point of jurisdictional difference between both countries and the U.K. is the absence in the former of a 'welfare checklist' identifying specific matters held to constitute components of a child's welfare interests, some of which are intended to have applicability across the public/private divide.

Adoption from state care

Adoption, traditionally the most private of family law proceedings, has steadily become less so as its essentially consensual nature fades and it acquires distinct

62 Ibid., at para 23.
63 CRC/C/DEU/CO/5-6, at para 15(a).
64 Ibid., at para 29(a).

public service characteristics. In that respect France and Germany are similar in that the proportion of total annual adoptions that originate in state initiatives to find homes for children in its care is markedly less than in such other developed nations as the U.K. and the U.S., where it is a much more pronounced aspect of public policy. For many children in France and Germany the default position of state care for the duration of childhood, rather than full legal and social integration into family life, must adversely impact their welfare interests.

CONSENT

In both countries, the legal presumption that adoption is a consensual process means that only if the consent of birth parents is unnecessary – because both are dead, or have abandoned their child and their whereabouts are unknown, or if a court has stripped them of all rights and responsibilities – may a child in state care become available for adoption. The child concerned – if aged 13 or older in France or 14 or older in Germany – must also consent to his or her proposed adoption.

POST-ADOPTION STATE SUPPORT

Adoptions in France[65] and Germany[66] share the same characteristic of being viewed as deserving of public support services. Curiously, in Germany adopters of a child from the public care system – unlike their counterparts in the U.S. and the U.K. – are not entitled to ongoing state financial support.

POST-ADOPTION INFORMATION ACCESS

Although the birth parent's right to veto information disclosure is most strongly associated with the maternal right to anonymity, epitomised by the *accouchement sous X* process in France, this traditional characteristic of adoption is in fact one that it shares with Germany. Anonymity rights for adopters (and by implication also for their adopted child) are enshrined in German law even if, since 2021, intermediatory adoption agencies are now obliged to promote openness between the adoptive and the birth family.[67] Also, the law in both countries now shares similar provisions allowing an adoptee to access personal identity information on reaching adulthood. This, of course, will be of no assistance in France to the children whose identity was hidden by the *accouchement sous X* process, which remains a distinguishing jurisdictional feature of French family law.

65 *Lois* n° 2005-744 of 4 July 2005.
66 The Adoption Intermediation Act (*Adoptionsvermittlungsgesetz*), as amended in 2021.
67 The Civil Code, ss 1747(2) and 1758.

Abduction

The phenomenon of parental abduction of a child has become a growing problem in international law. It inevitably leaves the child with a sense of loss, except in those few cases where the abducting parent is fleeing domestic violence. The disruption caused to the child – in terms of the abrupt absence of one parent; exposure to the stress of the other; loss of familiar relatives, other people, and surroundings; and enforced adjustment to a strange new context – compounded by anxiety and uncertainty regarding the future, must at least be damaging to the child's welfare interests. It may also be deeply traumatising.

Both countries share the fact that where the abduction is to another country then the legal proceedings for resolving this most extreme form of parental dispute will be governed by international law, specifically by the Hague Convention. Both adopt much the same approach by applying Hague rules subject to the caveat that the process is compatible with the child's welfare interests. There is evidence that there is undue delay in the resulting court proceedings in both countries, but this is particularly protracted in Germany. The net result is that domestic law displaces Hague requirements as delay works to the advantage of the abducting parent, forcing decisions to be taken on the basis of a child's welfare interests which have by then become compromised by a stronger attachment to one parent and weaker to the other: the *de facto* situation displacing the worthiness of any *de jure* claims.[68]

Commercial surrogacy

The international expansion of commercial surrogacy owes much to the many same-sex couples for whom this may offer the only means of creating a family, but it has also grown to become the preferred option for those who might otherwise have turned to adoption as it may provide them with the opportunity for a genetic link with the child.

However, this process does give rise to moral issues and to issues for international law. Moral issues most obviously arise from the basic fact of the arrangement being between rich and poorer people: the former, arguably, exploiting the latter in what some have termed a 'rent-a-womb' transaction, as morally repugnant as any other form of colonisation. Moral issues, reminiscent of Nazi tampering with eugenics, also arise from the discretionary choices available to the commissioning party: regarding selection of genetic material from a donor with particular physical characteristics, skills/aptitudes, etc.; and as regards the potential de-selection of characteristics through gene editing; not to mention choices as regards the number of 'parents' who are to be involved. This is a matter clearly more sensitive for Germany and one that can only grow more complicated for both countries and all others in terms of law and morals. Legal issues arise from UN CROC provisions where a baseline for the rights of a child born by this means are established by:

68 See, further, the editors of the EAPIL blog at: https://eapil.org/2022/11/24/german-constitutional-court-stays-enforcement-of-a-spanish-child-return-order/

Article 7, the right to a nationality and to know one's parents/origin; Article 8, the right to preserve one's identity; and Article 35, the right not to be sold or trafficked. Despite the sincerity of the commissioning prospective parents' motivation, and however propitious the outcome may be for the welfare interests of the child, there is an argument that in France and Germany, as elsewhere, commercial surrogacy may breach the Optional Protocol on the sale of children. Article 2(a) of the Protocol states that the 'sale of children means any act or transaction whereby a child is transferred by any person or group of persons to another for remuneration or any other consideration'. Arguably, commercial surrogacy constitutes just such a transaction.

The many citizens from both countries who travel abroad and successfully conclude commercial surrogacy contracts face similar legal problems on returning home with their child. France may be distinguished from Germany in that respect as French filiation rules raise unique complications. It is at least possible that such rules may conflict with the welfare interests of the child to the detriment of the latter.[69] It is also possible that the reliance the German courts seem prepared to place on the traditional maxim *mater semper certa est* (the mother is always certain) may have the same effect.[70]

IDENTITY AND ORIGINS INFORMATION

Article 8 of the ECHR includes the right to identity. Details of a person's identity and the interest "in obtaining information necessary to discover the truth concerning important aspects of one's personal identity, such as the identity of one's parents"[71] have been considered relevant to personal development. Birth and the circumstances of birth form part of a child's private life and related issues may arise in the context of surrogacy as also in adoption and IVF. The ECtHR has stressed that a state's margin of appreciation is narrow when it comes to determining parentage, because this involves a key aspect of an individual's identity.

Both countries share the same legal dilemma that, as commercial surrogacy is legally prohibited, to facilitate the official registration of a surrogate child's identity – as the birth child of the commissioning 'parent' – would be to violate their public policy and yet not to permit such registration would deprive the child of an official identity needed to access public services such as schools, etc.; further, to prevent him or her from accessing the factual information necessary to acquire an authentic identity would be to violate their Article 8 rights. It is probable that this area of hybrid public/private law is poised to undergo domestic and international revision.

Court orders

France and Germany, being civil law countries, rely more on encoding additional rules to supplement or adjust the existing law, rather than – as in common law

69 *C.E. & A.L. v. France*, Application No. 29693/19, (2022).
70 BGH, Mar. 20, 2019, Docket No. XII ZB 530/17, ECLI:DE:BGH:2019:200319BXIIZB530.17.0,
71 *Odièvre v. France* [GC], Application No. 42326/98, (2003), at para 29.

countries – promulgating a whole new self-contained set of legislative provisions, as the preferred means of addressing emerging social issues. This approach might explain the absence of a menu of free-standing court orders each addressing a specific legal function, and a reliance instead on flexible judicial discretion to tailor a broad use of authority to fit the circumstances and issues presented by each family.

The public/private divide

While family law 'orders' – or judicial uses of authority – tend to take a traditional form ('custody', 'contact', maintenance, etc.) they are now less likely to be confined, as formerly, to private matters (matrimonial disputes, etc.). The welfare principle is the driving force inducing a convergence across the public/private divide in family law and the two countries share a similar approach towards its role and weighting: in neither is the principle given an explicit paramountcy weighting and in neither is its application elucidated by means of a statutory checklist; in both the vestiges of traditional family values – such as family unity, parental status, and minimum state intervention – serve to counterbalance the effect of the principle. Not until the domestic law of either country interfaces with international law – on matters such as child abduction – does the significance of their more traditional public/private family law divide become apparent.

CUSTODY/ACCESS/PARENTAL RESPONSIBILITY, ETC.

In both France and Germany these orders, representing the heartland of private family law, may now well be applied in areas that cross the public/private divide such as abduction, commercial surrogacy, and adoption from state care.

GUARDIANSHIP/WARDSHIP/CURATORSHIP

These three forms of court-ordered protection are intended to entrust others with responsibility for the person and/or assets of someone deemed incapable of managing their own affairs. They are not specifically designed for the protection of children.

The concept or legal construct of 'wardship', as it is known in the common law nations, is unknown to German law. However, this legal status – *pupille de l'État* – is assigned to those children in France who are *né sous X*, or are orphans, or have been found abandoned, or are for whatever reason without anyone who has parental responsibility for them. Children designated wards of the state are eligible for adoption in France. This is a significant point of difference between the two countries.

Guardianship, on the other hand, is a legal status conferring a protective responsibility for a particular child, or an incapacitated adult, on a specific person or entity – and as such closely resembles its common law counterpart; it is equally well known to the law in both France and Germany. The appointment may be made by the Family Court or by a testator and although the appointment is most usually private – in favour of a relative or friend – it may be made to transfer responsibility for a child to a public body such as the ASE or the *Jugendamt.*

Curatorship is intended to supplement rather than replace parental responsibility if and to the extent that the parents or guardian are unable to undertake specific duties in respect of their child. While it is on occasion used in Germany – in cases where paternity or alimony need to be determined – it does not seem to be used in relation to children in France.

OTHER

While there is no equivalent to the statutory menu of orders available to common law judiciary, the courts in both countries enjoy a broad discretion under their respective Civil Codes to make such orders as the circumstances may require. In France, unlike Germany, there is specific provision under Article 515-9 *et seq.* of the Civil Code for the court to issue a protection order which, as the name suggests, provides for the protection of a parent and child from the unwanted/threatening or violent behaviour of a spouse or partner.

Conclusion

This chapter conducted a comparative jurisdictional analysis of the law relating to children, and the role of the welfare principle in that law, as currently applied in France and Germany. The analysis followed the structure adopted for profiling both countries.

The principle of subsidiarity, whereby state intervention is at the minimal level compatible with maintaining the primary responsibility of parents to care for the welfare interests of their children, is clearly a governing determinant of relevant law and policy in both countries. This deference to parental status, a key shared feature of their family law, probably impedes any prioritising of the welfare principle. It is noticeable, for example, that in France as in Germany the law emphasises the duty of the relevant authorities – including the judiciary in France – to work in partnership with parents in formulating a plan for addressing the needs or deeds of their children. It seems probable that in both countries the paramountcy principle would conflict with traditional presumptions – constitutionally protected in Germany – favouring family unity, parental status, and maintenance of the parent-child bond. Similarly, the relatively weaker reach of the principle would explain its lesser cross-sectoral capacity. There is a low level of legal activity in areas such as adoptions from state care and commercial surrogacy because of the corresponding weaker ability of the principle to prevail over other considerations. In neither France nor Germany is there an unequivocal statement in any area of law to the effect that the welfare interests of the child must be treated as of paramount importance in determining any particular issue. Arguably, this is because any such assertion would conflict with the subsidiarity principle.

Conclusion

Introduction

Although these two civil law countries have cultural and legal traditions that differ considerably from their common law counterparts, examined in other books in this mini-series, they share with them the same pattern of changes that have disrupted the definition of 'family' in recent years. The application of their domestic laws, like those of the common law nations, have also been similarly exposed to the moderating influence of the same international framework of legislative measures and court rulings. However, while the result has been a degree of convergence in the laws of both sets of nations, this book has shown that they remain differentiated in some important respects. As the brief audit below of compliance with the rights enumerated in the United Nations Convention on the Rights of the Child (UN CROC) indicates, the primary factor responsible for the continuing difference is, arguably, the paramountcy principle: the role, the weighting, and the application of this principle; in the public, private, and hybrid sectors of family law; to the welfare interests/rights of the child.

The United Nations Convention on the Rights of the Child 1989

This Convention, signed by both France and Germany, together with some 196 other nations, is the most relevant, the most well known, and the most far-reaching of all international treaties.[1] While it has no designated enforcement mechanism, the Convention has been adopted as a reference point for many European Court of Human Rights (ECtHR) rulings in which it is frequently cited. Primarily, it is represented by the Committee on the Rights of the Child (CRC) which makes recommendations to member states, on the basis of reports filed with it under Article 44, for improvements in national law and practice. Essentially, this functions as a 'name and shame' exercise as the policy, practice, and legal deficits of the country being reviewed are exposed to peer review and the resulting assessment, together with goals for any required remedial action, then become a matter of public record to be published globally.

1 Three optional protocols have since been added: Protocol to Prevent, Suppress and Punish Trafficking in Persons, Especially Women and Children; Protocol Against the Smuggling of Migrants by Land, Sea and Air; and Protocol Against the Illicit Manufacturing of and Trafficking in Firearms.

DOI: 10.4324/9781003415688-15

The Convention declares 42 substantive rights held to be vested in children and it binds judicial, regulatory, and administrative bodies to ensure that any decisions they take, on matters affecting the welfare interests of a child, are Convention compliant. All nations that have both signed and ratified the Convention are so bound. As such nations include the two currently being studied,[2] it would be remiss not to apply Convention provisions as an appropriate audit mechanism for conducting a final comparative sweep through the law currently governing the welfare/rights of a child in France and Germany.[3]

Article 1 – Definition of 'child'

This declares that for the purposes of the Convention, a child means 'every human being below the age of eighteen years unless under the law applicable to the child, majority is attained earlier'.

Interestingly, in Germany, youth offenders are treated as juveniles until they reach 21 years of age which is significantly extending the definition and protection assigned to the status of 'child'.

Article 2 – Non-discrimination principle

This directs that all Convention rights are to apply to children without exception and without discrimination of any kind. Article 2(2) requires that all appropriate measures must be taken to ensure that the child is protected against all forms of discrimination or punishment on the basis of the status, activities, expressed opinions, or beliefs of the child's parents, legal guardians, or family members.

The CRC has drawn attention to the continuation of discrimination: in France, directed towards Roma children, their families and communities,[4] and in Germany, against 'children in disadvantaged situations including asylum-seeking, refugee and migrant children, Sinti, Roma and other children of minority groups, children with disabilities, LGBTI children and socio-economically disadvantaged children'.[5] The discriminatory treatment of children with disabilities in educational settings has also attracted criticism.

Article 3 – Best interests of the child is a primary consideration

Article 3 states the most important principle in the Convention. It requires that 'in all actions concerning children, whether undertaken by public or private social welfare institutions, courts of law, administrative authorities or legislative bodies, the best interests of the child shall be a primary consideration': thereby conferring on a child

2 UN CROC was ratified by Australia in 1991 and by New Zealand in 1993.

3 Following the precedent set by Kilkelly, U., in 'Children's Rights in Action: Using the UN Convention on the Rights of the Child as an Auditing Tool', *Child & Family Law Quarterly*, 2006.

4 CRC/C/FRA/CO/5, (2016) at para 23.

5 CRC/C/DEU/CO/5-6, at para 15(a).

the right to have their welfare interests so treated across a range of fora; additionally, subsequent Articles then establish the particular rights held to be vested in a child.

As has often been pointed out, however, this statement of the importance to be attached to the welfare interests of a child is somewhat equivocal. It chooses to refer to 'best interests', which is open to subjective interpretation. It does not state that the principle is of 'paramount' importance. It does not even assert that it should be 'the' primary consideration. 'Primary' is itself suspect: other expressions indicating relative significance could have been used, such as 'most important'. So, also, with 'consideration' which is more indicative of a discretionary rather than an affirmative approach to the treatment of 'best interests'. In short, although often lauded as the gold standard that firmly establishes welfare interests as of paramount importance in matters concerning children, it is at least questionable whether it does so, or whether this was even intended.

In both countries the record of historical state-mandated child abuse against Jewish children and others from minority groups during the Nazi period, while clearly preceding UN CROC, nonetheless must constitute the most egregious breach of this fundamental principle.

Again, in both countries, there is some tension between Article 3 and their domestic law as it relates to children. In France, the law governing the age of criminal responsibility breaches Article 3. It is obviously not conducive to a child's welfare that: he or she is criminally liable for their actions according to when they are held to have reached such an indeterminate threshold as the 'age of discernment'; that he or she may be tried in a criminal court from the age of 10; nor that from the age of 13 he or she is to be treated in law as an adult and therefore eligible for imprisonment. In Germany, as mentioned above, the fact that youth offenders are treated as juveniles until they reach 21 years of age, while constituting a positive extension of protection to young persons, does distort the Article 1 definition of 'child'. From a common law perspective, the not dissimilar extension of the interpretation of 'adoption' in both countries to include adults again raises questions about the fit between Articles 1, 3, and legal proceedings.

Protection

The protective function establishes a baseline for state responsibility in relation to the best interests of a child. This is appropriately recognised in France by the universal mandatory requirement to report instances of child neglect or abuse to the appropriate authorities but, arguably, is not wholly satisfied in Germany by the lesser duty – restricted to those working with children – to make such reports. Unquestionably, France is in breach of the Article 3 duty to ensure protection as regards the high infant mortality rate and the levels of domestic violence against children about which the CRC has expressed deep concern.[6]

6 CRC/C/FRA/CO/5, at paras 27, 42, and 43.

Facilities

Article 3(3) requires States Parties to ensure that 'the institutions, services and facilities responsible for the care or protection of children shall conform with the standards established by competent authorities'.

In both countries, the relatively low recourse to foster parents and adopters, as against a continued reliance on residential care, for children in need of out-of-home placements, is a shared characteristic at variance with internationally accepted good practice favouring family-based care and one that has been a matter of concern to the CRC.[7]

Article 5 – Respect the responsibilities, rights, and duties of parents

The requirement that 'State Parties shall respect the responsibilities, rights and duties of parents … to provide, in a manner consistent with the evolving capacities of the child, appropriate direction and guidance in the exercise by the child of the rights recognized in the present Convention', is interesting in application to these two countries. France and Germany would seem to share a traditional culture of such respect which is reflected in their laws as they relate to children and parental status. There is an argument that at times undue respect for parents and their rights may obstruct a functional investigation into whether they are endangering the welfare interests of their children.

Article 6 – Right of the child to life

This requires that States Parties shall ensure to the maximum extent possible the survival and development of the child.

However, as mentioned above, there is an unusually high infant mortality rate in France. The CRC noted in May 2023 that the 'figures on violence against children were frightening. A child died every five days within their homes in France'.[8] This rate of child mortality by parental abuse is far greater than comparable estimates for the U.K. and other developed nations and is clearly in breach of France's Article 6 duty to its children.

Articles 7 and 8 – Right of the child to know and preserve their identity

These two Articles recognise the right of a child to information relating to their parents as the means of establishing and retaining his or her own identity. In relation to adopted children, this is a powerful legal acknowledgement that he or she has

7 See: for France, CRC/C/FRA/CO/5, at para 53; for Germany, CRC/C/DEU/CO/5-6, at para 26(a).

8 See Committee on the Rights of the Child's consideration of the sixth and seventh combined periodic report of France at: https://www.ohchr.org/en/news/2023/05/experts-committee-rights-child-praise-france-outreach-patrols-supporting-families

a right of access to information – in the form of agency records, etc. – that could potentially contribute to consolidating their sense of identity.

While it goes without saying that the *accouchement sous X* practice in France clearly violates this right, it should be added that the continued – if recently time-limited – anonymity granted to relinquishing mothers in Germany is similarly in violation, though to a lesser degree. In both jurisdictions, the right of birth parents to veto the disclosure of identifying information is equally in violation of Article 7.[9] Again, in both countries, as elsewhere, the complications arising from commercial surrogacy and the use of sperm donors means that for some children their personal identity rights will remain unrealisable.

Cultural identity

The right to a cultural identity – also given explicit recognition in other international instruments such as Articles 8, 9, and 11 of the European Convention on Human Rights and Article 27 of the International Covenant on Civil and Political Rights – specifically recognises the right of minorities to maintain their own culture, language, and religion. It is reinforced by Article 20(3) which states that 'due regard shall be paid to the desirability of continuity in a child's upbringing and to the child's ethnic, religious, cultural and linguistic background'.

Arguably, this right conflicts with the global practice of intercountry adoption and does so with greater potential for cultural disruption when the child is adopted from a non-Hague-compliant country. It is probably also breached, if not intentionally, in educational settings when Roma children – and others such as Muslims – are assimilated into generalised classroom learning programmes without regard for cultural sensitivities.

Articles 9 and 10 – Right of the child not to be separated from his or her parents

Article 9 requires States Parties to ensure that a child shall not be separated from his or her parents against their will, except when competent authorities subject to judicial review determine, in accordance with applicable law and procedures, that such separation is necessary for the child's best interests. Article 10 imposes a similar obligation on States Parties in relation to maintaining contact between parent and child living in different countries.

As in the U.K. and such other countries as the U.S. and Canada, this right is most severely stress tested when the issue arises as to whether rehabilitation with birth parents should be pursued in respect of a child compulsorily admitted to the public child welfare system. Under the provisions of UN CROC the authorities are required, from point of admission, to work towards returning a child to his or her

9 See: for Germany, the Federal Constitution, Basic Law, Article 2 and the Civil Code, ss 1747(2) and 1758; for France, Article 326 of the Civil Code and the provisions of Article L222-6 of the Social Action and Families Code, as amended by the Act of 22 January 2002.

family of origin, but for reasons such as lack of resources, hostile birth parents, the distances involved, and a 'play safe' strategy where there are child protection risk factors, it may be that steps towards rehabilitation are not immediately taken. Alternatively, from point of admission it may be decided to place the child in a concurrent placement, with a view to a possible adoption by the foster parent. In either case, the passing of time works in favour of the day-to-day carers and against the birth parents. Rehabilitation programmes are resource intensive, often requiring residential placement for parent and child in an intensive assessment/training facility, and/or day centre programmes; these are not always available when needed – and are more readily availed of in urban environments – nor can the stability of an initial foster placement be guaranteed. Disruption and drift in care can easily become the default reality resulting in disrupted or long-term separation from parental care, which would appear to be the outcome of most out-of-home placements in both countries, despite state obligations to the contrary under Articles 9 and 10.

This right has proven problematic in the context of transnational child abductions by parents, as illustrated in some particularly protracted German cases.[10] In addition, it might be noted that the availability of simple adoptions for children in France – but not in Germany – increases the probability that in France there will be continued contact with parents and other members of the adoptee's birth family; it also, of course, constitutes an important point of jurisdictional difference between the two countries.

Contact

Article 9(3) requires States Parties to 'respect the right of the child who is separated from one or both parents to maintain personal relations and direct contact with both parents'. Without the regularity of face-to-face contact, and regardless of whether the separation is a consequence of public or private proceedings, the parent-child relationship is likely to fade and thereby violate the child's Article 9(3) rights.

Contact arrangements are relatively easily managed when birth parents and foster carers are living in the same urban area and are respectfully attuned to any cultural differences, but can be problematic when – in either case – they're not. In Germany, a child is vested with a legal right of contact with his or her parent.[11] In France the contact right is clearly assigned to the parent rather than their child.[12] In both countries, kinship placements, step-parent adoptions, and 'open' adoptions have traditionally accounted for a large proportion of 'out-of-home' care arrangements and, as they all facilitate ongoing child and birth parent contact then, to that

10 See, for example, the 2022 decision of the *Bundesverfassungsgericht* (BVerfG) in respect of a nine-year-old German child abducted from his father in Spain when aged one and retained in Germany throughout the proceedings.

11 The Civil Code, s 1626(3).

12 The Civil Code, Article 375-7 para 2.

extent, both countries are more Article 9(3) compliant than others. Moreover, this is also more likely due to the fact that adoptees now tend to be older with established relationships to parents that may well be judicially construed as important for their future welfare and by the heavier onus on the state authorities in both countries to work towards the rehabilitation of children to birth parent care.

Article 12 – Right of the child to express an opinion in administrative and judicial proceedings

This Article states that a child has the right to express his or her views freely and the right to have those views taken into account in any matter or procedure affecting them, subject to the caveat that the child concerned must be capable of forming their own views. Due weight, in accordance with the age and maturity of the child, must then be given to such views.

Both countries have this right enshrined in domestic law. In France, the *juge des enfants* has a duty to hear directly from any child who wishes to be heard and is *capable de discernement* unless their age or state of mind does not allow it.[13] However, the CRC has expressed concern that in practice this right is subject to a written request which can be dismissed on flimsy grounds. It expressed further concern that children in vulnerable or marginalised situations, such as those in administrative placement and children with disabilities, were often not consulted in matters concerning them.[14] In Germany, a child of any age has a constitutional right to be heard in the Family Court on a matter concerning them.[15] In neither country is there any suggestion that the views so expressed would be determinative.

Representation in court

The only legally effective form of representation in court is that provided by a lawyer with relevant expertise. In France, the legal status of a parent is such that he or she is the legal representative for their child.[16] Where the interests of parent and child conflict – as in cases of parental abuse – then a lawyer will be appointed for the child. The latter has no automatic right to legal representation, and in proceedings the *juge des enfants* will normally act as their representative. In Germany, the situation is much the same except that the appointment of a *guardian ad litem* is mandatory in Family Court proceedings in all matters concerning the child, whenever necessary to protect their welfare interests,[17] unless those interests are adequately represented by a lawyer. This level of representation is quite similar to that provided in the U.K. and would seem more compliant with Article 12 than the French approach which may offer informality at the price of due process.

13 The Civil Code, Article 388-1.
14 CRC/C/FRA/CO/5, at para 29.
15 The Act on Court Procedure in Family Matters and Non-litigious Matters, ss 9(1) and 167(3).
16 The Civil Code, Article 389.
17 The Act on Court Procedure in Family Matters and Non-litigious Matters, s 50.

Articles 13 and 14 – Right of the child to self-determination, dignity, respect, non-interference, and the right to make informed decisions

There is a general absence in the law of both countries of any requirement to ensure that a child has the right to make informed decisions. Instead, the requirement is to ensure that the views of a child are heard and taken into account when decisions are being made on matters affecting their welfare. There are very few matters in relation to which a child, aged 16 or younger, can unilaterally give a legally binding consent. In neither country is there any equivalent to the unequivocal U.K. ruling in *Gillick*.

Consent

In both France and Germany, once a child has attained the age of 15 then he or she can normally give or withhold a valid legal consent in a range of situations – such as to dental treatment and to a sexual relationship – but any younger and their consent alone would be insufficient. There are a few anomalous exceptions. For example, in Germany a child aged 7 or younger can request and require the *Jugendamt* to take him or her into care[18] and the consent of the child is required in proceedings for his or her adoption: if aged 14 or older, the consent may be personal; otherwise the legal representative may do so on their behalf. In France, where the child is older than 13, then his or her personal consent is mandatory for both a plenary[19] and a simple adoption.[20]

Access to contraceptives or abortion services is determined by a combination of age and maturity; if 14 years of age or older there is likely to be a presumption of capacity in both countries.

Article 17 – Social media and a child's health

States Parties are required to have regard to the impact of media on the promotion of a child's social, spiritual, and moral well-being and physical and mental health and ensure the protection of the child from information and material injurious to his or her well-being, bearing in mind the provisions of Articles 13 and 18.

While this right was framed with a view to facilitating access to media-disseminated material with potential for promoting a child's welfare, its contemporary relevance is more in relation to protecting that welfare from possible harm emanating from international social media platforms that may expose children to pornography, grooming, violent images, etc. The General Comment on the Rights of Children in the Digital Environment, adopted by the UN CRC in February 2021,

18 Op. cit., s 42(1).

19 See Article 345 of the Civil Code.

20 See Article 360 *in fine* of the Civil Code: *L'adoption simple est permise quel que soit l'âge de l'adopté.*

(…) *Si l'adopté est âgé de plus de treize ans, il doit consentir personnellement à l'adoption.*

has established guidelines for addressing these issues. The domestic regulatory authorities in both countries, as elsewhere, are in the process of formulating policies for controlling the dissemination of material harmful to children. Presently the only known government initiative is that taken in Germany to deal with violent video games (*Killerspiele*) which prohibits the sale or the advertising of video games, movies, or other forms of media depicting extreme violence.[21]

Articles 18 and 19 – Primary responsibility for the upbringing of a child rests with the parent/s

Article 18 requires States Parties to render appropriate assistance to parents and legal guardians to facilitate the upbringing and development of their children. It is reinforced by Article 18(2) which requires the development of appropriate services for the care of children and by Article 19(2) which adds that such services should include 'effective procedures for the establishment of social programmes to provide necessary support for the child and for those who have the care of the child'.

In both countries, unlike the U.K.,[22] there is a relatively strong presumption favouring birth parents – all other factors being equal – as best placed to safeguard the welfare of their child. This is accompanied by legislative provisions requiring the state to provide, where necessary, support services enabling them to do so and is reflected in their joint approach both to non-consensual adoption and in the legal requirement to pursue rehabilitation in respect of children in state care.

Article 21 – Adoption shall ensure that the best interests of the child shall be the paramount consideration

States Parties are required to ensure that in their system of adoption the best interests of the child is the paramount consideration, that adoption is authorised only by competent authorities, with all necessary consents obtained, and that intercountry adoptions are properly authorised.

In both countries simple and plenary forms of adoption are legally available – though in Germany, children are restricted to the plenary form – but in neither is paramountcy established in the national law as the governing principle. The former has several characteristics which militate against the process being governed by this principle, including: the probability that most placements will be made directly by a birth parent, or by an intermediary acting on their behalf, either of whom may be open to undue influence; the absence of any objective professional assessment of the needs of a child relative to the coping capacity and related resources of the adopters; and the lack of any provision for post-adoption assessment of whether the placement has proven to be compatible with the child's best interests.[23] In nei-

21 See the Youth Protection Act, as amended in 2008.

22 See *Re W (A Child)* [2016] EWCA Civ 793.

23 However, as Jörg Reinhardt points out, simple adoptions are no longer available for children and since 2021 all adoption placements must be made by professional staff (note to author, 6 June 2023).

ther country, unlike in the U.K., does plenary adoption require application of the paramountcy principle. Moreover, the consistently high proportion of adoption orders made in favour of step-parents and relatives in France as in Germany – and the absence of alternative orders for such applicants – does in itself bring into question whether the principle is of any direct legal relevance.

The consistently downward trend in annual intercountry adoptions tends to reduce the significance of this Article's concern for related standards of practice. However, in France the CRC has expressed concern regarding 'the high number of intercountry adoptions involving countries of origin that are not party to, nor comply with, the safeguards of 1993 Hague Convention on Protection of Children and Co-operation in respect of Intercountry Adoption'.[24] In Germany, the 2021 amendment to the Adoption Intermediation Act has considerably tightened the safeguards for the welfare interests of children entering the adoption process whether by domestic or intercountry routes.

Article 22 – Right of unaccompanied migrant minors to receive appropriate protection and humanitarian assistance

This requires States Parties to take appropriate measures to ensure that any child seeking refugee status, whether unaccompanied or accompanied by his or her parents or by any other person, receives appropriate protection and humanitarian assistance.

In terms of scale, the social problem of unaccompanied migrant minors has become a challenge for France and Germany, particularly since 2015. In general terms it would appear that the response of both has been in keeping with humanitarian standards, though more could be done to ensure that children are not separated from their parents and to provide for reunification when they are. Nonetheless the CRC has expressed concern regarding 'the situation of migrant children, particularly unaccompanied migrant children' in France,[25] where there were some 41,000 in 2022. In Germany, the practice whereby the Family Court immediately appoints a guardian with a duty of care in respect of each child would seem a very appropriate means of ensuring migrant minors receive humanitarian assistance.

Article 23 – Rights of child with a disability

States Parties are required to ensure that a mentally or physically disabled child enjoys a full and decent life, in conditions which provide dignity, promote self-reliance, and facilitate the child's active participation in the community.

The practice in France of separating such children from others in educational settings has been condemned by the CRC as 'persistent discrimination against children with disabilities'. In particular, it urged France 'to take immediate measures

24 CRC/C/FRA/CO/5, at para 55.
25 Op. cit., at para 69.

to ensure that the rights of children with autism, especially their right to inclusive education, are respected'.[26] More recently, the CRC has been similarly critical of Germany, recommending that the root causes of discrimination be addressed 'with a view to eliminating discrimination against … children with disabilities'.[27]

Article 24 – Right of a child to the enjoyment of the highest attainable standard of health

While neither country can be said to be wholly compliant with this Article – probably no country is – the rates of infant mortality are abnormally high in France, which Article 24(2) specifically requires States Parties to address. Although alarming in itself, this failure may well be indicative of broader failures relating to access of children and communities to basic health intervention programmes. Indeed, the CRC and other bodies have expressed concern about matters such as migrant children's access to health care, the incidence of mental health issues, and the high level of teen abortions. Germany, in contrast, would seem to have a modern and efficient health system that caters adequately and appropriately for the health care needs of its children.

It is probable that neither country is achieving the requirement in Article 24(3) that they 'take all effective and appropriate measures with a view to abolishing traditional practices prejudicial to the health of children'. In particular, the practice of female genital mutilation is proving difficult to abolish in all developed nations as in others.

Article 27 – Every child is entitled to a reasonable standard of living

States are required to recognise the right of every child to a standard of living adequate for that child's physical, mental, spiritual, moral, and social development.

From the evidence provided by several recent reports, it is clear that France continues to have serious, apparently systemic, problems of child poverty.[28] Of particular concern is the reference to 21% of French children living below the poverty line in 2022.[29] Similar reports indicate that the situation is not much better in Germany where, in 2021, one in five children were considered poor or 'at risk of poverty'[30] causing the CRC, in 2022, to reiterate its concern regarding 'the

26 CRC/C/FRA/CO/5, at para 57.

27 CRC/C/DEU/CO/5-6, at para 15(a).

28 See, for example, *Break Poverty* (2021), at: https://breakpoverty.com/en/an-intolerable-increase-in-early-childhood-poverty-as-a-result-of-the-health-crisis/

29 See *Droits des Enfants en France* (2022), at: https://unicef.hosting.augure.com/Augure_UNICEF/r/ContenuEnLigne/Download?id=480588C0-E8CD-4A6A-B8D8-80AAA060B4C4&filename=SynthDroitsEnfantsFrance2022_final_pages.pdf

30 See the Bertelsmann Foundation report on child and youth poverty in Germany, at: https://www.wsws.org/en/articles/2023/03/01/fd97-m01.html

large number of children still living in poverty or at risk of poverty'.[31] As always, the burden of poverty falls heaviest on those already marginalised and it would seem that in both countries it is the Roma community, other minority groups, and migrants who are suffering most. The unavoidable conclusion must be that as both these leading developed democratic nations are unable to guarantee their children a reasonable standard of living, they are in breach of Article 27.

Articles 35 and 36 – Protection of children from trafficking and other forms of exploitation

Article 35 requires all States to take appropriate measures to prevent the abduction, sale, or traffic of children while Article 36 requires that they protect the child against all other forms of exploitation.

There is good reason to conclude that France is not succeeding in its efforts to deal with issues associated with migrants and the sex trade. The UN Special Rapporteur on Trafficking in Persons, Especially Women and Children was sufficiently concerned about the issues that arose in two cases concerning France to make an *Amicus Curiae* submission to the ECtHR in 2021[32] drawing attention to the sexual exploitation of women and children. The Rapporteur's concerns were supported by a 2022 U.S. country report on France which referred to 'the significant increase in children exploited in commercial sex in the past few years, which NGOs estimated to be between 10,000 and 15,000 predominantly French girls, in April 2021'.[33]

Given the volume of migrants that have flowed into and through Germany in the past few years, it is unsurprising that reports indicate similar problems in that country. Of the two main types of child trafficking – for purposes of cheap labour and prostitution – the latter is the more significant. The U.S. 2022 report on child trafficking in Germany[34] notes the reported increases in the number of child victims and that traffickers are targetting Roma and foreign unaccompanied children for sex trafficking, forced begging, and other coerced criminal behaviour. These observations were reinforced by the 2022 CRC report which expressed concern regarding the authorities' treatment of child victims of trafficking.[35]

Again, the conclusion must be that as both countries are unable to guarantee the safety of children from the predations of traffickers, they are in breach of Articles

31 CRC/C/DEU/CO/5-6, at para 34.

32 See Mullally, S., 'Submission by the UN Special Rapporteur on Trafficking in Persons, Especially Women and Children, in the Cases of *H.F. and M.F. v. France* (App. No. 24384/19) and *J.D. and A.D. v. France* (App. No. 44234/20) before the European Court of Human Rights', (2021). Available at: SSRN: https://ssrn.com/abstract=3933138 or http://dx.doi.org/10.2139/ssrn.3933138

33 See, further, at: https://www.state.gov/reports/2022-country-reports-on-human-rights-practices/france/

34 U.S. Government, *2022 Trafficking in Persons Report: Germany*, at: https://www.state.gov/reports/2022-trafficking-in-persons-report/germany/

35 CRC/C/DEU/CO/5-6, at para 41.

35 and 36, as are many others. As the volume of migration increases, involving many countries, so too do the dangers to children from trafficking.

Article 40 – Every alleged child offender to be justly treated

This Article requires States Parties to recognise the right of every child alleged as, accused of, or recognised as having infringed the penal law, to be treated in a manner consistent with the promotion of the child's sense of dignity and worth, which reinforces the child's respect for the human rights and fundamental freedoms of others and which takes into account the child's age and the desirability of promoting the child's reintegration and the child's assuming a constructive role in society.

There are several different aspects to this principle.

Firstly, just treatment or due process normally requires legal representation which necessitates legal aid and assistance for those who cannot otherwise afford the costs involved. On that measure, it would seem that both countries have an informal, investigatory – rather than inquisitorial – approach which most often does not strictly require legal representation, but that is available, and therefore both would seem to satisfy the Article 40 requirement.

Secondly, in both countries, the age of criminal responsibility is problematic: it is indeterminate in France and functions at too low a threshold in both countries to ensure just treatment.

Thirdly, the curiously opposite practice in each country in relation to a perceived correlation between age and culpability perhaps illustrates problems of ensuring due process. In France, the fact that a child aged 10 may be tried in a criminal court, will be treated in law as an adult from the age of 13, and could be imprisoned, represents a drastic contraction in the role of the welfare principle and is clearly in breach of Article 40. While in Germany, the fact that an offender may be treated as a juvenile until he or she reaches the age of 21 represents an expansion of that role and as such is clearly Convention compliant. However, both practices would seem to introduce uncertainty in the law regarding the definition of 'child' and its relationship with 'criminal responsibility'.

Finally, if the welfare interests of children are to be respected then the court needs to have a flexible menu of different orders to choose from so as to ensure an appropriate match between the disposal option, the needs of a particular child, and the gravity of the offence. In both countries, the fact that the civil law is not limited to a rigid, standardised set of disposal options – as in common law countries – but instead, as Reinhardt explains, 'basically, the judges have UNLIMITED possibilities, any case has to be decided individually and according to the interests and development of the juvenile delinquent'.[36] This leaves the court able to creatively customise disposal options to fit the needs/deeds of the child offenders appearing before it.

36 Note to author, 6 June 2023.

Selected Bibliography

Books & articles

Appel, G., 'An Attempt to Eradicate Deficiency in a Nursery', *Neuropsychiatrie de l'enfance et del'adolescence*, Vols. 4–5, pp. 257–262, (1982).

Bach, R., 'Von Kindeswohl und Kinderwunsch', (unpublished paper for adoption conference in Bad Boll, Germany, (2011).

Bell, J. and Lichère, F., *Contemporary French Administrative Law*, Cambridge Unuiversity Press, Cambridge, 2022.

Berger, M., *The Failure of Child Protection Services*, Paris: Dunod, (2003).

Botthof, A., 'Die Annahme als Kind als Alternative zur Dauerfplege', *FamRZ (Zeitschrift für das gesamte Familienrecht)*, p 768 ff (2016).

Bovenschen, I., Bränzel, P., Heene, S., Hornfeck, F., Kappler, S., Kindler, H. and Ruhfaß, M., *Recommendations of the German Research Centre on Adoption: Future Perspectives for Adoption Practice and Adoption Legislation*, Munich: German Youth Institute, (2017).

Dahme, H.-J. and Wohlfahrt, N., 'Hilfe und Kontrolle in der Jugendhilfe', in Böllert, K. (ed), *Kompendium Kinder- und Jugendhilfe*, Wiesbaden: Springer VS, (2018).

Dawson, J.P., *Oracles of the Law*, University of Michigan Law School (publishers), Ann Arbor, (1968).

Detloff, N. and Mariny, D., 'National Report: Germany', at: http://ceflonline.net/wp-content /uploads/Germany-Parental-Responsibilities.pdf

Dias, R.W.M., *Jurisprudence* (5th ed.), London: Butterworths, (1985).

Dünkel, F., 'Criminology and Criminal Justice, Juvenile Justice and Juvenile Delinquency', *International and Comparative Criminology*, (2016), at: 10.1093/oxfordhb/9780199935383.013.68

Eglin, M., 'Judicial Child Protection in France and England: A Comparative Approach', (June 2001), at: https://www.afmjf.fr/Judicial-child-protection-in.html

Eliacheff, C. and Masson, C., *La fabrique de l'enfant-transgenre* (*The Making of the Transgender Child*), L'OBSERVATOIRE (publisher), Paris, (2022).

Fuchs, R.G., 'Crimes Against Children in Nineteenth-Century France', *Law and Human Behaviour*, Vol. 6, pp. 237–259, (1982).

Fulchiron, H., 'Egalite, Verite, Stabilite: The new French Filiation Law after the Ordonnance of 4th July 2005', *The International Survey of Family Law*, pp 203–217, (2006 edition).

Galm, B. and Derr, R., *Combating Child Abuse and Neglect: Child Protection in Germany - National Report*, Deutsches Jugendinstitut e.V. (2011), at: https://www.dji.de/fileadmin/user_upload/bibs/DAPHNEGermanReportLayoutFIN.pdf

Gilbert et al, 'Child Maltreatment: Variation in Trends and Policies in Six Developed Countries', *Lancet*, (2011) at: https://scholar.google.com/scholar_lookup?hl=en&publication_year

=2011&author=R+Gilbert&author=J+Fluke&author=M+O%27Donnell&author=A+Gonzalez-Izquierdo&author=M+Brownell&author=P+Gulliver&title=Child+maltreatment%3A+variation+in+trends+and+policies+in+six+developed+countries

Golombok, S., et al, 'A Longitudinal Study of Families Formed Through Third-Party Assisted Reproduction: Mother-Child Relationships and Child Adjustment from Infancy to Adulthood', *Developmental Psychology*, (2023), at: https://doi.org/10.1037/dev0001526

Gosset, D., Hedouin, V., Revuelta, E. and Desurmont, M., *Child Abuse*, Paris: Masson, (1997).

Grevot, A., 'The Plight of Paternalism in French Child Welfare and Protective Policies and Practices', Paper presented at the Positive Systems of Child Welfare Conference, Waterloo, ON, (2002), at: https://scholars.wlu.ca/cgi/viewcontent.cgi?article=1014&context=pcfp

Guedeney, A., 'The Infant Protection System in France: How Does it Work?', *Infant Mental Health Journal*, Vol. 29(1), pp. 5–20, (2008).

Hoffmann, B., 'Adoption in the Care Planning Process – Case Workers' View', *JAmt*, Vol. 84, pp. 10–16, (2011).

Halifax, J., 'Why Are There So Many International Adoptions in France?', at: http://www.uea.ac.uk/swp/icar2/pdf's/Halifax99.pdf

Jehle, J.-M., *Criminal Justice in Germany* (7th ed.), the Federal Ministry of Justice and Consumer Protection (publisher), Berlin, (2019).

Kindler, H., 'Developing Evidence-Based Child Protection Practice: A View from Germany', *Research on Social Work Practice*, Vol. 18 (4), pp. 319–324, (2008).

Kindler, H., Lillig, S., Blüml, H., Meysen, T. and Werner, A. (eds.), *Handbook on Child Endangerment According to § 1666 BGB and General Social Service (ASD)* Munich: German Youth Institute, (2006).

Kiraly, M. and Humphreys, C., 'It's About the Whole Family: Family Contact for Children in Kinship Care', *Child & Family Social Work*, Vol. 21(2), pp 228–239, (2016).

Lammerant, I. and Hofsetter, M. (eds.), *Adoption: At What Cost?, Terre des Hommes* publisher*)*, Lausanne, (2007).

Lefaucheur, N., *Etude - Enfants nes sons X*, Paris: CNRS-IRESCO, (2000) and further, at: https://www.onpe.gouv.fr/

Leick & Darmois, 'International Children Abductions in France: A Review of the caselaw (2019)', at: https://leick-darmois.com/en/international-children-abductions-in-france-a-review-of-the-caselaw-2019-2/

Luckock, B., Vogler, R. and Keating, H., 'Child Protection in France and England: Authority, Legalism and Social Work Practice', *Child and Family Law Quarterly*, 8(4), 1996, pp.297–312

Mann, T., *Thomas Mann Diaries 1918–1939* (Hermann Kesten, ed.), Robin Clark Ltd (publisher), (1984).

Meysen, T. and Bovenschen, I., 'Adoption from Care in Germany: Inconclusive Policy and Poorly Coordinated Practice', in *Adoption from Care;International Perspectives on Children's Rights, Family Preservation and State Intervention*, (eds. Tarja Pösö, Marit Skivenes and June Thoburn), Bristol: Policy Press, pp 121–138, (2021).

Möller, K., 'Proportionality: Challenging the Critics', *International Journal of Constitutional Law*, Vol. 10(3), (2012), at: https://doi.org/10.1093/icon/mos024

Nanos, R., 'The Views of a Child: Emerging Interpretation and Significance of the Child's Objection Defense under the Hague Child Abduction Convention', *Brooklyn Journal of International Law*, Vol. 22, p. 437 (1996).

Norman, J. and Oborne, P., *The Conservative Case for the Human Rights Act, Liberty* (National Council for Civil Liberties), London, (2009), at: https://jessenorman.typepad.com/Churchills_Legacy.pdf

Nowak, M., *United Nations Global Study on Children Deprived of Liberty*, (2019), available at https://omnibook.com/ Global-Study-2019.

O'Halloran, K., *The Welfare of the Child: The Principle and the Law*, Aldershot: Arena/Ashgate Publications, (1999); *The Principle of the Welfare of the Child: a History*, Routledge, (2022); *Children & the Law: Shaping the Modern Welfare Principle in the British Isles*, Routledge, (2022); and *Children, the Law and the Welfare Principle: Perspectives from North America*, Routledge, (2023); and *Children, the Law and the Welfare Principle: Perspectives from Australia and New Zealand*, Routledge, (2023).

Papoutsi, E., 'The Protection of Unaccompanied Migrant Minors Under International Human Rights Law: Revisiting Old Concepts and Confronting New Challenges in Modern Migrant Flows', *American University International Law Review*, Vol. 3(2), pp. 220–258, (2020).

Renner, I., Saint, V., Neumann, A., Ukhova, D., Horstmann, S. and Boettinger, U. et al, 'Improving Psychosocial Services for Vulnerable Families with Young Children: Strengthening Links Between Health and Social Services in Germany', *BMJ*, (2018), at: https://www.bmj.com/content/363/bmj.k4786

Robcis, C., *The Law of Kinship: Anthropology, Psychoanalysis and the Family in France*, Cornell University Press, Ithaca, NY, (2013).

Robertson, J.A., 'Reproductive Technology in Germany and the United States: An Essay in Comparative Law and Bioethics', *Columbia Journal of Transnational Law*, Vol 43, pp. 189–227, (2004).

Rönsch, H., 'Effectiveness of Laws and Policies Governing Permissive Parenting in Pursuit of the Reduction of Severe Child Abuse in Germany', *Children and Youth Services Review*, Vol. 119, (2020), at: https://www.sciencedirect.com/science/article/pii/S0190740920307416

Schweppe, K., 'Child Protection in Europe: Different Systems – Common Challenges', *German Law Journal*, Vol. 3(10), (2002). This is the full citation (ie it would seem that the issue consisted only of that article)

Shapiro, J., 'For a Feminist Considering Surrogacy, Is Compensation Really the Key Question?', *Washington Law Review*, Vol. 89, pp. 1345, 1352–1353, (2014).

Walter, M. and Blandow, J., 'Foster Care in Germany', (2004) at: https://www.uni-siegen.de/foster-care-research/network_conferences/1st_conference/files/foster_care_germany_-_kindler.pdf

White, K.J., 'The Ideology of Residential Care and Fostering: Re-framing Children's Services', *NCVCCO Annual Review Journal*, Vol 3, pp. 231–242, (2002).

Wolf, K., 'Promoting the Positive Development of Foster Children: Establishing Research in Germany', *Adoption & Fostering*, Vol. 36(1), pp. 40–51, (2012).

Van den Berge, L., 'Rethinking the Public-Private Law Divide in the Age of Governmentality and Network Governance', *European Journal of Comparative Law and Governance*, Vol. 5(2), pp 119–143, (2018).

Zimmermann, R., *The German Civil Code and the Development of Private Law in Germany*, Oxford University Press, (2006), at: https://ouclf.law.ox.ac.uk/citation/

Reports

Bertelsmann Foundation Report on Child and Youth Poverty in Germany, at: https://www.wsws.org/en/articles/2023/03/01/fd97-m01.html

Break Poverty, (2021), at: https://breakpoverty.com/en/an-intolerable-increase-in-early-childhood-poverty-as-a-result-of-the-health-crisis/

Child and Youth Report, 'Between Freedom, Family, All-Day School and Virtual Worlds – Personality Development and Education for Young People', (2017), at: https://www.dji.de/ueber-uns/projekte/projekte/15-kinder-und-jugendbericht.html

ChildPact, *Putting Child Protection and Family Care at the Heart of EU External Action*, (2017), at: https://codeofgoodpractice.com/wp-content/uploads/2019/05/Lumos-Putting-Child-Protection-and-Family-care-at-the-heart-of-EU-External-Action.pdf

Commissioner for Human Rights, 'Positions on the Rights of Minor Migrants in an Irregular Situation', (2010), at: https://rm.coe.int/ref/CommDH/PositionPaper(2010)6

Corak, M., Fertig, M. and Tamm, M., 'A Portrait of Child Poverty in Germany', *Innocenti Research Centre (UNICEF)*, (2005).

Crime Report, (2018), at: https://thecrimereport.org/2018/04/10/in-germany-its-hard-to-find-a-young-adult-in-prison/

Fair and Just Prosecution Report, *Lessons Learned from Germany: Promoting Developmentally Appropriate and Rehabilitative Youth and Young Adult Justice*, (2022), at: https://fairandjustprosecution.org/wp-content/uploads/2022/06/FJP-Germany-Youth-Justice-Brief.pdf

Federal Ministry for Family Affairs, Senior Citizens, Women and Youth, *Family Today: Data, Facts, Trends – Family Report 2020*, at: https://www.bmfsfj.de/resource/blob/190146/7313bd244bf3b7d05b334afc70ce7e1c/family-today-data-facts-trends-family-report-2020-data.pdf

Fenton-Glynn, C., 'Adoption Without Consent: A Report for the PETTI Committee', (2015), at: https://www.europarl.europa.eu/RegData/etudes/STUD/2015/519236/IPOL_STU(2015)519236_EN.pdf

Global Slavery Index, at: https://www.walkfree.org/global-slavery-index/2018/findings/country-studies/germany/

Human Rights Watch Report, at: https://www.hrw.org/news/2021/06/08/germany-child-labor-rising-covid-19-supply-chain-law-even-more-urgent

International Working Group of the International Association of Youth and Family Judges and Magistrates, 'Guidelines on Children in Contact with the Justice System', (2016).

KiGGS [Study on the Health of Children and Adolescents in Germany] Baseline Study, at: https://www.kiggs-studie.de/english/results/kiggs-baseline-study.html.

Kuntz, B., Rattay, P., Poethko-Müller, C., Thamm, R., Hölling, H. and Lampert, T., 'Social Inequalities in Health of Children and Adolescents in Germany: Results of the Cross-Sectional KiGGS Wave 2 Study', *Journal of Health Monitoring*, Vol. 3, pp. 17–33, (2018).

Mignot, J.-F., *Child Adoption in Western Europe, 1900–2015*, HAL, (2019), at: https://shs.hal.science/halshs-02008838/document

Mullally, S., 'Submission by the UN Special Rapporteur on Trafficking in Persons, Especially Women and Children, in the Cases of *H.F. and M.F. v. France* (App. No. 24384/19) and *J.D. and A.D. v. France* (App. No. 44234/20) Before the European Court of Human Rights', (2021), at: https://ssrn.com/abstract=3933138 or http://dx.doi.org/10.2139/ssrn.3933138

National Academy of Medicine, 2002, report, at: https://segm.org/France-cautions-regarding-puberty-blockers-and-cross-sex-hormones-for-youth

Organisation for Economic Co-operation and Development, *Growing Unequal? Income Distribution and Poverty in OECD Countries*, Paris, (2008).

Permanent Bureau of The Hague, *A Preliminary Report on the Issues Arising from International Surrogacy Arrangements*, Preliminary Doc. No. 10, (March 2012), at: https://assets.hcch.net/docs/d4ff8ecd-f747-46da-86c3-61074e9b17fe.pdf

Secretary General of the United Nations, *Investigation on Violence against Children, Questionnaire for Governments: Responses by the Federal Republic of Germany*, (2005).

Thomson Reuters, *Practical Law*, at: https://uk.practicallaw.thomsonreuters.com/6-615-3545?transitionType=Default&contextData=(sc.Default)&firstPage=true

UNHCR, 'Global Trends: Forced Displacement in 2017', (2018), at: https://www.unhcr.org/5b27be547.pdf

UNICEF, *Droits des Enfants en France*, (2022), at: https://unicef.hosting.augure.com/Augure_UNICEF/r/ContenuEnLigne/Download?id=480588C0-E8CD-4A6A-B8D8-80AAA060B4C4&filename=SynthDroitsEnfantsFrance2022_final_pages.pdf

United Nations, Committee on the Rights of the Child, (2022), 'General Comment', at: https://www.ohchr.org/en/press-releases/2022/09/un-child-rights-committee-publishes-findings-germany-kuwait-north-macedonia

United Nations, *Guidelines for the Alternative Care of Children*, UN Doc. A/HRC/11/L.13, (2009).

United Nations, Report of the United Nations High Commissioner for Human Rights on Access to Justice for Children, Human Rights Council, Twenty-fifth session, Agenda items 2 and 3, A/HRC/25/35, online

U.S. Department of State, *2022Trafficking in Persons Report: France*, at: https://www.state.gov/reports/2022-trafficking-in-persons-report/france/

U.S. Government, *2022Trafficking in Persons Report: Germany*, at: https://www.state.gov/reports/2022-trafficking-in-persons-report/germany/

Index

For Product Safety Concerns and Information please contact our EU representative GPSR@taylorandfrancis.com
Taylor & Francis Verlag GmbH, Kaufingerstraße 24, 80331 München, Germany

www.ingramcontent.com/pod-product-compliance
Lightning Source LLC
LaVergne TN
LVHW021124300926
849160LV00010B/851
* 9 7 8 1 0 3 2 5 4 2 1 1 9 *